THE BODY CLOCK ADVANTAGE

Finding Your Best Time
of Day to Succeed in:
Love • Work • Play • Exercise

by Matthew Edlund, M.D.

Adams Media Corporation
Avon, Massachusetts

To my parents

Published by
Adams Media Corporation
57 Littlefield Street, Avon MA 02322. U.S.A.
www.adamsmedia.com

ISBN: 1-58062-789-7

Printed in Canada.

J I H G F E D C B A

Library of Congress Cataloging-in-Publication Data
Edlund, Matthew.
The body clock advantage / Matthew Edlund.
p.   cm.
ISBN 1-58062-789-7
1. Biological rhythms–Popular works. I. Title.
QP84.6 .E355 2002
612'.022–dc21

2002009817

This book is available at quantity discounts for bulk purchases.
For information, call 1-800-872-5627.

Contents

Acknowledgments

Time has obsessed me for many years, but it was only in the last ten that I realized how powerfully it underpins human biology—and how useful that knowledge is.

I owe thanks to many people but first to my patients, who have given me the chance to work and learn with them. To protect their privacy, I have changed names and details in the clinical vignettes. Dr. William Lose made my work easier. Many people encouraged me, particularly Dr. Gordon and Suzanne Stoltzner. Stacy Gillman, Dr. Larry Tancredi, Risa Schwartz, Enid Perll, Stuart Kaminsky, Pam Daniel, and Dr. Laurie Ossman helped with the manuscript. Lynne Lamberg gave it a particularly close and careful reading. Drs. Dan Oren, Rosalind Cartwright, and Daniel Weinberger were among many who provided scientific help, while Dr. Daphne Rosenzweig provided both artistic and culinary aid.

I also thank Peter Rubie for his faith. Let's hope it's fulfilled, and people learn how they are really built.

Matthew Edlund, M.D., M.O.H.

Good Timing

Time rules life. Yet there is never enough of it. The more time we need, the less we have. We feel enslaved by clocks. There is not enough time to do what we must, let alone what we like.

Or so we think.

The problem is not lack of time. The real problem is how we use time. Human beings operate on biological time, not the technological time of our society. Our bodies live by the rhythms of the sun and stars, our days and nights. They constantly change, shifting over the 24-hour day. Yet we try to force our bodies to live according to unchanging machine time.

People are not cars or computers. We're not machines. Trying to time ourselves as if we were machines simply does not work.

The costs to our lives and health are great:

- Americans complain bitterly of fatigue.
- Many of us never feel healthy.
- Obesity and diabetes are skyrocketing.
- Cases of depression have doubled over the past thirty years.

Many traffic and industrial accidents that cost time and lives could be predicted—and prevented. Why aren't they? Because we don't pay attention to our biological clocks, our inner time.

Did you know:

- That obesity and diabetes are connected with both what you eat, and when?
- That how much sleep you get, and when, affects how fat you'll become?
- That most drugs have markedly different effects on the same person at different times of day? That those differences have never been studied for the vast majority of drugs? That thousands of deaths in intensive care units and emergency rooms may occur because of the time drugs were given?
- That the most serious industrial accidents, such as at Bhopal, Three Mile Island, and Chernobyl, occur between midnight and 6 a.m.?
- That trucking fatalities may increase forty times during that same time period?
- That Americans are sleeping two hours less each night (and teenagers three hours less) than 100 years ago?
- That this chronic, partial sleep deprivation grinds us down and makes us more sluggish, more prone to diabetes and obesity, and less capable of learning and creative work?

Many of our relationships also are governed by differences in biological clocks. Whether we are morning or night people affects our work, our families, whom we choose as friends and spouses, and how much our kids drive us crazy. Many relationship conflicts can be traced to genetic differences between the two partners' biological clocks.

Some of the ills of our society and the struggles of our personal lives are simply due to bad timing. Yet they need not be. Learning about your own personal biological clock can make your life a lot easier, a lot healthier, and even a lot happier. Whether you are fat or thin, eighteen or eighty-eight, working with your biological clock should bring positive changes to your life.

This book is based on my clinical experience of the last ten years, working with people day by day, helped by the research of thousands of scientists who study biological clocks. The facts are often new, but the concept is old: use your body the way it is built. The LENS program (Light, Exercise, Naps, and Socializing) that I've developed is just one example of how to use clinical experience to ease people's lives.

As a physician and practitioner in the new field of Circadian Medicine, I try to teach people about "good timing." I want people to know which are the right times for them to eat, the best times to exercise, the most effective times for work, and the optimum time to enjoy lovemaking.

"Good timing" will vary according to you and your goals.
Do you want to time your eating to . . .
Lose weight?
Avoid family conflicts?
Are you exercising to . . .
Control weight?
Improve athletic skills?
Help you sleep?
Keep you alert?
When having sex, are you trying to . . .
Enjoy it the most?
Overcome impotence?
Become pregnant?
Not be bothered by the kids?

Today, our lives are complex and busy. Like the rest of us, you are probably trying to juggle job and family with the demands of friends and coworkers. You want to stay healthy, but you also want to enjoy what you eat. You want to sleep well and wake rested in the morning, while still being able to enjoy nighttime entertainment. In short, you want to balance the pleasures and requirements, the desires and fears of everyday life.

Fortunately, the basics of "good timing" are simple. These principles have been used successfully for infants and children, single mothers and fathers, adolescents and the elderly. You just have to know a few simple facts.

Let's start with learning how you're built.

Biological Time

"Star maps" lie inside every cell in your body. These program your life. If you live within their rules, you will live a more satisfying life.

Why?

Because time structures life.

Life on earth evolved by adapting to day and night. The earth turns on its axis, spinning like a top, flying across the solar system while elliptically orbiting the sun. These motions of earth and sun create the alternation of day and night, light and darkness, at regular 24-hour intervals.

Cells developed inner clocks to prepare for the environmental changes caused by day and night. Inner clocks helped sustain life on earth by predicting when the environment would change. Those animals and plants that were prepared for shifts in temperature, food sources, and climate were able to thrive. Within this basic structure of time, life evolved into hundreds of millions of different forms.

These inner clocks proved so successful that they soon timed all biological functions. Every aspect of your biology dances to 24-hour rhythms. There are rhythms for how well you remember (differing for short- and long-term memory), how well you throw a baseball, how efficiently your liver breaks down aspirin, and how quickly you metabolize food. Every process in your body runs according to its own 24-hour clock.

Once you know these cycles, you can improve your health, your performance, and your relationships.

The Need for Sleep

Over the years, several parents have come to see me because they could not sleep. Some thought they had sleep apnea, or difficulty breathing during sleep. Others thought they were depressed.

To my surprise, I discovered that the real reason they came to see me was grief. Each had had a young son who died driving at night. The parents could not understand how their sons had died, or why.

Each son was a "good kid." He did not use drugs. He worked a regular job. He was happy and looked forward to his future. Each had gone out for a quiet night with a fiancée or friend, and each had driven home alone.

Each drank one or two drinks. Just one or two.

At what time? I asked.

We're not sure, they'd told me. But we can find out.

Each time the answer was the same. Their son had not wanted to drink while driving. He "only had" one or two beers between 11 P.M. and 1 A.M. Unfortunately, this was enough alcohol to cause him to drive into a concrete culvert or to jackknife off the highway.

Would these tragic deaths have been averted if these young men had known that alcohol was more powerful after midnight? There is no doubt in my mind that they would have.

Biological clocks also affect the economy. Most major industrial accidents occur between midnight and 6 A.M., when sleep-deprived humans fail to properly keep watch over machines. For example:

Event	Time
Exxon Valdez oil spill	12:05 A.M.
Chernobyl nuclear accident	1:23 A.M. (the truly disastrous human errors began around 3 A.M.)
Bhopal chemical plant disaster	2 A.M.
Three Mile Island nuclear accident	4 A.M.

Unless you are a night person, your performance will decline from midnight on. The hours from 4 A.M. till around 5:30 A.M. seem to be the worst time for accidents.

Amazingly, this is highly predictable. Between 4 and 4:30 A.M. is when the human body temperature curve hits bottom. At that time, we are most likely to fall asleep, and sleep inertia may knock out our ability to rapidly respond to emergencies.

Training people to know the best and worst times for performance is essential for preventing transport and industrial accidents—including night driving. It is also, by the way, one key to preventing terrorist attacks.

Many workers in the transport and health industries perform shift work. They sleep one or two hours less per day than the already sleep-deprived general population. We have not yet even begun to recognize how widely partial sleep deprivation affects performance. We do know that sleep deprivation makes people more insulin resistant, perhaps more prone to obesity and diabetes, and less able to memorize and learn. In fact, there are many scientific studies showing that insomnia makes people cranky and irritable. Insomniacs don't think well. They feel (and often are) profoundly uncreative. They don't get along as well with other people.

About a third of Americans complain about insomnia, and nearly one-fifth of the population considers it a serious problem.

Over time many insomniacs become depressed. They snack at night and become heavier and heavier. They snap at others. Their relation-ships and family life suffer.

Timing your sleep and using a few simple behavioral tricks can change all that.

Biological clocks can also strongly influence sports. Until the National Football League wised up in its scheduling, it was easy to track who had the disadvantage for its Monday night football games: the team flying through the most time zones from east to west.

Yet biological clocks affect all of us who play any sport. Most people's athletic ability is fair in the morning, improves in the early afternoon, and is best in the late afternoon or evening. If you want to exercise to your highest level, especially as a competitive athlete, you may be better off working out in the late afternoon or early evening. (Fortunately, light boxes producing artificial sunlight can switch those times to almost any period you wish, if you know how to use them.)

The Power of Our Inner Clocks

How powerful are human biological clocks? We don't really know. Research is too new.

We know more about animals. Their inner clocks are remarkable. Monarch butterflies might normally be able to fly fifty miles before dying of exhaustion. Yet each year they manage to travel three thousand miles to the same small mountainous area in Mexico.

The monarchs know where the trade winds flow. They know where to ride them and where to turn. They perfectly navigate across swamps, mountains, and forests they have never seen before.

Nor had the previous generation seen those things before. Nor will the next. The journey takes more than one generation.

The monarchs are born with the star magnetic maps necessary to make the journey. Everything they need is inside them.

We, too, are born with star clocks and maps inside us. In this book you will learn what your biological clocks are, what they do, and, most important, how *you* can use them. Use them well and you can change your body shape, your ability to do your job, and your sensitivity to others. You can perform better at work and improve your relationships. You can protect yourself from potentially dangerous drugs and treatments and make the necessary ones work more effectively. You can wake in the morning feeling more refreshed and alert than you can remember.

To succeed, you need to recognize that biological clocks are powerful. Pay attention to them and they will help you. Ignore them and they may hurt you. It pays to live the way we are built.

Each one of us is unique. So are our inner clocks. Let's start by learning what kind of clock you have.

Chapter One

Are You a Lark or an Owl?

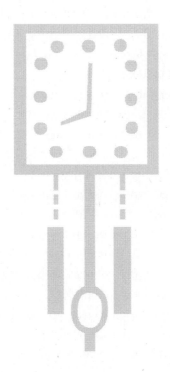

Jerry and Nancy are both twenty years old. They like the same music, the same clothes, and the same books. They also like each other. Yet they always fight.

Nancy likes to stay up with friends till 1 or 2 A.M., then study "while it's quiet." She goes to sleep at four. On weekends she stays up till six, getting up at noon.

Jerry has a hard time keeping his eyes open past 11 P.M.

Nancy thinks Jerry won't stay up with her because "he doesn't like my friends." Jerry says he *does* like her friends, but he can't remember their names because "I'm always half asleep when I meet them." He prefers to go out with Nancy in the evening, but that is when she has scheduled many of her classes. "The only time I get to talk to her is at lunch, and she's half asleep."

Nancy can't understand why he's "such a bore." Jerry tells her that it's not his fault, that he's just "made this way."

Jerry is correct. Just as we have different-colored hair and eyes, we have different inner clocks.

Scientists call morning people like Jerry "larks," named after the dawn twitterers who swarm across farm fields at the break of day. Night people are called "owls," named after those nocturnal carnivores that sense their prey with acute vision and hearing.

Many owls don't like to be called owls. They fuss about the title at scientific meetings. In many cultures owls represent dark, evil forces. Perhaps these night people would prefer to be happy as a lark. As a lark who envies the ability of owls to stay up late, I have some sympathy.

Owls must face an unpleasant truth: it is a Lark Work World. Much of the globe travels and toils between 6 A.M and 6 P.M. Many owls start the workday literally asleep. However, in some forms of shift work, night-loving owls have the advantage.

Not everyone is a lark or owl. Much of the world is made of switchers, people who attempt to be lark-like or owl-like depending on circumstance. The younger we are, the more we are able to switch our allegiance from lark to owl. That's part of the reason that Nancy, like many college students, can't understand why Jerry thinks 11 P.M. is a normal time to be asleep.

Age makes us more lark-like. Our body clocks move forward as we grow older. By the age of seventy, our clocks are an hour to an hour and a half earlier than when we were kids. That's why grandma gets up so early and telephones at that ghastly hour. Yet no matter what the circumstances, larks and owls must work with each other.

They also must live with each other. Many of the conflicts between spouses, lovers, parents and children, employers and employees, and bureaucrats and citizens have their origin in our inborn clocks. Unfortunately, hardly anyone recognizes such biological facts as the cause for endless disagreement. But *you* will.

One person who recognized the truth is my friend Martin. Martin has been a musician most of his life. He starts work, at the earliest, at 8 P.M.

Martin could not understand why we saw each other so little. Then I explained to him that I was a lark. I normally finish work close to the time he goes to work. And I'm asleep when he finishes his sets and feels ready to relax.

I asked Martin about his friends. Were they late-night people?

Almost all were. The people he worked with, the people he played with, were nearly all owls, including his wife. "I never realized it, but you're one of the few larks I talk to," he said.

Inborn biological-clock differences affect your choice of job as well as whom you select as friends and mates.

Part of the pleasure of learning about biological clocks is being able to understand truths you never recognized before. So many things we choose to do, so many of our work problems and relationship issues, become understandable. But first you have to understand how we're built.

Larks and Owls

Owls often think they are lazy and stupid. They have such bad luck, something about them must be defective. It's not hard to guess why they feel that way.

Tom walked into my office, or more accurately, was pulled into my office by his mother. A seventeen-year-old junior in high school, Tom was starting off the academic year failing more than half his classes. He had already seen several physicians and psychologists. His mother explained, "I'm bringing him here because I don't what else to do. I can't wake him up in the morning. I try. I really try."

I asked her if Tom and I might speak alone. Tom sat down and slouched in his chair, his long legs spreading across the carpet. "You know, I don't know what to do. I really don't. I mean, I like school, well, sort of. I can't do school in the morning. Can't. Like, it's hard for me to get going, you know?"

"What time do you go to bed?"

Tom looked sleepy as he considered the question. "Uhhh, pretty late."

"How late?"

"Oh, well, I try to get to bed around two or three."

Normal hours for his classmates, perhaps. American teenagers are world champions in chronic sleep deprivation. But Tom was merely *trying* to go to sleep.

"What time do you actually go to bed?"

"Maybe four."

"What time do you go to sleep?"

Tom looked ready to fall asleep in the chair. "About five, I guess," he said yawning. "Yeah, five. Maybe a little later."

"On the weekends?"

"Five or six."

He would awake on Saturdays and Sundays at two or three in the afternoon.

Tom was not lazy, nor stupid, nor depressed. Tom was a full-blown owl. He was more of an owl than his high school friends, who partly were his friends because they considered three in the morning an early bedtime. Their high school classes began at eight A.M.

Tom was physically present for his morning classes. Yet he was not awake. After his mother drove him to school, Tom found it nearly impossible to keep his eyes open. He would start to feel "a little alert" around 10:30 or 11 A.M. During morning study hall and English class he'd "crash" into slumber. Rarely was he alert until noon.

Almost all the classes he failed took place in the morning. Tom was sleeping through high school.

I talked with Tom about owls and larks. I pointed out that he was an owl living in the lark world. For Tom, every school day was shift work. His clocks were so late he began classes at the biological equivalent of 3 A.M.

"You mean I should start school at like noon?"

No. High school authorities would not be enthusiastic about changing his entire schedule in the middle of term. But I did point out to him that light, melatonin, and exercise all could be used to set his biological clock earlier. He could go to school on time. He could be alert for morning classes.

Exercise did not excite Tom ("I do that in PE"). Enticing him to take a morning walk proved an impossible chore. Melatonin helped him only a little.

But light therapy worked. Tom liked to eat. He was agreeable to sitting down for breakfast, a light box perched at the edge of his cereal bowl. He would begin that day's required homework at the breakfast table. Later on he moved the light box next to the computer in his bedroom.

Tom found it "kinda cool" that light could be used as a drug—a non-oral, non-injectable pharmaceutical that could change his inner clocks, make him feel awake and alert, and alter his immune functions and his mood. (See Appendix 3 for information on how to use a light box.) He was, however, shocked when Christmas recess arrived. Tom's idea of vacationing was to take a holiday from his light box. His decision quickly pushed Tom back into his natural owldom.

Your Biological Time Test

If you are an owl or lark you probably have a fair inkling of your own biological timing. Yet many people are neither lark nor owl. To know what you are, please take this short test. (If you want a more reliable but more complicated answer, check the questions of the Horne and Ostberg Morningness Eveningness Scale in Appendix 1.)

Please answer the next four questions and tally up the score:

1. Imagine you are greatly enjoying a permanent vacation. You have no responsibilities, no worries. You've got more money than you'll ever need. You can do whatever you like.

What time would you go to bed?

Between 8 and 9 P.M. . . . . . . 6 points
Between 9 and 10 P.M. 5
Between 10 and 11 P.M. 4
Between 11 and 12 P.M. 3
Between midnight and 1 A.M. . 2
Between 1 and 2:30 A.M. 1
After 2:30 A.M. 0

2. You're still enjoying your very pleasant, unlimited vacation. Considering only your personal desires,

When would you like to wake up?

Anytime before 6 A.M. . . . . . . 6 points
Between 6 and 7 A.M. 5
Between 7 and 8 A.M. 4
Between 8 and 9 A.M. 3
Between 9 and 10:30 A.M. . . . 2
Between 10:30 and noon 1
After 12 noon 0

3. Though still enjoying the vacation, you're beginning to feel a little stir-crazy. You think you want to begin a volunteer job. It's work you've

done before and that you really enjoy.

Of course, it is a job. You're not planning to overdo it. You will work only two hours at a time, continuing only if you find your tasks entertaining and rewarding.

When would you pick your two-hour shift?

Between 5 and 7 A.M. . . . . . . 6 points
Between 7 and 9 A.M. 5
Between 9 A.M. *and 1* P.M. . . . 4
Between 1 and 7 P.M. 3
Between 7 and 11 P.M. 2
Between 11 P.M. *and 1* A.M. . . 1
Between 1 A.M. *and 5* A.M. . . . 0

4. Your vacation is providing you great relaxation, rest, and a profound sense of peace. Remembering the very different circumstances of your previous life, you are reminded of times you felt free and at your best.

At those times you would have described yourself as:

Definitely a morning person . . . . 6 points
Probably a morning person 4
In between a morning and a night person . . 2
Very much a nighttime person 0

Add up your score and enter it here: _____

If you score 16 to 24 points, you are a lark. If your score was zero to 8 points, consider yourself an owl.

What if you score between 8 and 16 points? At least for the present, you are probably a switcher. Switchers find that they can be a bit like a lark or owl. It depends on their work and family situations.

If you're a switcher, do not fret. You're in the majority. Depending on your age, your job, and the relative larkishness and owlness of the people you live with, you probably shift frequently between living as a morning or a night person. For example, many 9-to-5 workers decide to become owls over the weekend. (Beware, however: Partly as a result of this shift in body clocks, Monday morning is the peak time of death in the United States.)

Unfortunately, our capacity to shift inner time lessens as we become older. It's the same as with many other biologically based abilities. It just grows more difficult to do things well as we get older. There are few marathon runners and swing-shift workers over the age of seventy.

Conflicts Between Larks and Owls

Fate sometimes chooses time spaces for us that conflict with those we love. Such was the case of Ginny.

Ginny worked in an office. In her mid-thirties she married a man "I really thought I would live with forever." At the age of thirty-eight, Ginny delivered a lovely baby girl, named Margaret.

Margaret was healthy and active. Unlike most infants, Margaret did not sleep fourteen to sixteen hours every day. In fact, she barely liked to sleep at all.

As Margaret grew older, she remained a short sleeper, and one with unusual habits. Unlike many three-year-olds, Margaret absolutely refused to go to sleep at 8 or 9 P.M. Instead Margaret preferred to "stay up with Mommy and Daddy." She'd laugh as her two parents fell asleep, continuing to amuse herself into the wee hours.

The major problems started in the morning. Often Margaret would not get out of bed until early afternoon. Threats, blandishments, and the loss of favorite meals and toys would not influence her.

Ginny accommodated Margaret by working part-time. She still had the time to raise her daughter while her husband worked his regular 8-to-5 job. Then he lost the job. Within a year, Ginny was divorced.

After the breakup Ginny's ex-husband could only find his particular line of work out of state. Ginny was forced to work full-time, leaving Margaret to stay most of the day with Ginny's mother. Like Ginny, Grandma was a lark, one who had turned more larkish with age. She could not adjust to Margaret's hours. Ginny kept going to bed later and later, arriving at work sleepy and exhausted. When she first met me she announced "I'm tired, I can't sleep, I'm about to lose my job."

We tried different bedtimes to gradually shift Margaret to an earlier sleep time. Success did not come. Margaret refused to do what her exhausted mother asked. Sitting in front of a light box was out of the question.

Margaret knew what she wanted. She was convinced that she was right. It was Mommy's fault that she got up so early and went to work. Why wasn't she still married to Father? And why couldn't Mommy go to work later, like all those people on television? Nobody on television went to work before 7 o'clock. Why did Mommy always disappear from the apartment when Margaret wanted to sleep?

With difficulty, Ginny tried different work times. Eventually she found a job on an evening shift. It allowed her mother to come and help baby-sit Margaret.

Not that Margaret was satisfied. She would go to sleep at 2:30 A.M. at the absolute earliest. Until she did fall asleep, Margaret demanded to spend every waking moment with her mother. Ginny thought she would die from her attempts to appease her daughter.

I asked Ginny to try exercise on her return each day from work. With Margaret in the same room, Ginny sat and pedaled on an exercise bicycle for a half hour. Exercise at this late hour made it possible for Ginny to stay up later. Eventually she placed a light box next to the exercise bicycle as she pedaled away. Exercising at night, light box at her side, Ginny lengthened her biological day, trying to answer her owl daughter's unending nighttime questions.

Margaret was growing up. She wanted to start school like all the other kids. But how to get her up and ready for kindergarten at eight in the morning? Ginny became very worried.

Fortunately nothing drastic was required. Abruptly Margaret began to adjust to the lark world. She was not willing to get up early for Ginny, her grandmother, or her father. But when her friends taunted her for sleeping through the first hours of class, she changed.

Margaret got up before kindergarten started, but she was hardly awake. She remained sleepy through the first hours of class until she and Ginny began walking together in the morning. Living in a balmy southern climate, Margaret could use both light and exercise to make herself more lark-like. Mother and daughter soon found one of their best times together was walking during the morning.

The Body Temperature Curve for Larks

Most people are not as difficult to adjust to as young Margaret. To understand why Margaret and Ginny are so different, it's important to know a little about our inner 24-hour body temperature clock.

This clock is not easy to study. Light, fitness level, food, and physical activity all change the measurement of our internal temperature cycle. But it is very helpful to understand your inner body temperature curve. **FIGURE 1-1** shows a temperature curve for a typical lark.

FIGURE 1-1: DAILY BODY TEMPERATURE CHANGES FOR A LARK

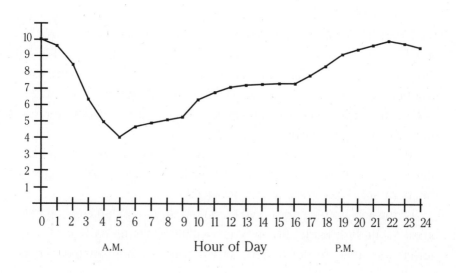

The body inner temperature curve helps determine many of our inner cycles, including performance. When body temperature is rising we are more alert. It's hard to fall asleep. When the body temperature declines we get sleepy. We sleep best as the curve goes down.

Perhaps the most interesting place in our body's temperature curve is the lowest spot. This time, the temperature nadir, is a critical period in our lives. It is the time when:

1. Light has its greatest effects. At the body-temperature low, or bottom, bright light can be used to shift our body clocks forward or backward, making our biological day much shorter or longer.
2. We experience our longest, most intense period of dream sleep. Dream (or REM, for rapid eye movement) sleep is important in making us feel rested and ready to face another day.
3. Human sexual function changes and male impotence is least likely (see Chapter 5, "Sex and Romance").

Let's take a look at the temperature curve of larks again. You'll see that the body temperature hits a peak around 10 P.M. Then it goes down, hitting bottom around 5 to 5:30 A.M. Notice that between 6 and 8:30 A.M., the curve is relatively flat. When the curve is flat, larks can remain awake or continue to sleep. You also see that the curve is quite flat in the early afternoon. Early afternoon is a time when lots of larks feel sleepy.

And many of them do something about it. Though our global economy is shifting basic cultural habits almost everywhere, over a billion people still take naps each afternoon. In Latin countries it is called the siesta. The afternoon siesta takes place for two major reasons. First, the body temperature curve is flat, making it easy for most people to fall asleep. Second, many people don't get enough sleep at night, as in some late-to-sleep Hispanic countries, and require naps to get through the day.

What happens in the evening, when the curve is rising? Larks and switchers become more alert. They find it harder to fall asleep (that's right—evening dozing is not normal for larks. It's a sign of sleep deprivation).

In the evening most larks and switchers experience a peak in physical abilities. If you're a lark and you want to perform your best at sports, late afternoon to early evening may be your time.

What would you expect to happen when the body temperature curve is diving fast, as it does around three or four in the morning? Ask any lark working the night shift.

Three or four in the morning is known in some countries as the "hour of the wolf." It is the time when many humans simply must sleep. This is when shift workers "hit the wall." It's when major accidents occur, and when people make terrible mistakes.

Larks don't want to be out on the road at three or four in the morning—not if they can help it. If they must be driving, caffeine may be useful (Chapter 7 discusses shift work). But it may be best to have a friendly owl drive for you.

The Body Temperature Curve for Owls

Now let's look at a body temperature curve for a representative owl (see **FIGURE 1-2**).

FIGURE 1-2: DAILY BODY TEMPERATURE CHANGES FOR AN OWL

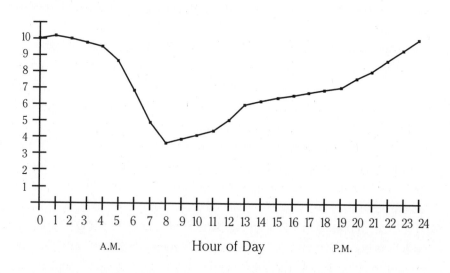

The same principles work for owls as well as larks. When the body temperature curve goes up, owls are alert and ready for action. When it goes down, owls like to sleep.

But these times are later for owls than larks. The forms of the curves are very close, often pretty much the same. Many owls like to do the same things larks like to do, except at later times.

Now let's superimpose the curves for Ginny and Margaret (see **FIGURE 1-3**).

FIGURE 1-3: DAILY BODY TEMPERATURE CHANGES

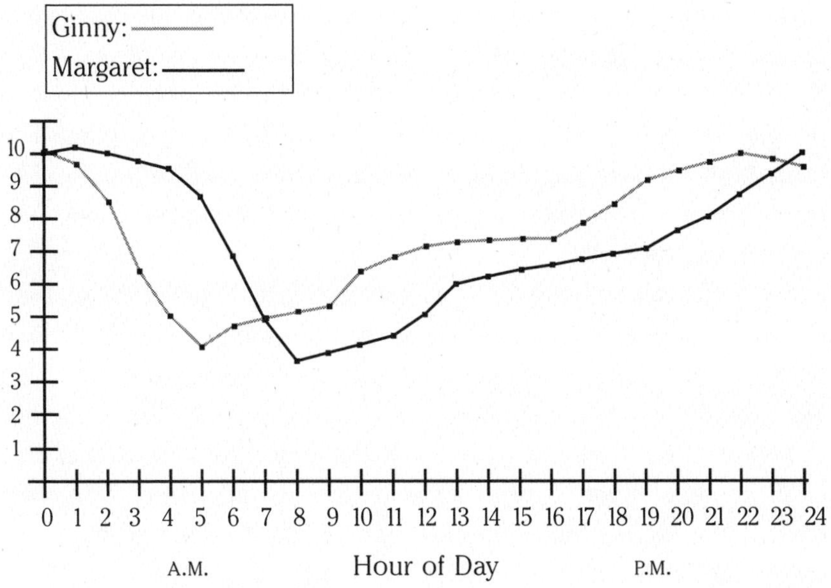

Ginny: ~~~~~~
Margaret: ————

Hour of Day

A.M.   P.M.

You quickly see that Ginny and Margaret are very different—so different that they are out of phase with each other for much of the day. Only in the late afternoon and early evening do Ginny and Margaret seem to get in sync. These times of synchronization of larks and owls are known as overlap times, and can be very helpful in planning family events and activities as well as important business meetings.

With Ginny and Margaret so terribly out of sync, one or both of them must accommodate the other. Three factors available to most of us—light, exercise, and melatonin—can change your body clock. The trick is to use them in a way that works for you.

Light—and How to Use It

Light sets the biological clocks for most of life on Earth. Whether you're a cockroach or a whale, an orchid or a Venus flytrap, light is the time-giver. Light times our lives.

In humans, sensing light is so important that it has its own pathway into the brain. This pathway is so important it exists outside our ability to appreciate light. Light can set inner clocks even when people can't see.

This discovery was spurred by studying the inner clocks of blind people. About half of blind people lack normal 24-hour rhythms. Their inner body clock is something longer, anywhere from 24½ up to 27 or more hours a day. For many of these blind people, their long inner clock makes life hell.

Blind people with inner clocks longer than 24 hours are often out of sync with the rest of humanity. Let's take the example of a blind person who has a 25-hour inner clock. She normally sleeps 8 hours out of every 24, but it isn't the same 8-hour period every day. Today she goes to bed at 10 P.M. and gets up at 6 A.M. But tomorrow, because her clock is 25 hours, she will want to go to bed at 11 and rise at 7. In twelve days, if she follows her inner clock, she will fall asleep at 10 A.M. and try to wake at 6 P.M.

Life for blind people is hard enough. Living with body clocks different from the rest of the world makes it extremely difficult to work, have normal family relations, and schedule times with friends. Many blind people end up disabled for work because of their abnormally long biological clocks.

Yet now there is something that can help. Dr. Robert Sack of the University of Oregon Medical School found that for many blind people, using melatonin regularly can normalize their clocks.

What about the other half of blind people, those who have normal 24-hour cycles?

It turns out that humans are born with a nerve pathway between the retina of our eyes and a small part of the hypothalamus, which is a critical regulation area in our brain. This pathway sweeps from the retina to a tiny, dense group of hypothalamic cells called the suprachiasmatic nucleus, or SCN.

The nerve cells of the SCN are perhaps the most important time-controllers in the body. Through an elegant chemical process, these few brain cells in the SCN beat out the 24-hour rhythms of our lives.

In normal-clock blind people, the pathway from the retina to the SCN is still intact. Light striking the eye creates signals that go directly to the SCN, *even though these people cannot see light.*

Light truly times life. Setting our internal biological clocks by light is so important that it can work without visual consciousness. Our brain "sees" light even when it can't see. In many animals, particularly birds, there are light receptors on the legs and skin. These light receptors also have direct nerve pathways to the brain.

How to Use Light

To get the best timing for your life you have to know how to use light. The important facts are:

The stronger the light, the more powerful the effect.

Sunlight, or the simulated sunlight of light boxes, works far more effectively than ordinary indoor electric lights.

Light before the temperature nadir makes you owl-like. Light after the temperature nadir makes you more lark-like.

Unlike most drugs, light *reverses* its effect depending on the time of day. The temperature nadir is a critical time. Light before that temperature nadir makes our inner day *longer*. Light exposure after it after makes our inner day *shorter*. At the body temperature nadir, light reverses its effect on your body time. You need to remember this simple rule:

Morning light makes you more of a lark. Evening light makes you more of an owl.

For people who live in sunny places like southern California or the southeastern United States, outdoor sunlight can be used to set their inner biological clocks. You need to be outside in the morning or evening, or close to a sunny window.

But what if it's a rainy day, or a dark, cold winter evening in the Midwest? What if you live in Seattle or Vancouver, and the sun regularly disappears throughout the year? People who live in darker places need not fear. They can use light boxes to harness the power of light.

Light boxes are special lamps that provide very bright full-spectrum light, similar in power to morning sunlight. They are more powerful than ordinary indoor lamps. Though often used to treat people with seasonal depression, light boxes are now coming into widespread use for many biological-clock difficulties, from shift work to delayed sleep phase syndrome (high school student Tom's problem) to shifting different family members more into sync. (See Appendix 3 for information on how to use light boxes.)

Though ordinary light is weaker than what we obtain from a light box, it also produces important effects. Electric lights are a large reason why people in industrialized countries now sleep far less than they used to (two hours less in America than 100 years ago).

That's because evening light makes us more owl-like. Ordinary indoor lights shift our inner clocks later. Electric light is a major reason why children, adolescents, and adults so often stay up late at night. It's not just that people prefer to stay up so they can read, watch television, or go to parties. Weak as it is, ordinary artificial light helps shift our inner clocks.

Simulated sunlight is powerful. Often thirty minutes of exposure a day is enough to shift us hours toward our desired bed or wake times. Light from light boxes can also be used to treat insomnia and keep us alert for a few extra hours when we wish to be sharp.

Fortunately, light is just one way for us to control our inner clocks. The second most effective used time-shifter is exercise.

Exercise

Exercise is what human bodies are designed to do. Particularly walking.

Most of human evolution was spent in hunter-gatherer societies, like the Aborigines of Australia. We still possess the biological bodies evolved under such conditions. Those bodies are built for physical activity. Our hunter-gatherer bodies are *not* meant to sit behind desks or lie on couches. Our bodies are meant to *move*.

When we do move, we are healthier. Exercise is a prime way of controlling weight and feeling fit. It can prevent heart disease and stroke, cut down the risk of cancer, and possibly prevent Alzheimer's disease. It can also reset our biological clocks and keep us alert.

Interestingly, the effects of exercise are of the same form and direction as those of light, although less powerful.

Morning exercise makes us more lark-like.

Evening exercise makes us more owl-like.

Exercise has the added benefit of making us more alert. It can also be used to help us sleep.

Exercise to Change Your Clock

From the standpoint of changing inner clocks, exercise has multiple uses. The simplest and most effective combination is walking outside in the sun.

- To move your inner clock earlier, walk, run, bicycle, or skate in sunlight (simulated or real) between 6 and 8:30 A.M.
- To move your inner clock later, exercise in light between 6 and 8 P.M.

- Exercising in the evening will also help larks get more restful sleep.

Exercise does not have to be complicated. Walking works well. Most of us can walk on the job. We can converse while walking, talking with family, friends, or coworkers. Walking is an activity helpful to both our physical and mental health.

And walking at the *right* times will make us more productive at work and play.

Melatonin

Lots of people have heard of melatonin, though not as many know what it does.

The pineal gland deep inside the brain, thought by the great French philosopher Descartes to be the seat of the soul, produces Melatonin. Melatonin is the light-dark hormone of the body. When darkness strikes, melatonin production begins. When we are young, brain melatonin levels peak in the early night. We continue to produce melatonin at high levels until morning. Shine a bright light at your sleeping eyes, however, and melatonin production ceases.

Melatonin acts as the biological counter to light. With bright light, melatonin production stops. Yet when we experience consistent darkness, we again produce melatonin.

In most mammals, melatonin sets the reproductive cycle. Unlike most animals, humans do not have mating seasons. We are able to enjoy lovemaking any day of the year.

Even though it does not control human mating behavior, melatonin still has its uses. It helps a third of the population fall asleep. And like light and exercise, it can be used to reset your biological clock.

- To make your inner clock move later, use melatonin in the early afternoon.

- To make your inner clock move earlier, use melatonin at night.

Melatonin's effects are almost 12 hours out of sync with those of light. Like light, its effects vary with dosage.

However, melatonin can have an important unwanted side effect: it makes some people sleepy. If you are using melatonin to prepare to fly to Europe, for example, you should probably use a low dose, perhaps a slivered half of a tiny 1 mg pill. If you don't mind getting sleepy, you can use it in a higher dose, like 3 mg, or in the sustained-release form at 1 to 3 mg. (For more details, see Chapter 11 on jet lag.)

Melatonin may be useful in helping us get over the "Monday morning blues." Many people like to stay up late on the weekends. We sleep in late on Saturday and Sunday.

Then Monday morning arrives. Many of us, already sleep deprived, are not prepared to resume activity so early.

Taking a 3 mg melatonin pill on Sunday night can reshift our rhythms, making it easier to get up and start the work week. It also can help many of us sleep.

SUMMARY

- Larks, owls, and switchers make up the world. Knowing your inner biological clocks can help you navigate most work and social worlds far more easily.
- It's easy to shift our clocks, and getting in sync with work and our families can make the lives of all those we deal with simpler and easier.
- Light and exercise in the morning makes us more lark-like, and light and exercise in the evening makes us more owl-like.
- Melatonin has the opposite effect: in the afternoon, it makes us more owl-like; at night, it promotes sleep and helps us to wake up earlier.

Chapter Two

Sleep Better, Live Better

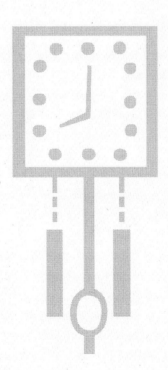

Sleeping and waking make up our lives. Biological clocks provide the timing and structure. We work, eat, and sleep following the eternal times set by the sun. Light sets the cycle of life and rest.

Sleep is still a great mystery. We do not know why we sleep, but we do know that we must. All organisms deprived of sleep will die. Personally, we recognize that if we do not get enough sleep we feel tired, cranky, slow, and fuzzy.

The Dangers of Sleep Deprivation

The real results of sleep deprivation are far worse than fatigue.

Americans are sleeping less than they ever did before. Sleeping fewer than seven hours on average, we have cut our sleep time two hours per night over the past 100 years. Much of this lessening of sleep has occurred in the last thirty years, which have also witnessed:

- A massive increase in diabetes.
- A markedly more obese population, especially among the young.
- A rapid increase in rates of depression.

Americans and many others around the globe have adapted to conditions of continuing partial sleep deprivation. We get some sleep, every night. But we do not get enough.

The effects of sleep deprivation are particularly underrated in the young. Among African-American and Hispanic youth, rates of obesity have doubled in the last twelve years. The rates have increased 50 percent in white children. The increase is usually blamed on children being sedentary; more television watching and computer game playing; and eating junk food.

Another part of the puzzle is sleep deprivation. Kids are eating junk food in front of the television set—at night. Nighttime is the perfect biological clock time for gaining weight. And children are sleeping less and less. Lack of sleep may also contribute to our children becoming fatter and fatter, through effects on insulin metabolism and many other factors.

Sleep and Mood

Another less well known effect is sleep deprivation's relationship to depression. Depression is not just feeling sad for a few hours or days. Depression is a syndrome, an illness composed of a group of several symptoms that last for months or even years. Overwhelming sadness is not required for the diagnosis of depression. Clinical depression involves loss of interest and motivation, fatigue, poor sleep, low energy, and lack of ability to enjoy oneself. Depression may also involve changes in appetite and a sense of guilt. It can but need not involve thoughts of suicide. Depression used to strike one in ten Americans. Now it strikes one in five.

Depression saps life of energy. It destroys the ability of people to adjust to the world around them.

One of the major problems with depression is recognizing it. Most of us, doctors included, think of health as the *absence* of signs of illness. We are "healthy" if we lack fever or high blood pressure, coughs and skin rashes, or tumors inside our bodies.

People with depression look fine. Often they act in a fashion that convinces others and themselves that nothing is terribly wrong. This may go on for months or years. The real costs of depression are frequently hidden from the public.

This is especially true in the business world. According to the World Health Organization, depression is far and away the world leader in economic disability. Its economic impact is twice as large as that of any other disorder. Because depression strikes many who are young, companies lose far more money from decreased productivity of depressed workers than from any other illness.

Many corporations, however, do not understand these facts. Their view of depression is often to ignore the problem; get rid of the worker; and make certain that the stigma of "mental illness" continues in all aspects of company life, including treatment. As most people with depression have found, insurance will cover their diabetes or heart disease but magically disappears whenever they become depressed. The fact that depression is also a major risk factor for heart disease and stroke rarely penetrates corporate consciousness.

Depression is not only treatable but also highly preventable. Insomniacs have much higher rates of depression, and so do patients with sleep disorders, like sleep apnea or narcolepsy.

Depression is itself a sleep disorder. Sleep in depression is horribly disorganized. The sleep changes are so characteristic it is possible to diagnose depression from doing a sleep study, observing the changes in the different phases of sleep.

Getting enough sleep each night probably goes a long way toward keeping us healthy and alert—and happy.

Sleep, Alertness, and Spirit

One of the most unusual recent studies was performed by Dr. Thomas Wehr and his colleagues at the National Institute of Mental Health. As part of the experiment, a group of young people were placed in a special work and living environment.

The environment controlled their exposure to light and dark. People were told to go to bed with the night and wake up at dawn. During the day they went about their planned activities. The idea in part was to have young people of today sleep like the hunter-gatherers of old.

During the study, people slept better and functioned well during the day. Some felt different than they ever had before. Many did not want the experiment to end.

When the experiment did finish, a surprising number of participants said they had never before known what it was to feel alert. They felt truly rested and mentally sharp. They perceived the world more clearly and brightly. People described a feeling of calm and relaxation they had not previously experienced.

Others underwent something wholly new: mystical experiences in the middle of the night. Possessing enough time to fully enjoy their dreams, they'd wake in the middle of the night with a sense of oneness and spiritual peace. They felt connected to themselves and to nature.

Many writers and anthropologists talk about the special spiritual connections available to people from "primitive" cultures. They describe their study subjects as possessing an astonishing recognition of the power of nature and an intense sense of perception. Many commentators tell of how these so-called primitive peoples feel more alive, more alert, and more at one with the world. These socially sophisticated observers normally lament the lack of such feelings in themselves. Some writers blame technological progress for the loss of this sense of wonder, of unity with the world.

The differences between primitive peoples and ourselves may not be only cultural. Far more than we do, primitive peoples live according to the cycle of night and day. Some of the heightened perceptiveness these writers admire may result from "primitive" peoples living in full harmony with their biological clocks. And getting enough sleep.

Why We Sleep So Little

We sleep less for a reason: electric lights.

Light resets the human body clock. Throughout our evolution, light set the times to sleep and to wake. Light determined when we were alert, tired, or sleepy. Light set the timing of our biology.

Today, electricity and electric lights reset our inner clocks. The power and presence of electric lights change sleep and waking throughout the world. First fire and then candles allowed humans to turn night into day. Yet these early man-made lights had far fewer effects on our biology than did sunlight.

Electricity allowed the development of powerful, inexpensive lamps. It changed our sleep and wake patterns in several important ways:

1. Evening light resets our internal clocks to a later hour. Though most electric lights are far less powerful than sunlight, they still slowly reset our clocks. Our hunter-gatherer bodies, faced with evening lights we did not evolve with, react to artificial light much as we do to sunlight. We go to bed later than ever before.
2. Electric lights made possible many more public activities at night. Work could easily be performed 24 hours a day. Shift work became a fixture of industrial societies.
3. Electricity made possible more private activities at night. Distinctions between daytime and nighttime activity wore down. Electricity allowed for new, varied types of amusements. Movies, radio, television, computers, the Internet, and video games are among the many forms of entertainment that can now be followed, night or day.

These devices are used throughout the night, particularly by the generation that has grown up with computers. The Internet is a tool that makes no distinctions about the 24-hour sleep-wake cycle. The attempt to create "Internet Time" of a thousand units instead of 24 hours shows how much the Internet is a creature of artificial, technological time. The Internet does not care about how human beings are internally clocked. As far as Internet timing and usage are concerned, humans might as well be machines.

Electric lights and technological progress now allow us to do almost everything we like throughout the entire 24-hour day. The natural response is to employ as many of these hours as possible. The result: we sleep too little, exercise hardly at all, and view nutrition as the fulfillment of temporary desire rather than a critical component of health. We wake up tired, caffeinate ourselves to get through the day, and glare at the mirror with alarm at our shape and appearance.

Life does not have to be this way. First we have to know what sleep is about, what sleep is made of. Knowing how sleep works can make your life a lot easier.

The Structure of Sleep

Sleep is a series of cyclical processes set by our biological clocks. In approximately 90-minute cycles all humans progress through several different states of consciousness.

Unfortunately, most of these states of consciousness are subsequently forgotten. Only our dreams are usually remembered.

Stage I Sleep

As the body temperature cycle hits its peak and begins its decline, we begin to sleep (see Figures 1-1 and 1-2 on pages 10 and 12). The first part of sleep, stage I, starts with slow rolling movements of the eyes and a change in brain electrical activity. Stage I sleep is often so close to wakefulness we often do not even notice that we are asleep. When people have been asleep for ten minutes and are then awakened from stage I sleep, half of them will tell you they were awake the entire time.

Why? Sleep itself causes amnesia. People in stage I sleep often don't remember falling asleep.

But you were asleep, their partners tell them. No, I was awake. No, you were asleep. The debate goes on and on, each side convinced they are right.

Many of us fall asleep and don't recognize it. People who fall asleep routinely without being aware include pilots, train conductors, nuclear plant operators, plus you and me when operating a car. Sometimes these sleeps are brief microsleeps, and we wake up quickly without any problem. At other times, we are not so lucky.

Stage II Sleep

After a brief period of stage I slumber, most sleepers progress into stage II sleep. Sleep researchers have little idea of the purposes of stage II sleep. The strange fact is that stage II constitutes the majority of time that humans sleep. People in stage II sleep are not completely unaware of their environment. Sometimes they recognize recordings they hear, or snippets of speech.

Stage II sleep, generally 55 to 60 percent of your sleep at night, may be useful for energy balance and control as well as learning. It may in some way be restful. If you selectively deprive sleepers of stage II sleep they will feel very sleepy in the morning. Yet so far scientists are stumped as to why we normally have so much stage II sleep.

Deep Sleep

Stage III and stage IV sleep constitute deep sleep. During crises or shift work, when people don't have enough time for sleep, deep sleep is preserved before anything else.

Deep sleep is a very odd time for our bodies. Brain electrical activity is taken over by slow, large waves. Deep sleep puts us as close to coma as we normally get. People in deep sleep are hard to wake.

Anyone whose child screams in the night probably knows what I mean. Night terrors generally occur in small children, who awaken their parents with piercing, blood-curdling cries. The screams are so frightening that people think their children are being murdered. Yet these children are engaged in a kind of sleepwalking. They are in deep sleep. When awakened they usually lack any clue about what they did.

Nor do they awaken quickly. A minute and a half or two minutes of touching, talking, or scratching their breastbone is needed before night terror screamers begin to recognize their surroundings.

Deep sleep seems to provide our most profound sense of rest. This blissful state of relaxation and resurgence is most common when young. Deep sleep declines with age, especially in men. It can be partly revived by circadian-timed exercise and hot baths. You have to use the proper body clock principles if you want to increase deep sleep.

REM Sleep

Perhaps the most unusual state of nighttime consciousness is rapid eye movement sleep, called REM or dream sleep. The term dream sleep is a misnomer. We can dream in all the different stages of sleep. However, the dreams we have in REM tend to be more vivid and complex.

REM sleep takes up more than a fifth of sleep. It is a time when large parts of our brain are turned off while others are activated. Our brain is then forced to make sense out of nonsense. For example, position sense is turned off during REM sleep. That is probably why so many of us "fly" in our dreams. In dreams we flit around the universe, hopping through space and time.

Many bizarre things happen to us in REM. During REM sleep our respiration and heart controls become ragged; most of our muscles are paralyzed, with the exception of our eyes and our diaphragm, which keeps us breathing; and in males, the penis normally becomes erect and stays so every time we move into REM. Finally, REM is the period when our inner temperature controls disappear, making us like newborn infants.

Losing temperature controls makes us drift into the temperature surrounding us. During a vacation in the Rockies long ago, I woke up dreaming at regular intervals throughout the night. I thought my waking was due to the fact that my sleeping bag was not fully deflecting the 30-degree outside temperatures. Only many years later did I recognize that all these mountain awakenings had occurred during REM.

REM is a state of consciousness with almost as much variety as waking life. Like deep sleep, REM is very important to obtaining a full sense of rest. Opposite to deep sleep, which occurs predominantly in the first third of the night, REM is most common and probably most useful at the end of the night. Most nights we experience our longest

REM period, sometimes an hour or so, right before we wake. This last REM period prepares us for the new day.

Sleep is not a single, homogeneous event. Sleep possesses at least four different phases, each with a biology as unique as our conscious, waking state. Each phase of sleep requires symphonic orchestration by the brain to control heart rates and nerve function, speed and type of metabolism, and use of oxygen and energy. If we could remember all of our different states of sleep, we might imagine ourselves to live several different lives. Used correctly, sleep can enormously enhance our daily, waking life.

Making Sleep Work for You

Understanding sleep is one thing, but the real question is, what steps can you take to make it work for you in the best way possible?

1. *Recognize that you need enough sleep to function.* Though indi-vidual sleep need is *very* variable, most adults need 8 hours of sleep each night to feel rested and refreshed. Most children and adolescents need at least 9½ hours of sleep each night. To restore your body, you need to sleep. Sleep requires time.

    Not all your time in bed will be asleep. The best sleepers usually sleep only 95 percent of the time they lie in bed (and that's trying to sleep). Healthy elderly people don't spend more than 80 to 85 percent of bedtime sleeping. So if you want 8 hours of sleep, you need more than 8 hours in bed.

2. *To rest us properly, sleep must be continuous.* Even superb sleepers wake fifteen to twenty times a night. Most of us will not remember these usually brief awakenings.

Sleep Amnesia

Sleep causes amnesia. That includes the periods where you wake up. Unless you were up for 6 or 7 minutes or longer, you probably won't remember waking from sleep.

Forgetting periods of wakening is very common. One night I was unexpectedly awakened around 2 A.M. to admit a patient, someone I did not know. I mumbled orders into the phone and went back to sleep.

I did not remember my new patient until eight o'clock the next night (fortunately he was not very, very sick). I rushed back to the hospital. The man was very friendly and polite, though his first words were "I thought you had forgotten about me."

I had. Sleep amnesia was the reason.

Amnesia after awakening is sometimes extreme. One afternoon I saw a sixty-nine-year-old woman who had suffered a mild stroke four years before. Her main complaint was insomnia. She was tired and sleepy every day. I suspected sleep apnea, often the result of certain types of strokes, and scheduled a night in the sleep laboratory. The lab technicians were rather skeptical. They did not think she merited a sleep study.

Her night in the lab horrified them. She woke up twelve hundred times. Many of her awakenings were due to leg kicks. She also averaged over seventy apneas per hour while asleep (apneas are period of ten seconds or more where we cease to breathe.)

She awoke in the morning with a smile. It was "my best night in years," she told the startled lab technicians. "I didn't wake up once all night."

Little awakenings during sleep are not something to laugh about. If you take a young, perfect sleeper, and play a little tone in her ear for a few seconds, she will perhaps wake up for a few seconds. She will not remember such brief awakenings.

But if you switch on the tone frequently enough, every 3 to 5 minutes, she will not feel well in the morning. Though she may have slept 95 percent of the time, she will not feel rested. Often such frequently awakened young sleepers will tell you they feel as sleepy, tired, and dejected as they do when kept up all night.

Sleep Continuity

People need to sleep in blocks of at least 5 or 10 minutes of *uninterrupted* sleep. Nighttime leg kicks, apneas, medical illnesses like Parkinsonism and diabetes, or even drinking an ounce of alcohol in a nightcap will cause us to awaken more. Smokers also waken far more than normal. Nicotine withdrawal occurs all through the night during sleep. Many a smoker will wake in the middle of night and light up before returning to bed.

Uninterrupted sleep may be important because only without interruptions does the sleeping brain have the time and resources to progress into the different stages of sleep. We do not achieve deep sleep and REM unless there are sufficient periods of uninterrupted sleep. And getting enough deep sleep and REM appears to be critical to waking up feeling rested.

Both deep sleep and REM sleep follow the body temperature cycle. REM can even be used as a proxy when studying our body's biological clocks. The longest REM period normally starts when the body temperature curve hits bottom, a very important time.

The body temperature bottom, or *nadir*, is the time when lots of biological changes occur that prepare us for wakefulness. It is also the time when shift workers "hit the wall," when our physical and mental abilities are at their worst, and terrible accidents happen. For both larks and owls, 4 A.M. to 5:30 A.M. is a period when you want to be asleep.

Though deep sleep is very restful, the amount we can get declines with age. Each year we obtain less and less. That is one reason so many elderly complain about insomnia.

We need lots of sleep to function during the day. What we especially need is deep sleep and REM sleep. If you're like most of the population, and can't take enough time for sleep, you really need as much deep sleep and REM as you can obtain.

Increasing Deep Sleep and REM Sleep

Think of deep sleep and REM as bookends for required rest. Though sleep runs in 90-minute cycles all through the night, most deep sleep occurs in the first third. The biggest REM period is just before we wake; in larks between 5 A.M. and 6:30 A.M., in late-running owls between 9 and 10:30 A.M.

Sleep is strongly influenced by changes in body temperature. Heating, as in a bath or exercise, or cooling, as in air conditioning or northern winters, can change sleep states. You can increase or decrease deep and REM sleep by manipulating temperature.

How to Increase Deep Sleep

Deep sleep is in many ways the most useful part of sleep. So it seems rather cruel that it decreases so rapidly with age, especially in men. Here are things to do to right the balance:

Exercise heavily (with sweating) 3 to 6 hours before sleep time. Sweating is the body's way of cooling off from too-high internal temperatures. Though anxiety and many ailments and medications can cause sweating, sweating while exercising is the result of inner heating. Push the human body up a degree or a degree and a half Fahrenheit, and most of us will sweat.

Many people do not like to sweat, but it can be very helpful. It is a sign of healthy exercise levels and a way to excrete toxic substances; and it helps our bodies regulate temperature and salt balance. Sweating can also help you sleep, particularly to provide more deep sleep.

Why exercise 3 to 6 hours before sleep time? Dr. Jim Horne, who also helped devise the most commonly used morningness-eveningness scale (see Appendix 1), wondered what exercise did to sleep.

He engaged a group of student athletes and ran them around a track. Running hard just before sleep time diminished sleep quality and amount. Exercise before sleep kept the athletes up and alert (a useful technique for larks who want to stay up late; see Chapter 9).

As with most human biological events, timing made all the difference. If the students ran 3 to 6 hours before sleep they had better sleep continuity. They also got more deep sleep.

But how did it work?

Horne thought the changes might be because of inner body temperature. So he took the same student athletes and again ran them around the track. And he made one change.

He got them wet.

As the athletes ran round and round and began to sweat, Horne passed them underneath a cold shower. Their body temperatures cooled under the flowing water.

Each night he put the young men into the sleep lab. The experiment was simple: Study sleep after running—with showers and without.

Running through the showers cut the students' percentage of deep sleep. Deep sleep went higher when the students ran normally, several hours before bedtime. (In my experience, many people can get better sleep after less sweaty exercise, such as walking in the early evenings.)

Horne and others wondered if there were other ways to increase deep sleep. There were.

Take a hot bath (passive body heating). You probably don't think that taking a hot bath is like taking a drug. It depends on your definition of "drug." If a "drug" is something that prevents and cures disease, or improves physical or mental welfare, a hot bath certainly qualifies.

The important word is "hot." Any non-Japanese person who first goes into a *furoba*, a Japanese ritual bath, knows what it is like to see your skin turn beet red as your brain contemplates imminent death. Covered in near-scalding water, you stop everything. You do not move *at all*. You are convinced the slightest twitch of a finger will cause a searing of flesh severe enough to burn.

Coming out of the *furoba*, fear is replaced by total relaxation. You feel you cannot move but entirely lack the desire. If the bath attendants let you, you believe you'll fall asleep standing up.

The same type of experience may occur with a true Finnish sauna. First your body is heated to a sweaty peak inside a wooden cabin, as your colleagues flay your skin with tree branches. Next you plunge into a lake's icy waters.

The old-style sauna produces intense calm. Manipulating body temperature affects both sleep and relaxation. Sauna and hot baths may work by returning to us energy-saving reflexes present in infancy. One example is the seal diving reflex that saves young children from brain injury after going underwater. Somehow these early reflexes are "forgotten" as we pass through childhood and into adulthood. Manipulating our inner body temperature may bring these early reflexes back.

Called "passive body heating" by sleep scientists, hot baths are similar to drugs in that they have different effects depending on how long they are given, and when. Hot baths even produce a proper "dose response curve" for sleep: the nearer the bath to the time you sleep, the more deep sleep and sleep continuity you obtain. The greater your sleep continuity, the more you will feel a sense of rest.

How to Take a Sleep-Inducing Bath

If you have a bathtub, determine the hour you want to go to sleep. About a half hour before you wish to sleep, heat up your bath as hot as you can comfortably stand. If possible, draw the blinds and turn off the lights.

Nestle yourself into the tub, sitting upright. Sit for a moment, then slowly descend into the bath.

Rest. Remember a beautiful, pleasant experience—a walk in the woods, a trek along a beach, a hike in the mountains. Visualize it in front of you. Then lie back, imagining you are making that trip again.

If visualization is difficult for you, you can try self-hypnosis or this variant of the relaxation response:

Lying back as far as possible in the water, breathe abdominally. Slowly breathe in. With each new breath, say a word in your mind, a comforting word like "home" or "peace." With each breath out, repeat the word.

Or try this: imagine you can breathe separately through each nostril.

You don't have to succeed at "single nostril" breathing, just make the attempt. For three straight breaths, breathe in with your right nostril, then out with your left. For the next three breaths, breathe in with your left nostril and out with your right.

Or just imagine the dreams you want to have that night.

All this time you are lying in the hot bath, heating your body. Soon you will feel tiny globes of sweat on your scalp and temples. Feeling yourself sweat from your forehead or ears means you have reached a body temperature high enough to help you sleep.

When you have spent fifteen or more minutes in the bath, or feel you have sweated enough (you'll discover how much through practice), turn on the lights. Towel yourself off.

You should feel relaxed—much more relaxed than when you started the bath. And if you can get yourself into the bed quickly enough, you should gain a more restful night.

How to Increase REM Sleep

Increasing REM sleep is mostly a matter of timing.

In normal sleepers, REM will recur throughout the night at approximately 90-minute intervals. If someone is depressed, or very sleep deprived, the first interval may occur early. Some people get their first REM period at 60 to 70 minutes after falling asleep. After this first period, REM tends to recur at 90-minute intervals.

As the night goes on, REM phases become longer. Finally, the controls determining how much we sleep reach a special balance. Our last REM period of the night begins.

Though not all researchers agree, these last REM periods tend to make people feel rested. They occur strictly by the clock. Keep someone in an environment without sunlight or time cues, and their longest REM period occurs when they fall asleep at the body temperature nadir.

Most of us will get our longest REM period just before we wake. To preserve REM sleep, don't get up too early. If you are a lark, make sure you can sleep at least until 5:30 or 6 A.M. For owls, try not getting up before 8:30 or 9 A.M.

But you can't sleep that late, you say. Your work/children/school schedule/parents/neighbors won't allow it.

The truth is many millions of people in this country and across the world get up too early to enjoy this last long REM period. Which may explain why:

- So many of us are cranky when we get up in the mornings.
- People imbibe abnormal amounts of coffee and tea to get themselves awake, and keep drinking them through the day to keep themselves alert. Unfortunately, use of caffeine beyond the morning often lightens sleep, perpetuating the whole process.
- Heart attacks and deaths peak in the morning.
- Starting times at work are so stressful.
- People watch morning television shows stuffed with witless banter and numbingly frequent commercials, dulled after a night of insufficient sleep.
- Morning commuters drive like sports car racers, trying to shave seconds to reach their workplace on time.

Though the 24/7 economy often refuses to consider human biological clocks, schools are now starting to recognize the problem. Many school districts now set schedules which start classes no earlier than 7:45 A.M., so that their REM- and sleep-deprived students do not sleep through the first two or three class periods.

It would all be easier if we followed the Rules of Sleep.

The Rules of Sleep for Larks, Owls, and Switchers

The Rules of Sleep are not the Ten Commandments. No criminal charges will be filed if you violate them. But you might want to try them, as most of my patients tell me they work.

Sleep Rule #1: Go to bed and get up at the same time every day.
Sounds pretty elementary. We have these biological clocks inside us.
They tick off the hours and days with extraordinary precision, day after
day and year after year. These clocks precisely time all the cycles in
your life. So it makes sense to go to bed and get up at the same times,
because that's how our inner clocks work.

If only your life was so easy.

First problem: Our population does not have the same desired sleep
and wake times. Families and workplaces are a mixture of larks and
owls and switchers. Larks and owls want to sleep and wake at different
times. Yet most spouses and many family members would prefer to start
the day (if not end it) at the same times.

Next, a quarter of American workers do shift work. For shift
workers, it is generally not possible for all family members to get up and
go to bed at the same times. Of course, people can still maintain regular schedules, especially if they divide up the labor of family tasks (See
Chapter 7 on shift work).

Finally, we run into a major social advance of our technological
society: the weekend. The weekend came about because workers fought
for their rights, demanding more than Sunday as a day of rest.

Saturday is now a day without school or work for the majority of the
population. Weekends have become "pleasure" times. With sleep viewed as
an unwarranted waste that cuts into time for normal enjoyment, and since
most "adult" entertainments occur late at night, sleeping in has become the
pattern for many adults. Teenagers have followed suit, with a vengeance.

Most healthy, normal people can probably shift weekend sleep an
hour or so later without upsetting their internal clocks too much. Shifting
more than an hour is a different story. Doing so probably contributes to
the Monday morning peak fatality time.

What can be done about weekend sleeping in?

1. Realize that biological clocks do not take weekend holidays. We
   did not evolve with weekends. Our bodies let us know when
   Monday rolls around.

2. Try to minimize the damage—don't go to bed late and sleep in late every weekend day.

3. Try using melatonin on Sunday night to phase-shift yourself earlier. Three milligrams of melatonin taken 20 to 30 minutes before Sunday bedtime can prepare you to awaken at your normal hour on Monday morning (light boxes also can help).

4. During the weekend, get up at your usual weekday wake time, even if you went to bed late. But set up a time in the afternoon to take a nap of half an hour to 45 minutes. Short naps won't kill your ability to sleep at night. (More on naps later.)

Sleep Rule #2: Make your bedroom or sleeping place comfortable, quiet, and dark. If possible, make it a bit cool. Making your sleep environment dark and comfortable is not as easy as it sounds. Though most Americans do not have to contend with elevated train lines or airplanes interrupting their sleep, as do many New Yorkers, Chicagoans, and other urban dwellers, nighttimes are often noisy. The neighbors are watching reruns of television game shows, and they don't like to wear their hearing aids; your teenage daughter has fallen in love with Ozzy Osbourne; giant trucks whoosh by your door in the wee hours, unconcerned about traffic regulations and minor speed traps; the tap in the bathtub is leaking; your spouse had two glasses of wine at dinner and can't stop snoring; and your nine-year-old son gets up at 3 A.M. and plugs in his GameBoy. The reasons sleep environments are difficult are as varied as human behavior.

Before you buy earplugs, negotiate. Your neighbors may not buy you earplugs, but they might agree to turn down the volume; your teenage daughter might accept a gift of headphones; you can call the police department about trucks illegally speeding through the neighborhood; and you can take your nine-year-old on a trip to the public library. If you keep an open mind, solutions *may* be found.

If easy solutions cannot be found, consider soundproofing the room, or buying earplugs (but not until you've sent your snoring spouse over to the local sleep disorders clinic to check for sleep apnea). Earplugs are not comfortable during sleep, but some of us have no choice. The cylindrical foam plastic versions seem to work best.

You may also want to lightproof your room. Blackout drapes are not just for wartime. They can be very effective in preventing morning light from waking us too early, especially with daylight savings hours. If blackout drapes are too expensive, night masks that cover the eyes can help us sleep into the morning.

Don't underestimate the stimulating effects of morning light. A closed human eye can still appreciate light at a level of just one-third of a lux, or light unit. The room you're reading this in probably has illumination of a minimum eighty to a hundred lux, perhaps thousands of lux if you're near a window.

Comfortable bedding is a very individual matter, as anyone who sleeps with someone else can tell you. In general, westerners like firm mattresses with enough room to roam and broad enough sheets or coverings to drape two people adequately even when one is a blanket hog. However, people can and like to sleep in thousands of different conditions, varying from wooden floors to carefully spaced futons. An important rule: if in *any* doubt, consult your bed partner.

Last is the matter of temperature. A cool room is again an individual matter, but heat is a problem for many of us. Summer heat waves are famous for causing insomnia, as many of us cannot sleep when the thermometer reaches 85 degrees Fahrenheit.

Coolness is not only a matter of comfort. Cooling off a room often prompts a shift into REM sleep, which preferentially occurs at lower temperatures. If you're unable to sleep in the middle in the night, turning down the thermostat often results in a return to sleep.

Sleep Rule #3: Minimize stimulant intake. This rule is kept vague for a lot of reasons, some cultural. The average Finn imbibes nine cups of coffee per day. Whether a response to dark, arctic climates or the result of their national obsession with saunas, telling Finns to stop drinking coffee would be unrealistic.

Stimulants come in many different forms, not just coffee, tea, cola, or chocolate. Many "diet aids," herbs for athletic performance, and even many mass-produced vitamins contain mild stimulants like ginseng or stronger ones like ma huang (ephedrine). These substances will not only make us temporarily more alert but will also cause us to urinate, cutting down our internal water content. Many of us have no idea how many stimulants exist in our vitamins, herbs, or restaurant meals.

Stimulants are everywhere, but they are not necessarily bad. Tea and coffee drinking is a great pleasure to billions. What is important is to use these drugs, like all others, wisely.

If you want to sleep well, restrict stimulant use to the morning hours. A cup or two of coffee or tea at breakfast will rarely harm nighttime sleep, but is well tolerated by most of us. Later doses may not be.

Patients diagnosed as narcoleptics have seen their diagnosis disappear when they stopped drinking afternoon coffee. Mountain Dew and other highly caffeinated sodas keep up many a teenager. People with schizophrenia or manic-depressive illness may hallucinate more frequently from drinking cola throughout the day. Conversely, properly timed caffeine can keep larks up at night for desired partying. The military uses caffeine to keep pilots and special forces up and alert during nighttime and prolonged operations (to stay awake for periods longer than 24 hours, see Chapter 8).

The problem with stimulants is that they last longer than most of us believe, and they directly interfere with nighttime sleep. Though a few selected individuals go directly to sleep when drinking coffee, afternoon stimulants often continue working into the night, lightening sleep, preventing deeper phases of sleep, and awakening us regularly for brief arousals we usually don't remember.

If you think stimulants are causing you inferior sleep, try *slowly* cutting down your intake over weeks and months. Caffeine can be as addicting as many other drugs. If lowering caffeine intake improves your sleep, fine. If it does not, consider morning or evening exercise as a way of naturally remaining alert without the dangers of drug effects.

Sleep Rule #4: Give yourself enough time to sleep. What is enough is sometimes not obvious. When in doubt, first watch what happens to your sleep on vacations. If you see vacations as a great time to get more sleep, you probably need more sleep time for all those nonvacation nights. Second, give yourself an hour more sleep time for five consecutive nights, and see if you wake more rested (if you are an insomniac, you may need fewer hours in bed; see below).

Remember, everyone is different. One of my best friends sleeps 2 to 3 hours a night, and he feels awful if he takes more sleep; another cannot obtain any sense of rest without 10 hours in bed. Most of us need around 8 hours to feel rested, but experience should tell you what you need.

Special Sleep Rules for Owls

Owl Sleep Rule #1: Make regular bed times and wake times a habit. Most owls are trying to adapt to the Lark Work World. To a typical owl, starting a job at 7 A.M. may feel like beginning work at 4 A.M., the classic "hour of the wolf" when most human beings shut down and perform badly.

One way out for owls is to use morning light and exercise to get ready for morning work. But do not sleep in on weekends.

It is difficult enough for most owls to adjust to common work schedules. Breaking those day-night patterns over the weekend makes them harder to re-establish on weekdays. To adjust to daytime life, workaday owls must become regularly timed sleepers.

Owl Sleep Rule #2: Consider afternoon naps. Many owls find themselves lagging at the end of the workday. If their work ends between 3:30 and 5 P.M., many owls can take a brief nap to refresh themselves. Following the nap with exercise can prepare them for the "free" hours of the evening, when higher energy levels will eventually return.

Owls can always use light boxes to shift as needed, though shifting inner clocks can take a while.

Special Sleep Rules for Larks

Lark Sleep Rule #1: Be wary of late nights. Most people like to stay up late. Electric lights keep us up later, shifting our inner clocks towards more late-night activity.

Larks must beware, as they have a great tendency to get up at the same hour each day. As the normal work world is a lark world, larks may have more orderly biological clocks than owls. Those clocks need to be kept regular.

Larks who stay up late, whether for parties, sex, family reunions, or to watch a favorite television show or movie, often wake the next morning at their normal 5:30 or 6 A.M. time with a feeling akin to a hangover. Alcohol is not required to give us a sense of sluggishness, frustration, and torpor.

Larks can adjust by exercising heavily the morning after a late night (such exercise will help wake them up, and maintain their early sleep times), and by taking brief naps (less than thirty minutes) in the early afternoon.

Naps

For many years sleep researchers declared naps out-of-bounds. People who slept well did not need naps. People who did not sleep well should avoid naps. Night was for sleep, day was for wakefulness.

We know a little better now. Naps are now a part of many night-shift schedules. The Japanese routinely prescribe 10-minute naps during night shifts. Scandinavian researchers find that naps of up to 45 minutes in the middle of a night shift can improve alertness for the rest of the night. Executives around the world take frequent, brief "power" naps. For a sleep-deprived society like ours, short naps make sense.

Short naps, or "catnaps," are the preferred form of sleep for people who cannot sleep very long as a matter of competition or simple survival. Such a group includes long-distance single sailing contestants. Research by the group at Circadian Technologies has found that the winners of these contests, which sometimes last several weeks, sleep only 4 or 5 hours per 24. And those hours are never in a single, unified period.

Long-distance competitors are natural catnappers. Among the leaders in the contests, the longest sleep varied from about 20 to 80 minutes. Most competitors were young. The most successful would wake at regular intervals, quickly find their sailing positions, reset their equipment, then return to sleep for 10 to 20 minutes.

Similar catnap behavior has been described among soldiers in wartime and among emergency workers forced to labor through prolonged crises. Our bodies adapt by taking brief naps, naps just long enough to preserve deep sleep.

Even if you're not sailing a race across the Pacific or trying to power down a runaway nuclear reactor, you still can benefit from brief naps.

As you know from the body temperature curves shown on pages 10 and 12, we normally fall asleep when our body temperature is going down, and are most alert when it is going up. But in periods like early morning to mid-morning and the middle of the afternoon, the temperature curve is pretty flat.

Brief naps can be remarkably refreshing. But they should be brief. Though most of us like to nap for 30 to 45 minutes, shorter naps are actually more efficient.

Research by Professor Leon Lack and others shows short naps of just 10 minutes refresh people more than do 30-minute naps. The results, like many involving sleep, seem to make no sense. You're tired, you haven't slept enough. How can less sleep be better than more?

There are reasons. Long daytime naps, even of 30 or more minutes, should not normally put us into the deeper phases of sleep—deep sleep, or REM. They often do, however. This is because so many of us are profoundly sleep deprived.

Waking from deep sleep, or even stage II sleep, is not always easy. Many of us wake up feeling a bit groggy or dazed. We are not fully alert for 5 or 10 minutes or longer. This groggy, dazed feeling on waking is called sleep inertia. It is extremely important to shift workers and the military. Employees or soldiers coming out of sleep inertia are not mentally sharp. They can easily make mistakes at a time when mistakes may prove fatal.

Brief naps decrease the risk of sleep inertia. A short nap is easier to get than it seems. Just use a kitchen timer, or the alarm on a digital wristwatch. Set the alarm for 15 to 20 minutes (which should give you 5 or 10 minutes to get to sleep). If you learn to fall into a nap immediately, put the timer on for 10 to 12 minutes.

People who take routine short naps often find they are able to wake up within seconds of the alarm. Biological clocks can precisely time naps, just as they can time every other activity in our lives. With practice, you may not need an alarm.

A final reason to nap briefly is that daytime is not the preferred period for human sleep. People who sleep in the daytime, like shift workers or those with mood disorders, invariably report that their sleep is not as restful as normal nighttime sleep.

We really are meant to sleep at night. Napping more than 30 to 45 minutes in the daytime will "rob" many of us of some nighttime sleep. Long daytime naps promote poor nights.

Still, as in dieting, a little cheating goes a long way. People whose jobs allow them brief daytime naps often find them refreshing and reviving, setting them up to continue working through the daylight hours and beyond.

Insomnia

Insomnia, the feeling of having insufficient or unrestful sleep, chronically afflicts over one-fifth of Americans, and over half of people over sixty-five. Rates are even higher in France and Germany.

Insomnia is a scourge with many causes. Any individual sufferer usually has more than one reason for poor sleep. Though insufficient time for sleep plagues much of the population, this is not a problem for the majority of insomniacs. Insomniacs are more than willing to give enough time for sleep (and often take too *much* time). Insomniacs usually can't get enough sleep. But they try and try.

The more they try, the less they sleep. Many worry about sleep, worsening their insomnia. Called "psychophysiological insomnia," this condition particularly afflicts hardworking, highly stressed people who need to juggle more than one ball at once. This secondary psychophysiological insomnia seems to hit anyone who has trouble sleeping, producing a "double whammy" that makes insomnia sufferers think they are in a vicious downward spiral with no way out.

Part of the problem is that insomnia itself seems to reset brain arousal controls, the mechanisms that keep us awake and alert. Keep a normal sleeper up all night and she will easily sleep the next day. Not so for insomniacs. Keep them up through the night and they still will not sleep the next day. Or night. Brief sleep deprivation often worsens their condition.

Common causes for insomnia include depression, which is a sort of neutron bomb of sleep and disrupts most of its normal mechanisms; alcoholism, which causes a fearful number of awakenings and is itself often a secondary result of chronic insomnia; unconscious nocturnal leg kicks, jerks of the legs or arms; psychophysiological insomnia, noted above; medical conditions like diabetes and Parkinson's; standard medications like those people receive for high blood pressure; and sleeping pills. Many people have more than one of these common causes. Treating insomnia is an art. But since insomnia is such a common problem, it makes sense to provide a few pointers for self-treatment. If you have suffered from insomnia, or know someone who has, here are some lessons that just might help.

Start filling out and evaluating sleep logs. Sleep logs (see the sample in Appendix 1) are records of when you went to bed, got to sleep, and got up. If filled out very quickly and subjectively at the time you wake up, sleep logs will help you evaluate your own sleep. However, make sure *you do not look at the clock during the night* (see the section on clockwatching below). *Guess* the times you woke up and got to sleep when you record your logs in the morning. Make sure you wake up to some kind of reliable, regular alarm.

Be especially sure to have regular bedtimes and wake times.
Get up at the same time each day. Insomniacs have disrupted sleep-wake
cycles and inner body clocks. The balance between alertness and sleep,
rest and arousal, is out of whack.

One of the best ways to start taking care of insomnia is to devotedly
attempt the same bed times and wake times. Don't give yourself 8 or 9
hours for sleep, however, unless you know you'll get them. Many insomniacs cannot manage to sleep 4 or 5 hours per night, let alone 8 or 9.

For those of you who find you are sleeping far less than you want
to, spend *less* time in bed. This process, called *sleep restriction*, is an
insomnia treatment validated around the world. It works for most of my
patients who are willing to stick with it. The point is to temporarily con-
solidate sleep by spending less time in bed.

Check your sleep logs. Let's say you find you are averaging 5 hours of
sleep per night. Take a 5-hour slot you prefer and designate that as your
sleep time. Allow yourself to sleep only during this period (say 1 to 6 A.M.)

Once you have slept 85 percent or more of that 5 hours for two or
three consecutive nights, give yourself another half hour for sleep. As you
sleep better, keep moving up the amount of time you can spend in bed.

The idea is to tell your brain that beds are for sleep and sex, *not* for
lying in while awake. Lying in bed without sleep sets up behavioral expec-
tations in the brain that makes it harder for many of us to fall asleep.

Consolidating sleep into certain times is usually effective because
the sleep produced is deeper and more restful. Forcing sleep into a
restricted period pushes the brain to become efficient at sleep, preserving deep sleep and REM. The experience is something like that of
an out-of-practice musician learning to play again by consolidating basic
skills, such as playing scales.

Sleep restriction takes much discipline and more than a little time. It
is unfortunate that many insomniacs find it difficult, as it works very well.

Exercise regularly and at regular times. For those who suffer
from chronic insomnia, frequent aerobic exercise can be a godsend.
Aim to exercise 3 to 6 hours prior to your sleep time, as late exercise
may arouse non-athletes. Regular aerobic exercise makes you more fit,

which helps you sleep, increases deep sleep and sleep continuity, and makes it easier to fall asleep faster.

Many insomniacs are tired. They feel fatigued, wasted. They can't imagine walking, let alone heavy exercise. They don't understand this very old principle: physical activity defeats mental exhaustion. Exercise generally does not exhaust insomniacs further. Instead, it makes them more alert and more alive.

Of course most of us can't start a heavy exercise program immediately. Gradually increasing one's walking speed and distance should help. You can start with just ten steps a day.

Take Mona. Over the age of eighty, she hardly left her chair most days. Or slept. She usually felt like a dishrag every morning.

Mona started evening exercise by taking ten steps. Gradually, she increased one, five, or ten more steps each day. Able now to walk a half to a full mile, she sleeps well most nights.

Don't look at the clock when you're trying to sleep. More than 24-hour rhythms flow through our bodies and brains. Though 24-hour circadian rhythms are paramount in many physiological processes, we also have 30-, 60-, and 90-minute rhythms; monthly rhythms, like menstruation; seasonal rhythms, which may cause depression in winter; and short rhythms, only seconds in length.

Entraining, or bringing these rhythms into action, is what clockwatchers do. Most times people have no idea they are entraining these rhythms all by themselves. I have been told thousands of times "I just keep waking up at 4 A.M." or "I wake up every hour on the hour at the same time."

Clockwatching is the unnatural behavior that makes us want to look at the clock whenever we wake up. Resist clockwatching. Put a cloth or towel over your alarm clock. Your alarm will still chime.

Watching the clock sets up recurrent rhythms that cause many people to wake up predictably throughout the night, night after night. For many it is a major promoter of insomnia.

But I want to know what time it is, people tell me. If it's close to the time I normally wake, I might as well get out of bed.

Not so. Such thinking is the result of living and working in a machine age. We have come to view ourselves as machines for which each minute of activity is equivalent to the next. Nothing like that is true of sleep. For many, deep sleep and REM are far more restful than the majority of sleep time, which is generally stage II.

Sleep is not a monolith. Not all sleep stages rest you equally well. The sense of rest obtained from sleep does not increase in a nice straight line as your sleep time increases. The last half hour of sleep may be the most useful half hour of the night, far more restful than the two previous hours of sleep. Watch the clock, and you'll sleep a lot less than you probably should.

When getting up during the night, remember: night is for sleep. There's plenty of time to watch clocks during the day.

Take a hot bath. Baths do cost money for hot water, and they take up time. But they are a remarkably easy way for many of us to obtain comfort and rest—and sleep, because heating the body affects our temperature regulation. Remember that sleep comes most easily when the inner body temperature is dropping.

Hot baths increase our body's core temperature. Our brain and spinal cord heat up. When we go to sleep immediately following a bath, our temperature fall is deeper and more acute. Many of us respond by falling asleep more quickly, and we experience deeper and more profound sleep.

To work, a hot bath must really heat us up. You should feel sweat flowing down from your earlobes and forehead.

Don't use showers. Showers rarely accomplish the goal of increasing your body's core temperature. If you only have a shower in your home, it probably will not help you overcome insomnia or markedly improve your sleep.

Making baths part of the before-sleep ritual sets a behavioral condition for the brain. Our bodies crave rest. As we are more successful at obtaining sleep, habits that increase sleep are reinforced. Exercise and hot baths before sleep become things we look forward to.

Make a pre-sleep ritual for yourself. Most of us have pre-sleep rituals, whether we know it or not. Rituals make it easier to fall asleep.

Standing in the kitchen, we finish our night with a few spoonfuls of ice cream, because somewhere we read that nighttime carbohydrates promote sleep. Then we go to the bathroom and floss our teeth—we need to get all that sugar out of those crevices so we won't get periodontal disease. We follow up with a rapid toothbrushing, wiping our faces clean.

Then it's off to bed. We take off our clothes and put on our most comfortable pajamas. We select our clothing for the next day. Our favorite romance novel lies on the night table.

We poke under the covers and deliciously check the last page we read last night, making sure we haven't forgotten too much of the plot. Then we read for ten minutes, transporting ourselves to a wonderful world of adventure and travel. Next it's a quick peck on the bristled cheek of our husband, a muffled good-night, and a short flick of the lamp switch.

Perhaps your sleep ritual is a bit different. It still pays to have one. Cleaning, undressing, preparing the clothes or makeup for tomorrow and engaging some pleasant, relaxing pastime, like reading or listening to music, gets us ready for something we rarely experience during the day: relaxation. Calming our brains gives our biological clocks a chance to throw us into sleep at the right time.

Over weeks and months, even severe insomniacs find that sleep rituals help them fall asleep at the same times night after night. Repetitive habits calm us down, preparing us for an extraordinary night of sleep and dreams.

Read before you sleep. Americans prefer television to reading as a way to spend free time. This policy is not necessarily best for your sleep.

Particularly in the age of the remote control, television must engage us every second to maintain our attention. Television by its nature must arouse us and keep us focused on its programs. Otherwise the program (and the programmer's job) may not survive.

The goals of your television station are often antithetical to helping you sleep.

In order to sleep, biological clocks must be given the chance to work. As the temperature curve falls we should find ourselves falling into slumber, like water descending a well. This can only happen if we are not too alert and aroused.

Arousal is a physiological term, not merely a sexual one. Organisms that are aroused are alert and quick to respond, which means they are not about to go to sleep.

For commercial as well as physiological reasons, television is an alerting mechanism. The clash of colors, sounds, personalities, and the movement of light and shadow engage the oldest and most emotionally powerful parts of our brains. And what typically appears on the 11 o'clock news? Often a litany of sensational events—murders, robberies, fatal disasters. For many this is not a good way to relax yourself into sleep.

Reading is much more helpful. When choosing a book to read to help you sleep, it pays to think about what you need. Thrillers do what television tries to do. Stories of suspense attempt to arouse and intrigue us.

Each person will respond to different books in different ways. For many, poetry is a way to calm themselves before sleep; for others, it is the most powerful emotional experience of their lives. Some thrill to books about history or art. Others read books that are serious and reflective, works that give them a better understanding of the promises of life and their own place in the world.

A quick rule of thumb for sleep-cravers: before sleep, try to read a book you should have read in high school but didn't. The book may be a great eighteenth-century novel, a history of England, the biography of a politician, or a great scientific text. Very often such a book is a classic, brilliant in style, but distant in time and culture from our immediate lives.

Reading a good book requires no defense. But reading books that tell us great stories, involve us in other lives, and bring us to places we have never been can relax us and calm us. Reading at night should not be only about entertainment. It should also help us relax. Sleep and dreams will take us from there.

Watch out for sleeping pills. It sounds strange that sleeping pills are a frequent cause of insomnia. But it's true.

Sleeping pills, whether prescription or nonprescription, can be wonderful to help us sleep if used temporarily. However, no sleeping pill is designed to be used for more than a few weeks at a time.

Pills that aid sleep, especially the long-acting medications like Dalmane and Valium, and their very similar shorter-acting cousins like Ambien and Sonata, have a fatal flaw. After a time, they usually don't work. They don't put us to sleep.

However, with regular use the potential for addiction grows. Over time, sleeping pills become insufficient but *necessary* for sleep. We can only sleep if we use them. Many governments have tried to ban sleeping pills, especially for people over sixty-five. The FDA some years ago tried to have sleeping pills given out only ten at a time, a proposal finally defeated by the pharmaceutical industry.

Sleeping pills have their place. Often they are used to decrease anxiety and daily stress. But if taken continuously, their biological sleep effects slowly lose their punch.

Researchers in Detroit did an interesting experiment years ago. They gave a group of long-term sleeping-pill users the chance to take blue or white pills. The group had taken sleeping pills every night for an average of ten years.

One of the pills was the sleeping pill they had always taken; the different-colored pill was a placebo. The group continued to take their sleeping pills. But they took equal amounts of each pill.

The message was clear: the brain needed some pill to sleep. It did not matter, however, whether that pill was a placebo or the real thing.

The pattern of "pill-sleep, pill-sleep" is a common one in the United States. Five percent of Americans use alcohol, a poor choice, as a knockout drop. This behavior is conditioned over time, repeated over and over.

Most prescription sleeping pills are not innocuous. Many of their deadening effects last well into the day. Sleeping pills sedate people and slow their reflexes while dulling their brains and washing out their memories. The classic sleeping pills like Dalmane and Librium are particularly noted for worsening memory.

Sleeping pills also make us think we are more physically adept than we are. Like alcohol, they give people the illusion that they are performing better at driving and other hand-eye coordination tasks than is actually true. The results are more accidents, more trauma, and more deaths.

Sleeping pills can be wonderful. But if sleeping pills become a permanent need, their best use is no use at all.

SUMMARY

- Most of the population is partially sleep deprived, especially teenagers and young adults, helping cause problems with alertness, work, and weight.
- Sleep is controlled by our biological clocks. When body core temperature is going down, we sleep. When it is going up, we are more alert.
- Larks and owls can manipulate body temperature using exercise and passive body heating (hot baths).
- The most effective single technique for overcoming insomnia is to have regular times of going to bed and waking.
- The most important and restful parts of sleep are probably deep sleep and REM sleep. Biological clocks can be used to maximize both.

Chapter Three

Eat the Right Foods at the Right Time

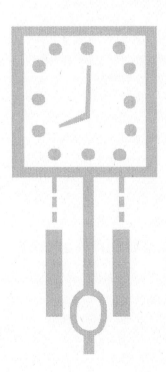

Diets, weight loss, and nutrition drive my friends and patients crazy. Even medical professionals who know better dive straight into every new diet fad. In a society where at least a fifth of the population is obese, even very slender people want to get thinner. The forty-billion-dollar diet industry has a great opportunity to make money.

Making money is what they do best. Ninety-five to ninety-eight percent of people ultimately fail to lose weight, and the few who lose weight don't necessarily become any healthier.

In fact, diets don't work.

In this chapter, I will explain why there is so much confusion about diet and nutrition. The field is filled with cant, deception, hucksterism, and outright lies. What you really need to do to get to your ideal weight is to learn how your body works—how it actually evolved, and what kind of nutrition it needs to operate most efficiently for your purposes. Unfortunately, despite its vital importance, what we understand about weight and human nutrition is appallingly little.

I will also show how using your biological clocks can make you fitter, healthier, and leaner, as well as more relaxed about what you eat.

The Diet Industry's Dirty Secret

The reason why most diets do not work is no surprise to biologists. It's all because of human genetics.

Because every human being is unique, diet and weight adjustment are very difficult to study. Here are some of the reasons:

- Our genetic makeup varies.
- Our pattern of parenting differs.

- Our social environment shifts from person to person, changing year by year.
- What we eat changes most days
- Different people eat different foods in different amounts.
- Exercise patterns differ from day to day.
- How we metabolize fat differs.

Furthermore, virtually every food you eat is made up of thousands of different chemicals (there are about ten thousand different substances identified in tobacco alone). Those components are not just fat, protein, and carbohydrates, but include many other chemicals that affect nutrition, such as vitamins, food additives, and carcinogens.

What you just ate and what you are about to eat (for example, having a tuna-fish sandwich followed by coffee, versus the same sandwich after a glass of milk) changes how you metabolize your food. And, because every meal represents hundreds of different chemicals, each will be processed differently depending on what you ate and when; how much you walk or move before and after you eat; your sex; your age; the time of day . . .

As you can see, studying diet is very difficult—though not impossible. To do it correctly involves enormous effort and a great deal of time. This partly explains why so little is accurately known about diet and nutrition. It also tells us why short-term studies by the diet industry report such wonderful results, and why so many of us who try these diets end up feeling distressed, convinced that we are dismal failures.

Performing accurate studies of diets often involves locking up people in hospitals for weeks or months at a time, where they are fed the same or similar meals day after day. The amount and timing of their exercise, sleep, and movement must be controlled.

Would you participate in a study like that?

Many diet studies are instead performed using epidemiology. Epidemiology looks at the rate of occurrences of specific events in large populations. Human studies inevitably involve thousands of variables, like weight, height, age, and sex. However, by studying many people in similar environments over a long period of time, scientists hope much of the variability will "wash out." Then useful conclusions can be drawn.

Even with epidemiological studies there remains the problem of human uniqueness. Each one of us is a separate genetic construct. Each one of us has our own individual biology—with unique responses to food, exercise, social engagement, and light (except, perhaps, for identical twins).

The Danish Twin Adoption Study

Europe, especially Scandinavia, was a logical place to do long-term genetic studies. In many European countries birth registries go back hundreds of years. Populations stay put. The same families may live in the same village for as far back as anyone can find accurate records, sometimes three hundred or four hundred years. People are more willing to undergo scientific surveys. Most don't demand the incredible bulk of legal paperwork that bedevils American researchers. In the 1950s, researchers in the United States and Denmark decided to do the legwork required to study populations and follow them over decades. The population they decided to track was composed of identical twins.

The genius of the Danish Twin Adoption Study was to look at identical twins who did not grow up together. The study looked at identical twins who were adopted out. These twins were biologically identical but had grown up in different families, studied in different schools, and lived under different physical, family, and social environments.

By looking at identical twins who were adopted by different families, researchers could study individuals who were genetically identical but otherwise different. Different parents, different foods, different lives—but the exact same genes.

The Danish Twin Adoption Study was created to address the thorny question of whether schizophrenia was genetically caused. The answer turned out to be yes, a hopeful result for the many millions of mothers and fathers who had been falsely told that their "inadequate, incomplete" parenting caused their children's illness. Prevention and care of the disease became easier.

One of the researchers working on the project was Albert (Mickey) Stunkard, a professor at the University of Pennsylvania Medical School. Stunkard wanted to study obesity, and he knew that the Danish Twin Adoption Study was a wonderful way to do it. He continued to follow his study subjects over many years. Finally, after looking at twins who had been tracked from birth into their twenties and thirties, he published his major findings in the New England Journal of Medicine.

The studies looked at statistical variance; that is, how much of the weight difference between fat and thin people is *not* explained by chance. What Stunkard found was that about 70 to 80 percent of the statistical variance in the twins' weight was apparently due to genes.

Human studies rarely find such powerful genetic results. Most "major" variables like cholesterol explain 5 or 10 or 20 percent of the statistical variance of a medical condition. In the Danish Twin Adoption Study, twin pairs with totally different diets and environments had virtually the same weights. Often the weights were uncannily similar.

When it comes to weight, genes are powerful. Most of us will never look like bone-thin media models unless we are literally starved.

Please do not despair. Genetics does not determine all our weight. More importantly, genetics does not determine what we look like. How we appear is powerfully affected by how we live, move, and eat, just like our ancestors' appearance was determined. How our ancestors evolved has a lot to do with how we look and feel today.

Your Hunter-Gatherer Body Goes to the Supermarket

Humans in versions resembling our present form have lived on earth for perhaps two million years. For more than 99 percent of that time our ancestors lived as hunter-gatherers. Our ancestors lived by hunting and foraging for food. Organized agriculture is a creation of our recent past.

Despite the rapid technological progress of the past two and a half centuries, hunter-gatherer groups still exist. Some live probably very much as they have for tens or hundreds of thousands of years. Peoples like the Kalahari Bushmen and the Australian Aborigines are very actively studied by scientists. We have a pretty good idea of how they live.

Hunter-gatherers spend a lot of their time gathering food. Normally there is division of labor, with hunting exclusively performed by men while much of the calories are gathered by women. People in hunter-gatherer tribes are physically active 7 or more hours a day. They subsist primarily on roots and tubers and other foraged plant products. They tend to spend a lot of time working together. Their diet contains a great deal of roughage, fibrous foods that are difficult to digest and require a lot of energy to metabolize and use. They usually have a hard time finding sources of important nutrients. Hunter-gatherer societies often go to great lengths to find and ingest foods with lots of salt, sugar, and fat.

Just like us.

Throughout our evolution, salt, sugar, and fat were probably hard to obtain, especially in pure form. Even the lucky hunters among the Bushmen and Aboriginals do not return carrying gazelles or antelopes packed with fatty, marbled meat. Meat from the desert would not interest most American consumers. The fat content of such meat on the hoof approximates zero. That's one reason why you find broken-up bones in the archeological sites of early man. Bone marrow was rich in difficult-to-obtain fat.

Fat, sugar, and salt were difficult to get but extremely important. Fat, often in the form of cholesterol, constitutes the lining of cells. The lining of cells, or cell membranes, is where many of our most important biological transactions occur. Much-maligned cholesterol is necessary for production of testosterone and estrogen. It is critical for communication between cells.

Glucose, a six-carbon sugar, is also critically important. Our brains and red blood cells run entirely on glucose. Brain and red blood cells cannot utilize fat for energy unless we are starved for days. Salt is equally necessary for life. The integrity of every cell in the body depends on it. Yet for most of our evolution, these essential nutrients were difficult to obtain. Often food of any kind was hard to obtain.

Because food was scarce throughout much of human history, we are extraordinarily good at maintaining our weight. In conditions of perceived starvation, our bodies have the capacity to scarf up every calorie and retain it. If they had lacked that capacity to retain calories, our ancestors would not have survived. Indeed, many—probably most—did not. This human ability to keep our weight stable helped to preserve us as a species, but it plays great havoc with most diet programs. It explains:

1. Why people who quickly lose weight often gain it back very quickly.
2. Why people whose weights "yo-yo" up and down often find it harder to lose weight with each weight dip and surge.
3. Why so many diets ultimately will not work. Many diets produce rapid weight loss. Such rapid weight loss convinces the brain that the body is in starvation mode that must be corrected by preserving every bit of nutrition that it can.

Weight gain almost invariably is a lot faster than weight loss. Worse, much of the weight that is lost by dieting and diet aids is not muscle mass or flesh. It's water.

Five-sixths of the human body is water. Control of water and salt is critical to our physiology. Even little changes in salt and mineral content can prove fatal. Salt and water metabolism is so important it is controlled by many different hormones and neurotransmitters in the brain and other organs. The system of checks and balances controlling salt and water is complicated, multiply controlled, and huge.

However, control of that water supply can be tricked by using diuretics, substances that cause our kidneys or gastrointestinal tracts to excrete water. Such substances include alcohol, caffeine, drugs like hydrochlorothiazide, and many of the herbs used in "diet aids." There is so much water in our intestines that weight loss can rapidly occur merely by getting rid of gut fluid. Many diet aids work that way.

These aids won't work for long, however.

Think about it. Your body, evolved in hunter-gatherer times, is made to survive famine and starvation. If it thinks it's about to starve, it will keep every calorie it ingests. Through millions of years of experience, it especially craves salt, sugar, and fat. Your body will seek to appease that craving with the intensity of a heroin addict looking for a fix.

Now imagine—your hunter-gatherer body walks into a supermarket.

Your body has been built for scarcity and famine. Grocers know what it craves. And they want to sell it to you. They want to keep selling it to you as long as you live.

Walking into a supermarket provides more food and nutritional abundance than your hunter-gatherer brain can normally process. The variety, the richness, and the forms are all overwhelming. From the standpoint of your hunter-gatherer physiology, they are also unimaginable.

Grocers and restaurateurs want you to enjoy yourself, and they want to make money. They make the most money by selling you foods that contain large and subtly varied combinations of salt, sugar, and fat, combinations that make your brain crave them more.

How much salt do you really need each day? Old studies proclaimed you only need 70 to 90 milliequivalents of salt per day. The usual American daily ingestion is 4,000 milliequivalents. Our standard foods are now so laden with salt it is difficult to ingest less than 1,000 milliequivalents a day.

Your body, built for nutritional scarcity, is daily assaulted by superabundance. The wonder is not that so many of us are obese, but how few.

One reason we are not hopelessly obese is that many of us are physically active. We burn off the calories by walking, strolling, bending, biking, climbing stairs, and fidgeting. Another reason is that we have a set point, a metabolic point in the brain that declares "Enough!" and maintains our weight at a certain level. That set point perhaps explains why identical twins, no matter where or how they are raised, have such similar weights.

To better understand what goes on in our bodies, why some of us are fat or thin, it pays to know a little about digestion.

What Your Body Does to Food

It's 6:30 in the morning. You bite down on your soy bar, hoping 90 seconds of munching will provide all the nutrients you need to avoid eating a real breakfast.

Crunched and gnashed, the scattered remnants of your soy bar are immediately attacked as they move across your tongue and the back of your throat. Enzymes rip into the carbohydrate parts of your meal. A series of quick gulps, and the frothing pieces descend with wormlike motions into your stomach, already filling up with acid provoked by just thinking of this glorious treat.

Other enzymes begin working, continuing to disintegrate your soy bar. So do stomach bacteria, which when they get out of hand produce the stomach ulcers that come with shift work and the everyday stresses of modern life.

Your soy bars sits in the stomach, sifting about in the acid bath, slowly digesting. A wonderful interplay of hormones, neurotransmitters, nerve discharges, and rolling muscle motions pass the silty mixture into your small intestine.

Now things get interesting. Already your food is partly separated physically and chemically. The 22 grams of soy protein have been liquefied. They are ready to be further macerated by a series of special enzymes secreted into your gut by the pancreas, a small organ slung under your liver.

The pancreas pops out digestive enzymes like an overworked chemical factory. The fats are picked up by agglomerations of salts and acids pumped from your gallbladder, which uses the dead matter of red blood cells and all sorts of ghastly things to create greasy green fat-catching molecules. These greasebag containers increase the working surface area for gut enzymes to chew through your fats.

Simultaneously, complex carbohydrates are being chemically crunched into nice, usable sized six-carbon glucose, the stuff that powers brain and red cells. The food additives, colorings, and petroleum-based gels that make your soy bar almost tasty (and allow it to stay on store shelves for years) flux in the same liquid mix, hoping they too will be ingested and put to some purpose. The whole batch then gets absorbed by the cells lining the gut. From there it is rapidly sucked into the bloodstream.

You might think these nutrients are then pumped by the heart to all the organs in the body, providing fuel, structural supports, and information molecules to keep our lives going. A logical prediction, but wrong.

Instead almost everything in the intestinal tract goes directly to the liver, which rapidly gets to work on it. After this "first pass" through the liver, most of what was ingested gets thrown right back into the gut.

The extraordinary process of all that semi-digested food going from gut to liver to gut is very important to your weight and health. The liver is the chemical factory of the body. It turns your soy bar into everything from wrapped up multichain glucose to the cholesterol lining your cells and the hormones, steroids, and large proteins that carry nutrients and drugs.

A very important part of the system is the glucose meters in the liver and pancreas, regulating whether there's enough or too much glucose, your body's main fuel, in your blood. The pancreas does more than secrete a stunning variety of digestive enzymes. Inside the pancreas are strange little clusters of cells called islets of Langerhans. There aren't many clumps of these cells, but they are important, because islets of Langerhans cells produce insulin.

The Insulin Hypothesis and Sugar

A consensus has been building over the last decade that insulin is a crucial factor in determining our shape and weight. Insulin is a hormone, a kind of special key that allows glucose to go from the bloodstream into our cells. Many cells can't live without the energy provided by glucose. Special sensors in liver and pancreas quickly calculate how much glucose is present in the blood.

If the liver and pancreas watch lots of glucose go by, insulin production is very rapid. If they see glucose dribble by, insulin production is slow and gradual. If you don't want to get fat, you want to make the flow of insulin slow and gradual, not fast.

Insulin turns out to do more than regulate how much glucose gets into cells. Some forms of insulin act like growth factors, the chemicals that make us produce more cells and tissue, and also make us bigger and bigger. And fatter. Cholesterol levels go up, too.

Many diabetics have learned the sad lesson: insulin makes you fat. Insulin production is powerfully affected by the speed and amount of glucose flowing through pancreatic blood.

To give you an idea of what happens, consider two different meals. First is what human evolution might consider the perfect food—ice cream. Ice cream is loaded with sugar, salt, and fat. The sugar is rapidly absorbed by the gut. The sugar-enriched blood then flashes by the liver and pancreas. The islets of Langerhans cells sense the high glucose content. Quickly they go to work.

It's not inaccurate to think of insulin production as something like a factory assembly line. The sugar from the ice-cream cone quickly flows by. The islets of Langerhans sense the huge increase in blood glucose. They respond by making insulin as fast as they can.

Pumping all that insulin into the bloodstream does much more than lower blood glucose. It sends word to the body that there are lots of nutrients out there. In fact there are so many nutrients it's time to convert some of it into fat, which is what happens to about 30 percent of the sugar you ingest.

Converting sugar into fat is not necessarily a good thing. A lot of quickly ingested sugar means more future fat. High sugar ingestion also stresses insulin-producing machinery. Many nutritionists believe in the insulin resistance hypothesis. They worry about the frequent, overpowering stresses caused by ingesting large amounts of sugars or starchy foods. Insulin production gears up, then wears down. So does the average cell's responsiveness to insulin. You end up needing more insulin to get the same amount of glucose into cells—insulin resistance. The end product is the epidemic of diabetes and obesity we see in America today.

Now consider meal number two, a snack of roasted soybeans. Soybeans will digest very differently from ice cream. Composed of soy protein and big carbohydrate and fat molecules, your soybean snack contains far less glucose than your ice-cream cone. Soybeans hold their nutrition in tightly held proteins and carbohydrate polymers. To digest them takes the gut much time and a lot of energy.

The big difference is that your soybean snack does not stress insulin production nearly as much as your ice-cream cone. Glucose flowing past the pancreatic sensors does not leap into the red zone. As your soybean snack is digested by your gut, blood glucose increases at a more even, steady clip. The pancreas has plenty of time to produce enough insulin.

Nutritionists write a lot about the glucose-increasing effects of different foods. They place a number on this tendency of foods to increase blood glucose, calling it the *glycemic index*. The standard for the glycemic index is 100, what you would get from table sugar. Interestingly, that's not the highest number. For example, a tofu-based frozen dessert has a considerably higher glycemic index, about 115. Protein and fats score zero on the glycemic index, since they do not contain glucose. Adding in the average density of food produces an even more useful measure, the glycemic load.

If you do not want to get fat, it helps to know the glycemic load of different foods. Low glycemic-load foods tend to not stress insulin production. They take time and energy to digest. Except for protein-filled foods like fish, lower glycemic-load foods often provide lots of fiber, letting your food pass through your system in a quick and timely manner.

We evolved eating high-roughage foods. We would do well to eat a lot of them. Increasing your bean, fruit, and vegetable intake may prevent hemorrhoids, diverticuli, gallstones, and possibly decrease colon cancer rates. Most of us need lots of high-fiber, low glycemic-load foods. They are the kinds of foods our bodies used throughout our evolution.

Now that your food has passed back into the small intestine, all sorts of nutrients like vitamins and minerals are quickly absorbed. In the colon the rest of your nutrients are ingested, as well as most of the remaining fluid provided by diet.

Remember: unless you are eating freeze-dried astronaut meals, most of your food, like you, is water. Diet-supplement makers cunningly use this fact. They add "proprietary" substances into their foods and diet aids, substances that quickly pass that water out of your gut. The weight loss they provide is temporary and illusory. It's not the kind you need.

Real Weight Loss

Barbara was thirty-six years old, and she had been depressed for two years. Antidepressants improved her mood, but they caused her considerable weight gain. One morning she happily told me she had she had lost eighteen pounds in the last two weeks.

How?

Diet supplements.

Having lost the weight, she decided to keep it off by severely restricting how much food she ate. She stopped the supplements at the same time. Within three weeks she gained back all her weight.

I explained to her how she could eat in a circadian fashion, following our body clock's 24-hour rhythms. Eating her largest meals at breakfast and lunch, and walking one to two miles a day, she lost the weight she had gained and kept it off.

The more you know about your body, the easier it is to take care of it. We did not evolve with ice cream and cupcakes. We did evolve ingesting complex roots and grass seeds, nuts, tubers, fruits, and stringy, not very fatty meat. Our bodies are not configured to take on the average American meal. Most of us pay for it.

Fortunately we have other options.

Different Diets: What Might Work for You

Low fat, low protein? High protein, high fat? High protein, low carbo-hydrate?

Any and all combinations of nutrients have been recommended by doctors and nutritionists over the last thirty years. All have been touted as potential "cures" for our society's weight problem. Sometimes the most popular diets are based on theoretical principles precisely opposite to one another. For a lot of people, including my patients and friends, it appears that the media diet gurus usually provide contradictory advice.

There are many reasons for our national diet confusion. Here are a few:

1. A lot of weight is related to genetics. Much of the weight loss obtained by these diets is from water and has little to do with decreasing body fat mass.
2. We don't know a lot about nutrition. What works in the short term may be a disaster in the long term. Long-term studies of different diets are rarely undertaken. Unless done carefully, such studies are difficult to interpret. Importantly, no one knows what high-protein diets do to us over many years.
3. People differ genetically in thousands of ways no one understands. A diet that works for your sister may cause you to gain weight, and vice versa.
4. Much of what controls weight is related to our exercise level. We did not evolve to sit all day in chairs, glued to desks and television monitors.
5. How we process food changes with exercise, age, gender, and our overall level of stress.
6. People have paid little attention to biological clocks and have not recognized that when you eat is often as significant as what.

Many diets obtain greater or lesser popularity over time. Ten to twenty years ago, the most popular diets were low fat, moderate to low protein, and low carbohydrate.

Popularized in varying forms by figures like Nathan Pritikin and Dean Ornish, these diets were studied intensively in cardiac patients. Most of these patients suffered from blockages in the coronary arteries that supply the heart. Heart disease was very much America's major cause of death. De-clogging coronary arteries with diet appeared a heaven-sent solution for a massive public health problem. Expensive, well-designed studies showed moderation or decreases in the narrowing of coronary arteries with strict low-fat diets. Millions of Americans leaped onto the dietary bandwagon of low fat.

Doctors terrified patients with measurements of their cholesterol, an important but far from overwhelming factor in our risk of heart disease. (There are at least 700 risk factors for heart disease in the scientific literature. The biggest cardiac risk factor is family history, so choose your parents wisely.)

Cholesterol came from fat, so fat became the enemy. Decrease your fat intake, decrease your fat grams, and get your dietary calories to 10 percent or less of total calories, people were told. Cut fat from your diet and you may live.

The U.S. Department of Agriculture promoted starch-based meals. Food merchandisers outdid themselves with declarations of "low fat" attached to every possible nutritional package, from factory-rolled turkey to defatted cottage cheese. Elders and adults, women and men, even growing children were exhorted to eat less fat.

The end result: the country got fatter and fatter.

Like most everyone on the planet, Americans try to find simple solutions to complex problems. They were told that all you had to do was stay away from fat and everything would be fine. No cardiac disease. You could prepare for a long, healthy life.

Instead of fat, people ate more carbohydrates, often much more. Suddenly there was no guilt attached to "fat-free" cookies or cakes. We could eat what we wanted and still lose weight.

Low-fat diets didn't work. The result was a national public health disaster. The population is fatter than ever.

Now the winds have shifted again. Americans became fatter eating lots of carbohydrates. Soon carbohydrates became the enemy. Don't eat bread, the headlines proclaimed, stay away from "white foods." Bust sugar and blast polysaccharides!

Many of my patients have joined this newer bandwagon, particularly the Atkins diet. Like many diets, the Atkins has not been objectively studied in large populations over time. Despite terrifying nutritionists with its relatively high animal-fat content, the Atkins diet is not entirely crazy, and often lowers weight—at least for a while.

The Atkins diet has evolved over the years. No longer does it appear like the Notre Dame football diet of the 1920s—steak for breakfast, steak for lunch, steak for dinner. Meat is still something you should eat, but vegetables are in, as long as certain hated carbohydrates are kept at bay. Lots of people find they lose weight, though most I know cannot stick very long with this high-protein diet.

Another diet plan that has many supporters is the Zone. The Zone accepts the insulin hypothesis as its centerpiece. It argues that the way to keep insulin production down is to make every meal 40 percent protein, 30 percent carbohydrate, and 30 percent fat. Every meal. I have found a lot of people who like the Zone, though most cannot live by zone bars alone.

Both the Zone and Atkins diets take insulin production very seriously. Both offer high-protein diets with lots of fat, and both place considerable restrictions on what people can and cannot eat.

These restrictions are sometimes a mistake, but it is the nature of most diet programs to go overboard. People like to think that some foods are good and others bad. They want the endless confusion of diet choices to be replaced with a single, simple plan. Many feel that if a diet is too complicated, they won't be able to follow it.

Do we know what high-protein diets do to us over time? Unfortunately, no. There are concerns that kidney function may worsen, leading to kidney failure, or that osteoporosis may increase. We really don't know what the Atkins, Zone, and other high-protein diets do to us over many years. Even if high-protein diets do result in weight loss, there is not yet sufficient evidence that weight loss is sustained. More important, there is not yet substantive evidence that health is enhanced.

Most of the long-term data we have comes from epidemiology. Epidemiologists have tirelessly gathered evidence from large populations in many different countries. These results sometimes assume that culture, work, and psychology are not large factors in weight control. They also may assume that genetic variations among populations ultimately wash out. Such assumptions may not be correct, yet epidemiological evidence points in useful directions.

A consistent result of scientific investigation is that the "Mediterranean Diet" is the choice of several healthy, long-lived populations. People in places like Crete and southern Italy suffer from fewer instances of heart disease than much of Europe, despite eating considerable amounts of fat and a fair amount of pasta.

Proponents of Mediterranean diets argue that what type of fat you eat does matter. They're probably right.

All Fats Are Not Equal

Fats are necessary molecules. We cannot live without them. Just like vitamins and essential amino acids, essential fatty acids are components that must appear in our diet. Or we die.

Fats, like carbohydrates, come in many shapes and sizes. It appears that saturated fats and trans fats, fats that have certain kinds of chemical bonds holding them together, may help cause heart disease and some cancers. Saturated fats are usually found in red meat and many animal products. Trans fats are artificially created in processed foods. They allow cakes to look "nice and moist," and they help keep baked goods tasty and chewy for months at a time.

Many epidemiologists, like Dr. Walter Willett at the Harvard School of Public Health, believe that trans fats and saturated fats are international culprits and should be avoided. They are however, partial to plant-based fats other than those from coconut and palm oil. Data on fats from foods like walnuts and canola oil have percolated in the scientific literature for years. There is considerable evidence that increasing these substances in your diet leads to less heart disease.

Fish are another popular food source among epidemiologists. Fish are usually high in protein, avoiding the "carbohydrate problem" posed by the insulin hypothesis. Fish also contain lots of interesting oils that are thought useful in preventing heart disease, cancer, even treating manic-depressive illness.

The present consensus is that nuts and most plant oils are supposedly healthy, and that fish oils are perhaps particularly healthy. The rest of one's diet is supposed to contain large amounts of whole foods without the added salt, sugar, fat, and chemical additives of processed foods. (Look at the items you eat at the supermarket. Virtually everything that is packaged or wrapped has some salt added to it.) Last, we are advised to ingest frequent, large helpings of vegetables and fruits.

Does this advice make sense? For the moment, yes. But perhaps not for you.

There is still a great deal of data that needs to be collected before there is any accepted belief about which diet makes sense for our population. And what makes sense for a national population may not make good sense for you. Just as drugs have very different effects in different individuals, so do foods.

Luckily for us, much of the real business of weight loss and health lies beyond what we eat.

Dieting Is Not About Diets

The general American pattern of dieting is to go too far. Take any idea, make it extreme, and sell it to the public. We have shifted from low fat/high carbohydrate, to high protein/low carbohydrate, to high protein/moderate fat/moderate carbohydrate. Just as with any fashion, soon we will see different variations on these themes. Various foods will become either heroes or villains, increasingly valued or strongly attacked.

We have gone too far again. Too much attention is paid to diet fads.

We have truly gone overboard by paying so little attention to activity.

Most diets don't work. People give them up for one of several thousand reasons. They don't like the food groups, they're bored with eating vegetables, they can't stand seeing another steak, the supplements cost too much, my son hates the way I now cook, etc. Frustration and anger are obtained, but rarely sustained weight loss, *unless you exercise.*

A consistent finding of studies is that an hour's worth of exercise every day is crucial if people are to maintain weight loss. The real trick of dieting is not in the diet. It's in getting the dieter to move. Otherwise lost weight will return.

When I tell people they should move their bodies an hour a day the reaction varies. Most often it is irritation or anger, sometimes bemusement. An hour a day? people say, staring at me with dismay. Impossible. I don't have an hour a day in my schedule. How could you possibly expect me to find an hour a day for exercise? And what about the time getting back and forth to the gym? For showering and applying makeup? What about when my kids come home? How will I spend any time with them?

Most of us are used to living a sedentary life. Trained from childhood through classrooms and movie theaters, buses and television sets, we have come to believe that sitting in place is the natural state of humankind.

That belief is wrong. Our bodies are meant to move. Hunter-gatherer societies average 7 or more hours of activity per day. Lying down is a campfire activity, not our normal, natural state.

The truth is we have our facts backwards. We should be moving, not sitting during the day. An hour out of each 24 represents barely minimal activity for the bodies that we have evolved.

Where some people make a mistake is their assumption that this hour must be rigidly spent in continuous, breathless aerobic activity. That an hour's worth of exercise somehow requires gyms and high-tech sports equipment, or painfully enduring marathon running and biking. This is not the case. Our bodies are trained to move, yes, but they are not meant to move particularly fast, nor necessarily for a long, sustained effort.

Movement does not usually mean desperate, frenzied aerobic sports, though certainly the pleasures and benefits of such maximal activities are multiple and healthful. Movement may just mean walking.

Human beings are built to walk. If we are allowed to wear comfortable footgear, most of us can walk long distances, though not particularly quickly. Against lions and cheetahs, even jackals, we don't have a chance. Fortunately, outrunning predators is not a problem of present-day life.

Moving an hour a day means walking, not running, an hour *total* during the day. It includes our morning stroll from bedroom to kitchen, our brisk sprint from the office garage to our workplace, even pushing the cart through the supermarket.

The problem with these activities is that most engage us all too briefly. To move a full hour a day requires that we become a little creative. It means parking the car far away from the office entrance and walking up the stairs two or three flights to our office. It means getting up in the morning to enjoy the morning air, watching the sun rise over the landscape, enjoying the power of light that sets our clocks and brightens our mood. It means getting out with the whole family, putting the youngest kids in a stroller and letting the nine- and ten-year-olds keep up on their bicycles.

Moving an hour a day means recognizing that is how our bodies are made, that strolling, walking, marching, and strutting are part of what makes us human, part of what makes us feel healthily alive. It demands reconfiguring our views of what we are. We should see ourselves as active participants in our environment, people whose bodies are defined by their graceful motions rather than by how they look in an office chair. Once people recognize that their bodies are meant to move, they find myriad ways to do it. And they enjoy moving. They particularly like physical activity when it is social. We can walk, bike, or run in groups.

The Right Foods

Vegetables or fruits? Animal or plant products? Soy protein or skim milk?

All or none of the above?

These are the wrong questions.

People make a major distinction between food and drugs. Foods are supposed to be substances we eat for nutrition, to deliver the energy sources and structural components we need to live. Drugs are expensive medicines prescribed by high-priced doctors. They appear inside little hard-to-open plastic bottles grudgingly doled out after long waits at the pharmacy. Drugs cause extreme and often dangerous side effects even when they do what they're supposed to do.

Many foods have medicinal properties. Tea, coffee, and cola drinks are used liberally by many of us as drugs, to stimulate us and keep us alert. But foods as varied as blueberries and turkey breast have pharmacological properties, changing our immune function and our awareness, shifting attitudes and moods.

It makes more sense to look on food and drugs as similar. Both food and drugs are ingestible chemicals. All such ingested substances can affect our health and welfare.

Foods should be regarded for what they are really are, substances that can change our body shapes, emotions, and chances of avoiding cancer or heart disease. Foods are also powerful engines of pleasure. If we regard foods with the seriousness with which we view drugs, we can then begin to consider our own personal diet. Are we eating a particular diet for our health? To keep us awake? To make us lose weight? To build up our muscular bulk? To help us sleep?

Most of us would like foods to do several things at once.

It's apparent then that any diet is about much more than weight. Food helps make us healthy or ill. What we eat, how we eat, and when we eat affects our bodies, our minds, our moods, and our views of who we are.

Keeping in mind how we evolved, it makes sense to recognize that throughout human development, sources of nutrition were multiple. Nutritional diversity is a good principle. One of the many problems with popular diets is that they heavily restrict what we are supposed to have— don't eat this; cook lots and lots of that.

Variety is more than the spice of life. Food diversity keeps us healthy.

Human agricultural activity is remarkably inventive. In our supermarkets we have a great array of foods to choose from, foods that can help us in many ways. Trying different foods, increasing the sources from which we obtain nourishment, is also a good idea—and a difficult one. Most people are bred to a particular diet and set of food groups. Many of us prefer meat and potatoes, pasta and salads. Every day at lunch or dinner many of us dine on the same or very similar meals.

Just as there are many different cultures, there are many different cuisines. The world is filled with extraordinary varieties of grains and vegetables, fruits and fowl, fish and dairy products.

Certainly some food groups seem to produce unhappy results. Trans fats and saturated fats are probably negative factors for health and longevity, but mainly if they provide a large and consistent part of our food intake. When it comes to different foods, everything has its place. We have evolved to crave sugar, salt, and fat, and all three are all still required for our survival. Eating these "forbidden substances" in moderation, and through a wide combination of foods, is the healthy response.

The next time you sit down to a cereal breakfast, think of combining several grains. Put the oats together with the bran and rye. Add soy milk to the skim milk you pour into the bowl. Eat lunch salads made of many different vegetables and fruits. Try walnuts and Brazil nuts, cashews and peanuts. Until we learn a lot more about combinatorial nutrition, it pays to hedge our bets. It makes sense to put together many different foods, in very different ways.

Three thousand years ago the Chinese learned that combining different cereals could prevent major vitamin and protein deficiencies. Now we know that eating different cereals together allows us to pick up all the essential amino acids. Essential amino acids are building blocks of protein we must obtain from our food. We cannot make them ourselves, as we do with most of the substances used in our cells.

We have come a long way in three thousand years. Now we have the means to eat thousands of different foods. We need not restrict ourselves. Just as diversity is useful in healthful ecology, diversity is helpful in what we eat.

Brain Food and Calming Food?

It is important to recognize that food and drugs overlap in their effects. That does not mean we know what most of those effects are.

Many claims are now made for certain foods. Some are supposed to improve brain function, while others are said to calm us or help us sleep. There are arguments that foods high in the amino acid tyrosine help keep us alert, while carbohydrates, particularly starches, make us sleepy and calm.

There is some merit to such positions. Tryptophan, found in turkey meat, does help some people sleep. Unfortunately, however, most studies of food and alertness are at a very early stage. They often do not take into account the differential effects of combined foods, the effects of time of day, age and sex, relative fitness and physical activity, and cultural experience.

People differ widely. For many, a high-protein breakfast is a weak energizer. Milk (containing tryptophan) and cookies at night mildly sedates some of us.

What about you? For you, a high-protein fish breakfast may be ideal. For someone else, it may be unpleasant or unpalatable. Psychology is strongly involved in our food choices. We are taught from birth what is tasty and what is not. This is one reason why changing diets is so difficult for us. Just as we are used to living a sedentary life, we are used to certain foods—and certain times for eating these foods.

Changes can't be made overnight. Changing one's diet and exercise habits may be a product of months and years of steady, gradual effort. Similarly, the healthful results of diet and exercise changes often are slow to appear.

Nonetheless, few of us will try any diet or exercise regimen unless we understand why. One of the things to know is how biological clocks affect food.

Circadian Nutrition: The Importance of Breakfast

Periodic, temporary starvation is our normal way of life. With the exception of patients being fed intravenously and people who snack while sleepwalking, very few of us eat while we sleep. Nor do most of us eat during the two hours prior to sleep, nor in the middle of the night.

Primed by our biological clocks, our bodies prepare for morning. Sleep does not take as much energy per hour as do waking activities. But sleep's energy "saving" is small. The theory that we sleep to save energy is feeble. Sleeping 8 hours rather than staying awake saves us at most 200 calories. The energy saving is the equivalent of a small hot dog. Sleep had better do a lot more for us than save a couple of hundred calories. Fortunately it does. In fact, *not* sleeping enough may be a cause of obesity.

Since we do not eat during sleep, we draw down our energy sources. Much of the energy in the body is supplied in the form of glucose. The liver has a store of multichain glucose that allows us to keep functioning through the night. This multichain glucose polymer, called glycogen, is usually about 50 grams' worth. That's enough to produce 200 calories of energy. The brain and red blood cells use only glucose for energy under all but extreme conditions.

As we sleep our glycogen stores are drawn down, bit by slow bit. By 5 or 6 A.M. they have mostly disappeared. With that energy store gone, where can you turn to keep yourself going?

The answer is an odd one: your muscles. The liver starts taking up protein, often from skeletal muscle. Laboriously and expensively it converts muscle protein into glucose. Turning muscle into sugar is not an easy task.

Each morning before we wake, our body is digesting itself to create enough fuel. By the time breakfast rolls around, ideally in the first hour or two after waking, we are literally starving. We are digesting our muscles, and must search for new energy sources to power us for an active day.

Morning is almost always a time of relative starvation. Weight and fluid control become very important. The set point in the brain that controls weight recognizes a need to preserve fat stores. All energy sources must be preserved to tackle the fuel requirements of the waking day. Breakfast is critical to providing enough energy for us to work and move. By the time we eat breakfast, many of us have gone twelve to fourteen hours without any food.

So when breakfast time rolls around, we *really* need food. We are starved, we are digesting our muscles, and our bodies need a lot of fuel. What do people do?

Eat a doughnut or a tiny bowl of cereals packed with salt, sugar, saturated and trans fats, and petroleum-based additives. Untold millions of us eat nothing at all. To the extent anything is eaten, breakfast is usually the smallest meal of the day.

Is this nutritionally crazy? Absolutely. If the insulin hypothesis has any validity, we are in starvation mode *every* morning. Our brain will try to keep every calorie we've got. Eating little or no breakfast gives the brain the message that starvation is continuing while fuel need increases. The brain responds by making sure fuel stores are protected, and no calorie will be given up without a struggle.

Not eating breakfast is probably a great way to *gain* weight.

More galling, metabolism is highly efficient in the morning. Part of the reason is that we produce more insulin in our bodies during the morning than at any other time. The increased insulin floating through our bloodstream moves glucose into our cells. More important, our insulin sensitivity is highest, making what we eat quickly and efficiently metabolized.

The time to eat is in the morning. What we eat in the morning we mostly use up. We don't put it into fat stores as readily as we do at night. If you want to lose weight, your biological clocks tell you eat in the morning, not at night.

The average American eats her biggest meal at dinner, when insulin sensitivity is low and insulin resistance is high. When it is hardest to satisfy our craving for food. When food is inefficiently metabolized, and is more preferentially used for fat stores.

Most of us eat in a manner precisely the opposite of how we should. Eating large meals at night will not keep us fast and lean.

Don't blame agricultural progress for putting us into this mess. Farm families traditionally eat huge breakfasts. They know the large fuel demands required by physical work.

Our strange nutritional behavior is more likely the result of industrial society and our odd sleep, wake, and work habits. Americans often rush around like crazy in the morning. We wake from shortened, sleep-deprived nights and zoom off to school and jobs. There just isn't time for breakfast, people tell me. All I can manage is a Danish or a doughnut—and that's if I'm lucky. Coffee is the only necessity, required so chronic sleep deprivation can be overcome long enough to get to work on time.

What do you think that morning coffee with sugar does to *your* insulin production? What if the insulin hypothesis is true?

Another crazy result of our bizarre morning meal patterns is that many people believe skipping breakfast helps them lose weight. They think that starving themselves for sixteen to eighteen hours out of each twenty-four is somehow virtuous. Skipping breakfast allows them to keep their calorie count down. After all, they are "only" eating one or two meals a day. Many of my patients are often dismayed that "eating so little" does not cause them weight loss. Instead, breakfast haters often gain weight.

They don't understand how biological clocks work. They don't understand that breakfast is the most necessary meal of the day, the one meal that should not be skipped. They don't understand that metabolism peaks in the morning for larks and in the early afternoon for many owls, and that the food they eat in the morning will be much more efficiently disposed of and used than the food they eat at night. Emphasizing the evening meal, as most North Americans and Europeans do, is exactly what you need to do to gain weight and store fat.

Scientific study of biological clocks and nutrition is only about twenty years old, but popular knowledge of how to eat has existed for centuries. An old adage is correct.

Breakfast like a king; lunch like a prince; Sup like a pauper.

Naturally enough, most of us do the opposite. A nation filled with crazed, unhappy dieters is one result.

Breakfast for Breakfast Haters

Hundreds of patients have told me they hate breakfast. I'm not hungry when I wake, they say. I can't stand food in the morning. The whole idea of eating at dawn is nauseating. I only want to eat when I'm hungry, and I don't feel hungry until lunch. Isn't it natural that I should only eat when I'm hungry?

No, it's not natural. Just as we have trained ourselves to believe that the hours of the clocks on the wall are all equal, that our biologically clocked bodies can be made to work without regard to night or day like cars or telephones, so we have trained ourselves to a ruinous schedule of eating. Unfortunately, any doctor can tell you that changing the habits of a lifetime does not occur overnight.

Humans are not machines. To make any diet work, you have to know how to cheat.

Americans and Europeans are not going to go out and eat huge breakfasts because doctors and nutritionists say they should. Many work and school schedules make it difficult or nearly impossible to take time to prepare or even eat breakfast. When breakfast does occur it is often a solitary occupation, with children munching multicolored, overrefined cereals while their harried parents try to find lunch boxes and errant jackets, occasionally twisting over to the coffeepot to gulp down a slug of "instant" mudwater whose main nutritional ingredient is a medicinal dose of caffeine.

The main place I now witness the civilized, large breakfast of the past, where the entire family gathers to dine on a large, healthy conglomeration of protein, fat, and carbohydrate, is in old movies on cable television networks. These days not eating breakfast is a sign of modernity. It demonstrates the power of work over our lives, even a measure of self-importance: I have far more significant things to do than eat breakfast.

Perhaps you do. But you will do them more efficiently, more easily, and with far less anxiety if you eat *something* for breakfast.

One solution to the problem is to find a technological fix. Most breakfast haters are not going to microwave a batch of oatmeal, let alone cook it on the stove. They will eat, if they will eat any morning meal at all, only if food ingestion time approximates that of injection by syringe.

Industry has responded. Just as there is instant coffee, there are instant meals. Most of these are based on only three materials: eggs, milk, and soy.

Eggs receive a bad rap these days. Quick to fix, cheap, abundant in protein, eggs contain sufficient amounts of cholesterol and fat to gag some physicians and clinical epidemiologists. However, in an age of anticholesterol drugs and anorexic teenagers, eggs are an excellent food, especially for children. Eating an egg or two each day often will not increase your cardiovascular risk.

Nevertheless, in a country where people compete over lowering their cholesterol, eggs will not become the breakfast choice for breakfast haters. Egg whites, lacking most cholesterol, have a better chance. Egg whites can also be prepared very quickly.

Some of the breakfast haters I see have grown used to egg whites. They like the idea of eating something solid which is also high in protein. Most will even eat egg whites with a glass of orange juice and toast, demonstrating a willingness to spend at least four minutes on breakfast preparation and eating time.

Milk products, often as part of "instant breakfasts," are also frequently used quick breakfast meals. Most of these "instant" products add water to a dehydrated milk mix to which some vitamins and minerals have been chemically applied.

In most cases, people would be just as well off and need less preparation time taking a multivitamin pill and downing it with a halfpint of skim milk. Eight ounces of skim milk contains 9 grams of protein, about twelve grams of sugar, and 90 calories total. A glass of skim milk is not a "hearty" breakfast. Yet it is enough to stave off hunger and help prevent the body from breaking down muscle protein for fuel.

A better choice than skim milk may be low-fat soy milk. Low-fat soy milks do contain fat, but it is primarily the polyunsaturated and monounsaturated fats that may help prevent heart disease. Soy milks contain no cholesterol, and have 4 or 5 grams of protein. Often they are vitamin fortified. They also provide a little bit of dietary fiber.

Let me divulge the experience of one of my patients, an executive who has detested breakfast all his life. Thinking about eating a morning egg made his skin crawl.

Skim milk was something he was willing to consider. His wife normally bought two gallons a week for herself and their children. Habituated to whole milk as a child, George felt skim milk tasted like "chalk sludge."

I persevered. After a couple of weeks, a cup of skim milk struck George as possessing the taste and consistency of "liquid straw." He returned to his breakfastless existence.

Next we tried soy milk. He liked the fact that it was sweeter than skim milk, though "it doesn't taste like anything I remember." After about ten days, he also gave it up.

Our next move was to breakfast bars. He tried five brands before he finally settled on a soy-based confection created to taste like carrot cake. "It's not anything like carrot cake," he told me, "but at least it has *some* taste." He liked the fact that the bars came in many different sizes, affording him the chance to eat "twenty-two grams of protein in less than ninety seconds" and still listen, if not speak, on the cell phone dangling from his ear.

Over the following months George became interested in walking each morning. Exercise fortified his appetite. Soon he felt the need for a more substantial breakfast. Fortunately, he was now used to soy. Having received a blender as a Christmas present, he decided to experiment. First he tried low-fat soy milk mixed with nonfat or low-fat yogurt. Enjoying the energy it gave him, he continued for several months eating breakfasts that alternated soy milk "smoothies" with soy bars.

These days he generally blends 8 or more ounces of soy milk and yogurt with large helpings of multiple fruits. To make his morning preparation easier, he blends his breakfast at night, puts the large glass in the refrigerator, and downs it quickly on awakening in the morning.

If you are a breakfast hater, you can try any of these combined ingredients.

- Egg whites
- Skim milk
- Soy milk
- Protein bars (soy bars)
- Yogurt (active cultures, please)
- Soy milk smoothies, made of soy milk plus anything else you like and can put in a blender. Bananas, apples, pears, oranges, and grapefruit work, as do smaller fruits like blueberries or figs—but watch out for pits.

If you get used to a little breakfast, someday you might become interested in a real breakfast, the kind that can keep you healthy and promote weight loss.

Circadian Nutrition: Some Useful Principles

Circadian nutrition works for a lot of people. Among its principles:

1. Not very much is known about diet, but it pays to use what is known.
2. Metabolism is more efficient in the morning for larks and early afternoon for owls, and pretty slow at night for both.
3. Humans need protein, fats, and carbohydrates to survive, and we appear to do best when eating a large variety of foods.
4. Diets based on plant sources appear to be healthiest for avoiding heart disease and cancer.
5. We evolved eating lots of whole, fibrous foods. Fiber and plant cell walls smooth out insulin rises and speed food through the digestive system, perhaps decreasing cancer risk.
6. The real basis of diet control is total energy balance. Ingested calories have to be balanced by energy expenditure. Exercise is as important as what you eat. If you want to keep off weight, you have to move. Walking is the easiest way to keep moving at pretty much any age.

7. The recent diets that are the most popular are relatively high in protein. Their long-term effects on health are unknown.

8. Most Americans eat in a fashion that is opposite to circadian principles: large dinners, often heavily laden with protein; quick, sandwich-based lunches; small, carbohydrate-based breakfasts.

What to Eat—and When

Most people are not going to shift their eating habits overnight. Here are samples of what has worked for many patients of mine.

Breakfast

Though some national medical organizations recommend diets that are 50 percent carbohydrate, 30 percent fat, and 20 percent protein, try to eat a relatively large amount of protein at breakfast. Also try to eat a large part of your total daily food intake.

Breakfasts should be hearty but balanced. The typical American breakfast, a bowl of processed cereal, has much of its protein component made up of the milk you're supposed to add to the cereal. Try to make your breakfast relatively protein rich through:

- Soy milk or soy products. Soy bars can be used for those who must eat very quickly. Soy smoothies take more time, but can add a nearly limitless variety of nutrients to your meal in the form of fruits, yogurt, nuts, and grains.
- Skim milk or nonfat/low-fat yogurt. Some people have problems with dairy products. Milk, however, is an abundant and cheap source of protein and sugar, particularly when added to cereals. Milk also contains some essential amino acids. Yogurt has the additional element of active bacterial cultures that can often aid digestion, and perhaps it helps with bone formation.
- Eggs or egg whites can be used more liberally than the campaigns against cholesterol would make you believe.

- Other sources of protein, particularly nuts like walnuts, Brazil nuts, and cashews, have their place. They are expensive but easy to eat, and can be added to virtually any breakfast meal, especially cereals.
- Try to at least imagine adding fish to your breakfast. Though not popular in the United States, fish is a routine breakfast food in much of Europe and Asia.

Next we need a source of carbohydrates and fat. An ideal choice is whole grains.

Whole grains possess many advantages over processed cereals. They contain less pure sugar and provide much more fiber. Whole grains cause far lower peak insulin production. They are also far cheaper than processed supermarket cereals.

The main problem people have with whole grains is palatability. We have been trained to enjoy meals with lots and lots of sugar, as well as added fat. Whole grains often contain quite a lot of useful fats, particularly polyunsaturated and monounsaturated fats. But for our tastebuds, it is hard to compete with the pure sugar of most processed cereals.

This need not be a problem for you. Two relatively easy solutions can be tried:

1. **Mix cereals.** There is no religious dogma proclaiming that only one cereal can be eaten at breakfast. Mixed cereals have been a staple of Asian diets for thousands of years. Mixed cereals provide a far more diverse mix of vitamins and minerals. They also have more taste.

   Experimentation helps. Some people mix oatmeal and bran, often adding rye or granola mixes from health-food stores. Combining many different cereals is nutritionally more advantageous and more delicious.
2. **Mix your milks.** There is no law proclaiming that soy milk cannot be mixed with skim milk. Almond and rice milk can also be used.

For younger children, where saturated fat content is less of a problem, adding 1 percent, 2 percent, or whole milk can be tried.

Mixing different milk types adds different sorts of sugars beyond the galactose and lactose found in cow's milk. Adding varied milks to mixed cereals provides more protein. Mixing milk forms also provides a more balanced meal, and very often a far tastier one.

For people on the Zone diet, adding soy and skim milks to cereals may not provide sufficient protein. Other sources, like protein bars, eggs, or small pieces of fish, may top off a meal.

Finally, after having this hearty breakfast it pays to walk or exercise. It is worthwhile to exercise before or after *every* meal. Exercise is the key to energy-balanced nutrition.

Coupling eating with exercise, before or after a meal, is very helpful in increasing metabolism and promoting alertness. The old saws we were taught in school declared we should not exercise following a meal. They are wrong. You can walk after a meal. Coupling exercise and eating in the minds of your children may go a long way in preventing cardiac disease and cancer in their future. Start early.

The same principles also work for elderly parents, particularly elderly women with osteoporosis. They need to walk to prevent bone loss and future fractures.

Larks have fewer problems with morning exercise surrounding mealtimes, but owls may benefit more. Morning exercise makes owls more lark-like. It can help many owls to adjust to the conditions of day jobs in our Lark Work World.

One of my owl patients hated the very idea of breakfast until he began walking in the morning. He felt he had no choice. Without a morning walk he could not shift his body clock to get himself to work at 9 A.M.

Once he started to walk he discovered that exercise built up his appetite. Following his morning walk, breakfast became more and more of a possible, and then a reasonable, idea. Eating a quick, high-protein soy and oatmeal breakfast, he normally gets to work on time and feels far more alert.

Lunch

Most Americans cannot train themselves to make breakfast the biggest meal of the day. Many can adapt, however, to eating larger lunches.

Lunch is an ideal time to have a large meal. For meat eaters, lunch is the time to really enjoy yourselves. Combining meat or fish with large helpings of vegetables may help maintain alertness as well as potentially keep off weight.

There is the further benefit of lower cost. Many Americans eat out. Though restaurants must emphasize salt, sugar, and fat to stay in business, restaurant lunches are often less expensive than dinners. They are also meals in which large helpings of vegetables may be indulged.

Following lunch with a walk is a good idea. For those who have post-meal dips in energy, taking a walk can prevent mid-afternoon wooziness and fatigue.

For owls whose peak afternoon fatigue comes toward the end of the work day, finding a few minutes in the late afternoon to walk inside or outside your workplace can make the rest of the work day far easier to complete—and enjoy.

Lunches may contain:

- **Lots of protein.** Fish and legumes and fish oils are preferable to red meat.
- **Lots of vegetables and fruits.** Pulses—items like beans, lentils, and peas—are ideal sources of food for lunch. The proteins they provide rival or better those obtained from meats and fish. Pulses also contain large amounts of fiber, which does not provoke the high insulin surges that come with starches and sugars. These insulin surges may also help create those post-meal dips in energy and alertness. Vegetable oils, particularly carolon and flaxseed oil, are also useful.
- **Lots of water.** Most people do not drink enough water during the day to promote digestion and "flush out" the gut and kidneys. Several glasses of water, drunk periodically throughout the

day, can help people with gastrointestinal tract problems. Staying fully hydrated also helps to keep us alert and sharp.

Dinner

Dinners are usually the pièce de résistance, the culinary specialty of the day. At dinner people feel they finally have time to relax, meet with their families, and enjoy the taste of their food.

Enjoying your meal is important to successful dinners. Superb tastes, however, need not require large helpings. Dinners are times to unwind, to take the time to eat, to enjoy a varied, multicourse repast. Make them select and make them small.

As a family sits down to dinner, small food portions combining varied tastes and sensations should make dining more memorable. So will conversation. Meals are best when they're social affairs. In our culture, dinners provide an opportunity for families and friends to meet and take time together.

A few rules may help you enjoy your dinners:

1. If you love starches and sugars, dinners are your meal. All reasonable diets employ "cheating." For those who are forbidden "white foods," carbohydrates at dinner *may* make you more relaxed. They may also help you get a good night's sleep.

2. Use meat and fish as aids to taste, not main courses. Ideally, the majority of your daily protein calories have been ingested at breakfast and lunch. Dinner is a time to use protein sources as condiments. Small slices of meat added to pasta and vegetables make for a completely different meal—usually a healthier and less expensive one—than does a 16-ounce steak.

3. Dinner is a time for dessert. In the early evening, larks are as alert as they ever get. Owls are beginning to overcome their late afternoon dips in sharpness. If you love sugary, salty things, the time to indulge them is at the dinner table—but in moderation.

Once again, exercise after or before a meal is something you should do. Evening exercise, particularly a walk with the family or friends, is a good way of continuing dinner conversation. It may also aid digestion and even help you fall asleep at bedtime. Exercise 3 to 6 hours prior to going to bed appears optimal in helping many people have restful, continuous nighttime sleep.

Eating the circadian way is difficult for many. We're not used to big breakfasts. We don't normally combine all sorts of different foods, and we don't mentally put together eating with exercise. But if these steps are taken one at a time, even a half a step at a time, they often become habit.

The reason they become habitual is because people feel healthier. They lose weight and keep it off. Knowing how our biological clocks work, how we eat and digest food, can make your body your friend, never your enemy.

What to Do in Restaurants

Many people spend months following a particular diet. They count calories and exercise as if preparing for a personal Olympics. Then they stroll into restaurants and forget every piece of nutritional advice they ever heard.

Restaurants are refuges. You go to a restaurant to escape kitchens, nosy neighbors, and dreary television programs. To dine out is to enter a sanctuary.

Restaurants like to encourage these fantasies. When possible, restaurateurs try every way to distract and entertain. When I ask patients about their favorite restaurants, they describe gilded armchairs and rococo plastered ceilings, linen whiter than the snows of Kilimanjaro. They proceed to describe service fit for an empress, queen, or princess, all accompanied by meats that melt while still on their fork, hors d'oeuvres of visual splendor and exquisite delicacy, and pastries and cakes that transport them to heaven.

Virtually no one mentions the nutritional quality of this grand restaurant meal. The few who do are usually health professionals, with a disproportionate number of them graduates from our endangered schools of public health.

Why is it that when people enter a restaurant they act as if their diet and exercise program no longer matters? Because the experience is meant to be theater. However, please don't lose yourself completely in the role.

Restaurants, whether vegetarian or carnivore, English, Egyptian, French, or Chinese, urban or rural, survive by catering to our finicky taste buds. Those taste buds have evolved to desire sugar, salt, and fat in extraordinary quantities. Restaurants cater to our desires and try to satisfy them to the full. That's why customers come back.

There is little point in blaming chefs and restaurateurs for culinary habits that ignore or deride what little we know about nutrition. They want to make a profit, as do most businesses. And what they especially desire is to give people a sense of ease, the promise of happiness.

To survive restaurant fare, particularly on the regular basis required by many businesspeople, is not impossible. It requires a new way of addressing the owners and chefs of restaurants—as partners rather than servants.

Many people enjoy the personal aspects of restaurant dining. Almost anyone who has waited tables for more than two hours can tell you about patrons who adore demonstrating their lordly power on wait staff. There is also a servile cast in many diners. We pick up the menu. Then we choose. We do not ask how the food is prepared. We don't ask about the specific ingredients, nor the way they are cooked. To enjoy the fantasy, most of us don't want to know.

People with food allergies, especially those allergic to items like peanuts, are not so compliant. They have to know what's in the food and how it is cooked. Otherwise they will become sick.

They ask.

Many of the people I talk to consider it rude to ask waiters and chefs what the food materials are, how the restaurant obtains them, and how it prepares them. Such questions are considered rude, probing, impolite. Personally I do not see why clients cannot ask restaurant workers about their fare. You are not accusing them of dirty dishes or vermin in the pantry. You just want to know what you are eating. In many ways it is no different from asking a pharmacist what is in a drug and what it is likely to do. Foods are ingested substances that often contain drugs (alcohol from wine and beer, caffeine); allergenic substances that can kill (peanuts, blue cheese, mushrooms); and other nutritional components that powerfully affect your health.

Most of the time a few questions about ingredients will tell you more than you want to know about saturated fat and salt content. Trying to understand what you are fed demonstrates an interest in dining that many food workers greet with surprising relief. Many enjoy talking to educated consumers. If the waiters don't know the answers to your questions, they usually can find out.

There's an even easier method than asking what is in the food you're being served: simply tell the people in the restaurant what you want to eat.

Many folks I treat are scared silly to tell chefs what they really desire. They feel they will be ripped off, that the chefs will be annoyed when asked to prepare something different from their routine.

Rest easy. Many chefs like the opportunity to preparing something to a patron's designation and taste. Quite a few chefs I've treated grow bored preparing the same foods and sauces day in and day out. They like variety. They also come to appreciate that their customers are consumed by interests of health as well as taste.

Health and taste are not in any way incompatible. Many of the "finest," which usually means fanciest and most expensive restaurants, have changed. Today they cater to a health-conscious clientele. They use plant oils rather than animal ones. They steam vegetables to perfection. They prepare fish and meat with only the subtlest and lightest of sauces and spices.

Going out to eat does not have to waste your pocketbook and your waistline. Asserting yourself with restaurant personnel can make it possible to be fed well and healthily. It makes it possible to regard required business lunches and dinners as neither a fantasyland where health no longer matters nor an ongoing nutritional disaster. Constant dining out for work need not provoke weightiness and heartburn, nor increase your fears of an early grave.

The next time you eat out, ask the waiter a few questions about what you plan to eat. If you want to have more vegetables or grain products, ask for them. Explain how you would like them prepared. If wait staff becomes defensive, explain you are asking for the information under medical advice. If they act haughty and derisive, consider dining somewhere else the next time you eat out.

You have a right to know what is going inside your body. By asserting yourself, you assert your right to a healthy life. The people who ask about food in restaurants also ask questions at home. They pay more attention to what their bodies really need, and when they need it.

Sleep Your Way to Weight Loss?

Like most weight-loss claims, it sounds too good to be true. This time, however, it may not be.

No one is sure why we sleep. Hundreds of reasons for the existence of sleep have been advanced.

Now it appears that at least one purpose of sleep is insulin and nutritional regulation. Studies by Dr. Eve Van Cauter at the University of Chicago and by other researchers are opening little windows into what the great mystery of sleep does to our body's energy use.

Americans today are sleeping about 2 hours less per day than they did 100 years ago. This great and unheralded biological experiment has produced a new national budget deficit—the great American sleep debt.

Working with the standard American laboratory subject, healthy male university students (though females are finally getting some attention), these studies demonstrate that partial sleep deprivation is not good for you. Partial sleep deprivation is here defined as sleeping 2 hours a night less than one's "ideal." Most of the time the ideal is said to be 8 hours a night.

Such an ideal is only a fantasy for the majority of American high school seniors and undergraduates. To them, 8 hours is a long weekend sleep. The average undergraduate is now crawling up from the mattress after 5 to 6 total hours of rest per night. In the first years of university, it's often less.

So when Van Cauter and others studied the physiology of the young men they allowed to sleep 8 hours, 6 hours, or 4 hours for several nights, they were actually looking at how undergraduates normally sleep. The results were surprising.

A few nights of 6 hours' sleep pushed the young men into insulin resistance. Greater amounts of insulin production were required for them to get glucose into their cells. More insulin means more insulin growth-factor effects and greater placement of nutrients into fat stores. Brief partial sleep deprivation caused these young men to temporarily appear physiologically like diabetics and obese people.

Such studies are difficult to do reliably. They require strict control over movement, diet, timing, sleep amounts, and light exposure. That's why most studies of this type last only a few days or weeks. These studies need to be redone with longer periods of partial sleep deprivation. Because so many undergraduates are already depriving themselves of sleep for years and years, epidemiological studies may provide some answers.

Do these results help explain why we have so many more diabetics and obese people with each passing year? Probably.

My experience with "full sleep" as an antidote to weight gain is limited. However, several patients of mine told me they had a much easier time taking off weight once they got sufficient sleep. Some of them were insomniacs. On average, they claimed to get only 3 to 4 hours of sleep per night. They were successfully treated with standard, nondrug treatments to obtain more sleep. Others utilized exercise in the evening as a way to help them sleep. All said they lost weight more easily when they consistently got 7 to 8 hours of sleep.

Sleeping your full complement, which varies from person to person but is usually 8 hours or more, is something most of us no longer have "time for." Yet there are many benefits to getting enough rest. Avoiding diabetes and obesity may just be the beginning of what sleep does for our health.

SUMMARY

- Much of weight is genetically determined (as seen in the Danish Twin Adoption Studies).
- An hour a day spent walking or moving appears to keep weight gain at bay.
- Plant-based diets seem to make the most sense for overall health and fitness.
- When you eat may be as important as what you eat. A substantial breakfast may be crucial to weight control. Morning is the time when food is most efficiently metabolized.
- The evening meal should be the smallest meal. Metabolism is most efficient in the early to mid-morning for larks, late morning to early afternoon for owls.
- Getting a full night's rest may be necessary for many people who want to lose weight.

Chapter Four

Living Longer

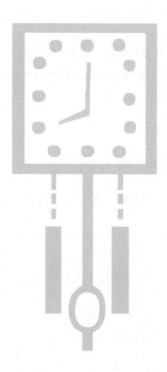

Asked what his goal is in life, Woody Allen responded "immortality." People are hard to satisfy. We not only want to look young, we want to live forever.

We won't. Even with science-fiction-quality preventive health and medicines, aging is a part of all life on earth. In 1990 a well-known aging researcher predicted the average human life span would peak around age eighty-five. So many illnesses occur before this age, including half the population suffering from Alzheimer's disease, that eighty-five looked like a reasonable final point for human life.

Japanese women have already reached that level. Progress has been made on many fronts in keeping people alive and healthy longer. Knowing about biological clocks, effects of socialization and caloric restriction, plus keeping our lives smoothly regular may help us last a long time.

How Long Could We Go?

If we were able to arrest aging to the lowest level we presently have, how long would we live?

In the United States the population with the lowest mortality rate is young girls from the ages of ten to twelve. If a group could maintain such a low mortality rate permanently, some of them would live about 1,500 years.

It's not about to happen soon. People age. We break down. Aging researcher Gordon Stoltzner talks about the "Automobile Theory of Aging." Our parts wear out. The leading causes of death are cardiovascular disease and cancer. If somehow we could last longer, other, presently rare diseases would probably kill us.

But perhaps not immediately. More than 1.6 percent of Americans born before 1897 became centenarians, lasting till age 100 or longer. The numbers look much better for those of us born more recently.

Genetics plays a major role in aging. Many centenarians have sisters and brothers who are centenarians. But aging is also affected by exercise, obesity, diet, stress level, social support, medical care, your sense of humor, and being born female. In 1997, there were 3.2 women aged 100 or more for every male.

With partial decoding of the human genome and the growth of proteinomics, the science of how proteins fold, move, and work, there is great hope that genetic treatments will dramatically extend human life spans. If genetic engineering follows other technologies, such recent hype will fade. Major technological additions to human life span will probably not occur anytime soon.

Though promising technologies often do not *immediately* deliver, they may succeed admirably over time. The full impact of electricity, telephones, cars, and trains took decades. Even with our speeded-up version of life, the same will probably prove true of present leaps in genetics, nanotechnology, and neurobiology. Great advances take a while.

And we must not expect that the diseases of today will be the killers of tomorrow. In 1900, accidents killed five times as many Americans as they do now. Infectious diseases killed twice as many people as does heart disease today. Most health improvements took place (and still take place in most of the world) as a result of changes in sanitation and nutrition, *not* advances in medical care.

There still is a lot that you can do. A life span of a century is no longer a fantasy for many of us. There are things you can do now to improve health and longevity. They may give you enough time to become beneficiaries of the major technological progress trumpeted so often in magazines and television.

Lessons from the U.S. and Other Countries

Life spans have been rising. In 1949 the average American could expect to live 58.9 years. By 1997, white females could expect to live 79.8 years, white men 74.3; black women averaged 74.7 years, black men 67.3 years.

Americans are of course not the longest-lived people in the world. Figures in Japan for 1998 were 84 years for women, and 77.2 for men.

Japanese differ from Americans in many ways. While heart disease is easily the leading cause of death in the United States, cancer deaths in Japanese men equals the total for strokes and heart disease combined.

Smoking is probably part of the reason cancer deaths are so high, as Japanese men smoke ferociously. But genetics is probably not the only reason the Japanese live so long.

Japanese society is homogeneous and organized. By American standards, Japanese social structure is rigid. Yet there is a sense of belonging in Japan that Americans rarely experience. The sense of "yamato-e" or "Japanness" experienced by the Japanese is difficult for Americans to understand. In the 1980s, when it was thought that Japan was quickly building the world's largest economy, Americans wrote with fear and envy about "Japan, Inc." Japan looked better organized, more cohesive, and better planned than anything we could muster. Japan appeared unbeatable. Despite what has long been a lackluster economy, Japanese life spans continue to increase. Part of the reason may be social support.

Looking just at measurable elements in social support, Lisa Berkman and S. Leonard Syme studied young and middle-aged women and men in California. Those with the greatest number of social connections had mortality rates one-third of those with fewer connections.

Friends count. Feeling that you belong counts. Involvement in social organizations, even without much emotional attachment, counts. All these factors can help you live longer and healthier.

Americans wistfully recall a different era of greater community spirit and involvement during World War II. Social connectedness still differs much from region to region.

In 1996, the United States as a whole had an age-adjusted death rate of 492 per 100,000. In other words, about one in two hundred people die each year. Rates in Utah and Minnesota were much lower, 406 and 413 per thousand. Rates in Utah might reflect Mormon practices of not drinking as much tea, coffee, or alcohol. Minnesota has many people whose ancestors were long-living Scandinavians. But higher rates of social connection may have something to do with why death rates in these two states are nearly 20 percent less than for the nation as a whole.

Social disintegration certainly leads to increased death rates. Since the end of the Soviet Union, the average Russian male is living on average five years less than before the breakup. Economic conditions have been harsh, but people have not starved. Alcohol and hopelessness are much more important factors in the Russian public health tragedy, a country which has lost, it's hoped for only a temporary period, much of its social cohesion and hope for the future.

It is not possible for you to go out and make ten new friends tonight. But paying attention to social connections, meeting people, talking to and enjoying people both at work and play, is important. Social connectedness pays large dividends in physical and mental health. Exercising socially is a particularly good way to promote your health.

Differences Between Men and Women

The twentieth century saw more improvement in women's longevity than in men's. In 1900 there were 1.3 women living to age 100 for every man. By 1950 the ratio had risen to 2.4. Now the ratio is 3.2.

Why do women live longer? Many explanations have been offered. Anthropologist Ashley Montagu wrote about the "natural superiority of women." He had a good case. Yet women in developing countries, like India, tend to have life expectancies similar to those of men.

Lifestyle probably has much to do with it. American women do not drink as much as men. They smoke far less tobacco. Their rate of death from accidents is half that of males.

Despite much higher rates of depression, probably twice as high as that of men, women commit suicide only one-quarter as often. Their rate of suffering homicide is one-fifth that of men.

Do women have lower stress levels? There is little support for such an idea. So many women are now in the workplace that occupation can no longer be viewed as a major factor killing American men more rapidly than women.

Some of the difference in male versus female longevity may lie in exposure to health care. Women visit doctors two or three times as often as men. Many of these visits occur in younger age groups, as women regularly visit their doctors for obstetrical care.

Unlike some other parts of medicine, much of obstetrical care is preventive. Obstetricians are on the lookout during pregnancy for obesity, diabetes, hypertension, high lipid levels, and the use of tobacco and alcohol. Much of pregnancy care is public health screening and advice, like avoiding tobacco and alcohol while carrying a baby. Women may be educated to consider and protect their health far better than men, particularly at younger ages when lifestyle changes count.

If you want to live longer, choose your parents wisely. And try to live your next life as a woman.

Weight and Aging

Most Americans, even thin ones, want to lose weight. Throughout our media and culture, Americans are exhorted to lose weight, rather than given the saner message of trying to get fit (see Chapter 3). From the standpoint of living longer, does it really make sense to always become leaner?

The answer is no. But first you have to know how to calculate adjusted weight.

Adjusted weight is usually studied scientifically through the term "body mass index" or BMI. If you have a calculator, figuring out your body mass index is not hard.

The difficulties in calculating BMI appear mostly for Americans, because BMI is calculated in the metric system used almost everywhere except the United States.

Here's what you do: write down your height in inches (5 feet is 60 inches, 6 feet is 72 inches, etc.). Now divide that figure by 39.37, the number of inches in a meter. This number, probably between 1.5 and 2, is your height in meters.

Now take your weight in pounds and divide it by 2.2. (There are 2.2 pounds in a kilogram.)

Body mass index equals:

Weight in kilograms divided by *height* in meters *squared*.

Let's say your weight is 145 pounds. That's 65.9 kilograms. You're 5' 3" (63 inches), which works out to 1.6 meters.

1.6 times itself is 2.56.

The BMI is 65.9 divided by 2.56

Your body mass index is 25.7.

(You could instead determine your BMI with a calculator found at the Web at *www.nhlbisupport.com/bmi/bmicalc.htm*; it's sponsored by the National Heart, Lung, and Blood Institute.)

According to the National Heart, Lung and Blood Institute, you're in a little bit, but not much trouble. For women, the lowest mortality statistics occur with BMIs of 19 to 24.9. For men, the range 20.5 to 27.9 has the lowest death rates. The so-called "average" 5' 9", 170-pound male has a BMI of 25.1.

Neither extreme is good. Men and women with a body mass index above 30 are likely to die earlier than they should. But extreme thinness may not be healthy either. People with very low BMIs tend to die early. Though that number includes people who are medically ill, it also includes most of the nation's female models, many of whom have BMIs of 17 or less.

However, overall leanness may be helpful. When autopsies are done on people older than 100, lots of cancer and sclerotic arteries are commonly found. Diabetes, obesity, and evidence of stroke and high blood pressure are less likely conditions among the very old. Diabetes and high blood pressure are very much correlated with weight.

The lesson: first, get fit. Worry about your weight only if your BMI is above 25.

Caloric Restriction

Environments have powerful effects on longevity. The largest factor in animal life span is nutrition.

One of the major focuses of aging research for the past forty years has been caloric restriction. Caloric restriction, usually defined as 30 to 60 percent fewer calories per day than the average an animal eats, does not mean that a similar percentage of carbohydrates, proteins, minerals, and fats are reduced. Under caloric restriction, basic nutrients—like vitamins, essential amino acids and fatty acids—are kept at high levels.

In almost every species of animal looked at, caloric restriction extends life. Mosquitoes may live twice as long, mice and rats 25 to 50 percent longer. Mice eating less food over their lifetimes have a lower incidence of cancer, and they appear to age more slowly.

Research work is ongoing in monkeys. So far the results appear to be the same. Monkeys reared with 30 percent caloric restriction are showing less age-related decline than normal-diet monkeys.

The jury is out on whether primates like man and gorillas live longer with caloric restriction. Even if caloric restriction does work in people, it will be hard for most of us to accept such a life. Checking out in detail every meal we eat, making sure the number of calories is kept to what we perceive to be starvation level, is not something most of us will relish.

Eventually the data will come in. Presently hundreds of people across the United States are trying to use caloric restriction in their daily life. There are even cookbooks for those who practice caloric restriction. Over time, we will be able to see if it works for humans.

However, caloric restriction is probably much more a research tool than a practical way for us to eat. It does point out that nutrition is a very important part of aging. It also highlights that long-lived individuals have one striking similarity: their aging is gradual and fairly uniform. People who live a long life appear to have the same breakdown of organs and joints as the rest of us. Those breakdowns just occur at a slower, more regular rate.

And many long-lived individuals have led very regular lives, an idea that we'll explore in the next section. For those who cannot consider caloric restriction, vegetarianism may help. Vegetarian populations, like Seventh Day Adventists, do live longer. Plant-based diets may also be a sound ecological policy for our ever-increasing population.

Living Long the Circadian Way

Long-lived populations have many things in common. They include:

1. Active physical lifestyle
2. No use of tobacco
3. Use of alcohol only in moderation
4. Plant-based diets
5. Social connectedness and cohesion
6. Positive outlooks on life

There is another factor too often overlooked: the regularity of life's pattern.

People who are long-lived often work hard and have large families, enjoy their work and care about their communities. But whether they are vegetarian Michigan farmers or generations of doctors in Düsseldorf, a strong element in their life is regular patterns.

Walking every day. Eating regular meals every day. Seeing their families at the same times each day.

The biological clocks that program and prepare our lives work best under patterns as regular as the clocks themselves. Year in and year out, the people I see who have survived long and happily have, with very few exceptions, hewn to a regular pattern of daily life. They have done similar things at the same times most days. They go to bed and rise at the same times each day. They regularly exercise. Many have worked consistently and long, and have kept their friends. They have not tried to hurry their lives and careers but have paced themselves, using their time as a resource not to be wasted.

Many people, especially teenagers, reject regularity of lifestyle and life tempo. They see it as stifling, antagonistic to freedom and liberty. To many young people, waking at the same times, working at the same times, and sleeping at the same times is boring and stupid. They think such regularity restricts their ability to do anything they want anytime they want.

Many long-lived people find that pattern frees them, rather than restrains them. Time provides the structure of life. Living life according to a predictable pattern allows greater opportunities to try the unexpected, because the basic elements of life are always there.

If sleeping well involves going to bed and rising at the same hours; eating well, a regularly timed but diversely sourced diet; living well, a sense of one's purpose and place in the world; then consistency should make life easier and more fulfilling. Our biological rhythms are precise and regular. That is how we are made. It is pleasurable to live our lives in ways consistent with our inner forces.

Most great tasks take long, consistent effort to fulfill. Having a consistent life allows the body to work at it its best, to produce the performances required to sustain and fulfill our imaginations.

SUMMARY

- People are living longer and healthier lives than ever before. Living to age 100 is no longer impossible for many Americans.
- Caloric restriction might allow an appreciable increase in our lives but is difficult for most of us to follow.
- To remain healthy longer requires lots of friends and social connections; a regular pattern of daily life; a plant-based diet; regular, consistent exercise; and keeping moderately fit.

Chapter Five

Sex and Romance: Getting in Synch

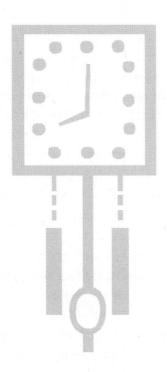

Bob and Linda, both in their late sixties, had been married forty years. Their relationship had experienced many ups and downs. When the children grew up and left the house, many of their frustrations disappeared. Bob began to think about Linda and her concerns more than he had since youth. As she aged, Linda felt greater fondness for her husband. Both eagerly looked forward to retirement, hoping to have "enough time together."

For many years of their marriage, Bob and Linda had intercourse once a week. When young they had usually had sex on Saturday night, shifting through the years to late Sunday mornings after sleeping in. Advancing into their early fifties, the frequency of sex declined, as did its regularity.

Bob especially looked forward to retiring. When younger he had enjoyed sex more than Linda did, but as they grew older, their relative enjoyment grew more equal. Bob confided that he thought he could enjoy sex more when retired, because "nobody would be around and nobody could tell me when to do anything." He imagined long nights holding his wife without worrying about neighbors, children, and job schedules.

It was not to be. As Bob grew older he found it harder to ejaculate and hold an erection. As his frustration increased, his attempt at any kind of sexual activity diminished year by year.

Linda was less concerned with achieving orgasm than Bob was. Linda regarded sex as a way of expressing and reasserting her fondness and love for husband. In time she realized that sex also made her feel wanted. Slowly she became frustrated with her husband's lack of interest. Though still enjoying each other's company, lack of a sex life left a lingering feeling of ill ease between them.

They both left their long-time home in the upper Midwest and decided to retire to Florida. For the first few months of living in the

South, Bob felt "more alive." He showed greater physical affection towards his wife. Gradually, his attentions declined. Bob and Linda remained the "best of friends," but were only occasional lovers.

Both Bob and Linda kept up with medical news. Each year they went for regular medical checkups. Bob never showed evidence of diabetes. His mild high blood pressure was handled with drugs that were not expected to affect his sexual performance. When his internist suggested he try Viagra, Bob agreed, surprised by Linda's enthusiasm.

Bob tried Viagra at 50 mg. No result. He tried 100 mg. When he achieved only the smallest of erections, Bob gave up. He soon recognized that Linda was even more disappointed.

Bob did not smoke or drink. He did not suffer from peripheral atherosclerosis or other illnesses expected to decrease sexual function. He did, however, snore at night. His wife noted that he stopped breathing during the night "a bunch of times," and that his breathing had worsened with increased weight or "especially when he had a beer."

When I told Bob about sleep apnea, an illness of daytime sleepiness, loud snoring, and missed breaths throughout sleep, he was concerned how it might affect his mortality. I told him it might possibly shorten his life by promoting higher rates of heart disease and stroke. And when I told him sleep apnea might affect his sexual function, he quickly asked to have an overnight sleep test.

Bob had a few apneas, or missed breathing episodes, every hour. The number was not very high, particularly for his age. I then pointed out to him that he had, as did most every male, several REM periods during the night. I explained that REM is a special time when the body does remarkable things. Temperature controls disappear. Muscle tone disappears, except for the eyes and the diaphragm. And the penis.

Testosterone had cycles like everything else in the body. Just before the start of every REM period testosterone would markedly rise, falling after the end of REM sleep. The highest levels of testosterone would occur during his longest REM sleep at the end of the night, at the time of his body temperature bottom. Before and during each REM period his testosterone would increase, and his penis should become erect.

"Does mine?" Bob asked.

I didn't know. Tests for nocturnal penile tumescence, or normal sleep erections during REM, are rare these days. Insurance companies don't pay for them, and Viagra has made many unnecessary. But there was an easy way to find out.

REM Sex

I talked with Linda and Bob about REM and sexual activity. Physiologically, female sexual interest *and* pleasure peak at ovulation, generally the middle of the menstrual cycle. That was of no use to them, as Linda was far along into menopause. Not as much was known of female sexual change with REM, though there were a few studies suggesting that lubrication increased.

Like many older people, Linda and Bob were larks. Both went to bed at 10:30 P.M. He liked to get up at 6:30 A.M., she at 7. In the lab, Bob's REM cycles had not clocked out in pure 90-minute rhythms. However, his longest REM cycle was typical, occurring right before waking up.

I asked Linda if she would be willing to wake up at 5:45, when Bob should be towards the beginning of his last REM cycle. She was willing. Not Bob.

"What if it doesn't work?" he asked.

Sex was a sign of affection, I told him. There were many different ways to make love. Linda was quite prepared for erectile "failure." If he was erect, fine. If not, he should still try to enjoy lovemaking. Many couples enjoyed early-morning sex. Though some felt "hardly awake," others felt more playful and less inhibited. Often they surprised themselves with how much fun they had, even if sexual "performance" was minimal. Pleasure, fondness, and mutual affection were the goals. I emphasized that enjoying the process often took time and repetition.

A good thing I did. The first time Bob and Linda tried REM sex they both felt so sleepy that they embraced each other, touched each other, and stopped. Linda had fallen asleep.

Bob felt more frustrated than usual, but he was willing to try again. I told them to try awakening early, but only when they were both interested.

A few weeks later they tried REM sex again. Linda was surprised and happy to find Bob almost fully erect. Though the erection did not hold, they were able to hold each other and talk about old times.

Bob discovered his sexual interest increasing. He tried to relive some of the romantic experiences of their earlier lives. Sometimes the results were more comic than sexual, but Bob and Linda felt closer to each other.

I told them to try simple tasks before they went to bed. They could watch a romantic movie they remembered from their youth; hold hands and fondle each other before going to sleep; visualize having sex together, past or present. Bob and Linda were surprised to learn that dreams could influence waking thoughts. I explained that dreams often were created from experiences and ideas while awake. Women often dreamed of sex when menstruating. Thinking of romance, remembering good times, and visualizing ways of enjoying themselves could change what happened in the night.

Bob said he rarely dreamed. Yet he began for the first time in many years to have sexual dreams. On nights when he experienced sexual dreams, he found his ability to maintain an erection improved.

Though he rarely achieved orgasms, and then only briefly, Bob again enjoyed sex. He loved being with his wife, holding her, talking to her about his love, what she meant to him. Linda especially found herself looking forward to the early morning, saying it gave her a "kind of peace." I encouraged them to walk together both in the morning and evening, to talk about what had happened and was happening to them.

REM sex is not just for seniors. Testosterone in men and estrogen in women declines as we age past thirty. REM-related erections are more common in young men, but still occur through a large part of the night for men in their seventies.

REM sex is part of the reality of human sexuality—sex is a brain event. Most of what goes on sexually occurs in the cerebral cortex as well as "lower" brain centers. Sex is more about thought and feeling than simple physiologic arousal.

Unlike other mammals, humans can have sex throughout their days and nights, 365 days a year. Americans, however, tend to talk about sex, think about sex, fantasize about sex, and watch sexually focused media far more than they engage in sex. According to some national surveys, young couples of 25 to 29 average intercourse only once a week.

Timing Sex for Pleasure

For many, sexual intercourse represents the most intensely pleasurable experience of their lives. Is it possible that there are best times for sex?

The answer is highly individual. Larks and owls prefer different times for sex. When larks and owls are together, considerable negotiation is often required, aided by having sex at overlap times. For many owls and larks, 9 or 10 P.M. is a period when both are at least moderately alert. Yet most people do not have sex around times when it will be most pleasurable—they have sex when they can.

Most sexual activity in the West takes place between 10 and 11 P.M., prior to going to sleep. Why do people generally have sex when, with the exception of owls, they are most tired, sleepy, and exhausted?

The answer is socially required convention, married to convenience. Late-night sex is more the result of necessity than desire. The children are, it's hoped, off sleeping in their rooms. Spouses or partners are already together in bed, preparing for sleep. Often this is the only time couples spend together without social or work interruptions.

Another reason for end-of-the-day sex is the belief that sex improves sleep. Psychologically, this may be true. Being able to spend time with your partner, to feel that deep, intense connection, and to have the experience of sexual release prepares people for the expectation of a good night's sleep.

Laboratory studies do not support the belief that sex improves sleep. The way these studies have been conducted may have prejudiced the results, however. Having sex with your partner in the sleep laboratory is not everyone's idea of a great time. Following sex with a night or nights in the sleep laboratory, hooked to wires and oxygen sensors, is not quite the same as sleeping in your own bed.

The other time when people have sex is in the mornings, particularly weekend mornings, generally at 8 or 9 A.M. The standard pattern of weekday sex at night and weekend sex in the morning is common among families both with and without children or elderly parents to care for.

In general, my patients who are larks tend to like morning sex. Owls seem to have a preference for nighttime sex. Each can accommodate readily to morning sex, particularly REM sex, if their partners are reasonably in sync. Interestingly, while on vacation, both larks and owls find their choice of times for sex expands beyond the narrow late night and early morning range of ordinary life.

Sexual pleasure changes dramatically with ovulation. This is exactly what would be expected from our evolved bodies: The best time to have sex is also the best time to continue the species. Sex is most enjoyable for women, and most desired, when they are ovulating, the time when women are most likely to become pregnant. This is true even for gay women, who usually are not attempting to attain pregnancy.

In a 28-day menstrual cycle, ovulation, or release of eggs, tends to occur right around the middle. The hormone estradiol peaks and the egg or eggs is released into the fallopian tubes. Women also try to initiate sex around these times, when eggs are being prepared for possible pregnancy. When ovulating, women report their senses are heightened. They reach orgasm more often, and more intensely. Birth control pills can take away this effect.

Men are also more inclined to seek sex around the time when women are most fertile. As women's interest and pleasure in sex is sparked by estradiol, men's interest changes with testosterone. Yet testosterone is far more variable through the day than is cyclic estradiol production. The primitive limbic lobe of the brain, where human sex, aggression, and food are partially controlled, seems to have a lot to do with male sexual interest.

When men win at sports, testosterone surges. Losses cause testosterone to decrease. In keeping with the health implications of social connectedness, male sports fans' testosterone will increase or decline with wins or losses by the local team. Invitation or decline of sexual interest by women has similar results on male testosterone.

What is clear is that underlying rhythmic testosterone secretion peaks in males with their last REM period. This is also the time of their body temperature bottom—and the time when most men of any age have their REM-induced penile erections.

Sex is always a psychological event. Intimacy and togetherness, along with the sense of being understood and appreciated, are critical to enjoying sex for all of us. This is particularly true even when issues of pregnancy arise.

Timing Sex for Pregnancy

Tomas and Jane were very much in love. Yet the inability to conceive a child was driving both of them crazy.

They had married four years earlier, in an emotional ceremony recognizing their different ethnic origins. Tomas was an immigrant to the United States. He had been overjoyed to meet Jane, an American who appeared to understand his different background and celebrate it. They both shared the same faith, which made their otherwise wary families more relaxed.

Both Tomas and Jane had good jobs. Both enjoyed their time with each other a great deal. They lived a life of relative comfort, possessing most of their material wants even though they were only in their early thirties.

What they wanted most was a child. That had been denied them.

The usual suspects were investigated. Jane had normal menstrual function and hormonal levels. Tomas' sperm count was more than adequate.

Trying to have a baby warped their lives. Sex changed from an adventure and a pleasure to a job. Jane would check her temperature chart, carefully following from month to month her relatively regular cycles. Use of commercial kits to determine estradiol levels demonstrated that her temperature charts were fairly accurate. She knew when her eggs were being released.

So did Tomas. Three to five days of the month were spent in planned sex, carried out with almost military deliberateness and precision. Each month that Jane menstruated she felt she was a failure. She would go to work, see other women who were pregnant, and weep.

I told them that I thought they were doing many of the right things, but in what might be the wrong spirit. Sex should be about joy and affection, not a chore. Making sex important only to procreate destroyed much of the pleasure of life. It would also come to burden the relationship between them.

Tomas nodded. He understood what Jane was feeling, he said. He knew how desperate she was to have a baby. But he hated feeling desperate every time he had intercourse with her, every time she would look at the thermometer and place a mark on her charts. He would love her forever, he said, whether they had children or not. But he could not stand her continuing sense of failure, her sense of disappointment—with herself and him.

Jane told Tomas how sorry she was. She could not help herself. She wanted a child, and she wanted *his* child. But she could not conceive. She felt she was a "total failure." At times she wondered if God had abandoned her.

I told them that I had seen many people who had been unable to have children. Many of them planned to adopt children, and just before they did, conceived. Others had had several children after adopting one or two.

Many things about conception were unknown. Sexual pleasure, however, was clearly part of the process. When people really loved one another, felt great sympathy for each other, and experienced great sexual pleasure, they appeared to have a greater chance to become pregnant.

I asked Tomas and Jane to "cool off." It was time to give up the temperature charts, at least for a while, and enjoy sex whenever and wherever they wished.

Though both Jane and Tomas were natural owls, they had adjusted to the Lark Work World, and often were fairly alert in the morning. I suggested they try dawn REM sex. Both said they didn't have enough time before work, but I told them to try to wake some mornings a half hour early, when Tomas was generally tumescent.

I also suggested they try greater daytime bright light exposure. Some studies demonstrated increased fertility with increased time under bright light. (Was it due to the higher mood that comes with greater light, or simply entraining the times of menstruation? I didn't know.) But getting more light during the day was relatively easy for both of them.

Finally, I suggested mini-vacations. I asked them to try different conditions and situations at the times when ovulation was expected.

For those few days, home involvement with work should be shelved. Any activity that relaxed them, like movies or sports, should be engaged in as much as they liked. They should go for walks on the beach or in parks, feeling as close to nature as possible.

And they could engage in sex whenever and wherever they liked. I asked them to view sex as one form of play. They could go to a hotel or out of town if they wanted, but sometimes sex should be a little bit of a game. They might try different rooms in the house, different conditions, and different times.

Tomas and Jane found they liked weekend mornings best. They would wake, look at each other, and start to tell jokes. If they were both in the mood, they would have sex in different parts of the house, using different positions. Often they forgot about the time, feeling a sense of flow, an engagement with one another that made both of them feel more complete.

Jane did not become pregnant for months. She, did find, however, that her mood lightened. As the summer months came, and their work time decreased, their times together became happier and easier. It took almost a year before Jane became pregnant. Long before that, she felt more confident in herself.

The child came in early spring, not the most common time. Despite the impact of light on fertility, sexual activity is usually greatest in the fall.

Worldwide, pregnancies peak in summer. Like increased sexual interest around ovulation, summer births should be expected from our hunter-gatherer bodies. Though today we live with supermarkets, we did not evolve with local groceries. Timing our children to appear in summer, when food should be most abundant, makes good evolutionary sense.

Sex and Romance: Larks and Owls in Love

An old joke among biological-clock researchers goes like this: what do larks and owls have in common?

They marry each other.

We met Jerry and Nancy in Chapter 1, which explores the differences between owls and larks.

Jerry met Nancy as a junior in college. He loved her from the start. The way she talked, her interest in her friends, her fascination with politics, enthralled him. He wanted to be with her every minute, more than he ever wished to be with anyone.

Unfortunately, Nancy was an owl. When Jerry was going to bed, around 10 or 11 P.M., Nancy was waking up. So were almost all of Nancy's friends.

Jerry and Nancy's romance nearly did not get off the ground.

The same is true of many other lark and owl couples. Larks and owls often do not get along. Several studies suggest that lark-owl couples have more trouble staying together than lark-lark or owl-owl couples.

Yet Jerry had no idea of these facts when he first met Nancy. All he knew was that he was in love. That he was a biologically different type than the woman he loved was not something he could guess.

At first, Jerry and Nancy went out at late hours. He tried staying up with her. He discovered he was so worn and tired in the mornings he could neither study nor work.

Jerry was ambitious. He wanted to have good grades to be able to enter graduate school he might choose. He imagined that school and career considerations came first.

But he liked Nancy so much he could not get her out of his mind. He tried to go out with Nancy only in the evenings and early night, on those days when Nancy was not taking her preferred evening classes.

Nancy liked Jerry. She wanted him to meet her friends. Jerry found his schoolwork slipping as he tried to stay up till 1 or 2 A.M., hours when Nancy's friends were just going out to start their nights. He started taking naps in the daytime. Short naps helped a bit, yet not enough.

To stay up with Nancy, Jerry began drinking brewed coffee. Soon he was drinking pots. With these high doses, Jerry could stay up late. What he could not do was fall asleep and stay asleep.

Caffeine was stimulating him, arousing him too much. His sleep was wrecked.

Jerry was at his wit's end. Nancy was telling him he was a killjoy. All he knew was that his brain hardly functioned from morning through the afternoon. Only come evening was he able to do any difficult or creative work, and normally he was too exhausted to try.

I told Jerry about the biological differences between larks and owls. Then I suggested to Jerry that he try evening exercise. Was it possible for him to go to the gym and work out on the machines? Pedal an exercise bicycle, or run on an indoor track?

It was possible. He started exercising between 9:30 and 10 P.M. Soon he could stay up with Nancy till 1 A.M. and still feel half alive. If he wanted to go out until two or three on the weekends, he would sometimes add small amounts of caffeine: a tiny flick of a Vivarin pill, perhaps one-tenth of its 200 mg dose, or a few ounces of cola. Walking around or dancing through the late hours also helped keep him awake.

With this evening and nighttime exercise Jerry found he could sleep past his usual time of 6 A.M. He slept in till 7 or 7:30 A.M., but rarely could he sleep past 8 A.M. He was getting the same 6 hours sleep as many of his classmates, but Jerry was feeling, as he put it "wasted."

Here Nancy came to the rescue. She told Jerry that she wanted to be with him. She saw how much he was trying to become an owl like her.

Nancy told him she would try to get up earlier. With considerable effort, she did. Nancy quickly realized there were "overlap" times when she and Jerry would both be alert. Late morning and early evening were times both felt at ease.

Nancy still went to bed late. However, with time she realized her grades were not as high as she liked. Instead of going to bed at three or four, she eventually settled in to sleep at 2 A.M., sometimes 1 A.M.

Nancy and Jerry are together more now. They don't try to do *everything* together, however. They recognize there must be some "division of labor."

Jerry wakes about two hours before Nancy. He studies while she sleeps, and he prepares her 10 A.M. breakfast. She cooks the evening meal.

When they go out, they usually pick the evening well in advance. Nancy tries every day to get lots of morning light, but still feels like an owl. On weekends she will sometimes stay up till 3 A.M. with friends. Jerry usually leaves parties around 1 A.M., waiting for her to join him later in bed.

Nancy still likes to have sex late at night, while Jerry prefers morning. They usually compromise by spending weeknights together between 9 and 11 P.M. Jerry then goes off to sleep, while Nancy studies on.

Many couples survive by developing distinct tasks for each other. Interestingly, lark-owl couples often find child-raising makes their relationship oddly easier. They take care of the children at different times of day, meeting each other at day's end.

Sex and romance are often most engaging and powerful at the beginning of relationships, when both partners care very little about the hour. Couples want to be together all the time, from daytime through white nights.

Eventually our hunter-gatherer bodies rebel. We need sleep to survive. To think. To create. To keep our metabolism in order. To function socially, and not feel crabby all day and night.

Both in love and in work, it pays to know your colleagues' time spaces—lark, owl, or switcher. Once Jerry and Nancy knew their differences were inborn, they were able to adjust. That was when their love for each other truly took over. They accommodated and changed for each other, making their lives easier. Young as they were, it was "okay" if one slept while the other studied.

It pays to know your clocks.

SUMMARY

- For most working couples, especially those with children, sex is timed by necessity, usually just before or after sleep.
- Often sex is most enjoyable toward the end of sleep, as in REM sex. And sex in the afternoon, while rare, is often greatly pleasurable.
- Many larks and owls are deeply attracted to each other, but to stay together they must learn to respect each other's time spaces. Properly timed light and exercise, along with the division of labor, helps keep couples together.
- Proper timing of sex may make pregnancy more likely.

Chapter Six

Peak Performance at School and Work

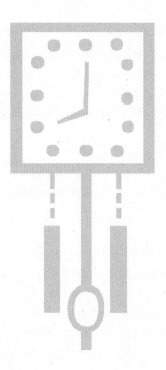

Sally felt that she was a failure.

She was always an excellent student. Her grades were far better than her brother's and sister's. Both had obtained admission to famous universities. Sally's guidance counselor had told her she would have "her pick" of schools—if she did well on the SAT.

Sally did not. Not that she did poorly. But her scores were far below her performances in practice exams. She had always studied. She had worked hard. Now, she thought, I'll go to a lousy school. The world will think I'm a dummy.

Her parents asked me for advice. I told them the stories of Dr. Mary Carskadon's "Sleep Camp" at Stanford in the 1970s. Students took a series of tests. They were then asked to sleep an extra 2 hours each night for several days. Their test scores went up.

"But Sally gets enough sleep," her father told me.

"How much?

"Oh, eight hours a day."

They asked me to talk with their daughter.

Sally is a very likable kid. She was interested in sports and music, and she had lots of friends. Unfortunately, she was convinced that if she did not attend a "top university" she would have no future.

I explained to her that I thought that was bunk. Where you went as an undergraduate mattered, but not as much as the connections you made. How well you did in college was usually more important than where you went. Her grades were good enough that she would have no trouble attending any of her state universities.

But Sally's older friends had gone to the Ivy League. She wanted that kind of experience. She was sure it would never be hers.

I told Sally that America is a land of second, third, and fourth chances. When people are likely to go through three or more careers during their lifetime, where you go to college matters less and less. I told her that her ability to get along with and persuade others would be much more important, at least to her future financial success, than her college choice or grades.

What I really wanted was for Sally to relax more. Anxiety and test performance are intimately linked. Sally was tighter than a drum.

Sally finally let out that she wanted to go to the same school that her boyfriend wanted. "He's a genius," she said. She would be heart-broken if she could not join him.

I changed the subject.

"How much sleep do you get?" I asked.

"Oh, about eight hours."

Unfortunately, this was not so. If Sally went to sleep when she went to bed, she might sleep 8 hours. Instead, she watched television for a half hour to one and a half hours, depending on whether one of her "favorite shows" was on that night.

Sally was a lark. She normally tried to go to sleep between 10:30 and 11 P.M., waking around 6 A.M. But when she was anxious and worried, she took a half hour or longer to get to sleep.

I asked her if she wanted me to give her a personalized study program. Without hesitating, Sally said yes.

"Okay," I told her. "I want to keep it very simple. The week before the test I want you going to sleep at 9:30 and getting up at 6:15. And you can't watch television."

"No television?"

"That's right."

We negotiated quite a while. I provided fuller explanations for my suggestions. First, the SAT was more a test of "reasoning power" than one of memorization. She could study till she was blue in the face, but whatever she remembered would not much affect her test results.

Then I explained the effects of anxiety on test performance. I wrote down an inverse U-shaped curve. "Zero anxiety" situations, in which people were told to take a test with no consequences as to whether they scored 0 or 100, mostly led to poor scores. Providing people a little anxiety, by making test scores matter, generated better results.

But when people were told that their test scores would matter a great deal, many became too anxious. Their ability to think dropped, just as it does for many of us during emergencies. Some panicked, and their scores sank. Average scores plummeted.

I told Sally anxiety was her biggest problem. She had taken exams most of her life. She had virtually always done well.

Now she was giving the SAT too much power over her life. Her future was bright no matter what she did on her next SAT.

"You have to be pleasantly distracted, refreshed and relaxed. I want you to enjoy yourself the week before the exam."

"Then you better let me watch television."

Television can overarouse us before we go to sleep. Sleep was absolutely necessary to learning and good performance. "I want you to read," I said.

"Read? Read what?"

"Poetry."

Sally liked many poets, but not as much as she liked television. We compromised. Right up to the exam I told her she could watch her favorite shows. But she could not watch television during the last 2 hours before sleep. If she wanted, she could watch her shows earlier, on tape.

Sally became a whiz with the VCR.

After our negotiations, Sally followed many, if not all, of my suggestions. The last two weeks before the SAT, she tried out practice tests, but not for very long. She continued her sports training, but took extra time for sleep each night. She read a few short poems and parts of classic novels prior to sleep (though after watching her regular television programs). And she made sure not to study, but to see a favorite movie the night before the exam.

"How was it?" I asked her after the exam.

"It was bad," she said. "I was thinking about the movie."

Sally did very well on this last SAT. She got in to the school she wanted, though her "genius" boyfriend did not. By then they had broken up, though they still liked each other's company.

Learning and Partial Sleep Deprivation

Several years later I learned better why sleep was so important to test results and overall learning. Researchers at Harvard took a group of undergraduates and modified their hours of sleep. Some slept an average of 8 hours, others 6. Then they tested their ability to remember and learn.

The students who slept 6 or fewer hours learned far less well. They had much more difficulty remembering material. Their overall test scores correlated with how much deep sleep and REM sleep they received.

As you read in the chapter on sleep, deep sleep and REM appear in some ways to be the "business end" of sleep. Though they take up only a minority of sleep time (especially with age), deep sleep and REM seem necessary to help us remember and lay down memories. And to learn.

Partial sleep deprivation makes us learn less well. One reason is that we remember less well.

Memory has two major parts. One, short-term memory, is the ability to fast-forward facts into a special mental compartment. It's the kind of memory you test when you meet people for the first time at a party and try to remember their names.

However, short-term memory is quite different from long-term memory. After a period of minutes to hours, memory gets moved in the brain into a sort of long-term segment. This long-term memory is the kind we tend to keep most if not all our lives.

People who want to understand long-term and short-term memory can learn about the differences by observing people afflicted with Alzheimer's diseases. When Alzheimer's disease appears, one of the first things to go is short-term memory.

Alzheimer's victims will remember their weddings, their college dances, and their vacations with the kids. Ask them to remember your name and they may not have a clue.

Deep sleep and REM appear to work differently in maintaining different strands of short- and long-term memory. These brain functions are poorly understood. But getting enough deep sleep and REM appears to be critical to maintaining memory and learning.

Deep sleep and REM are like bookends. Both occur at approximately 90-minute intervals across the night. Deep sleep is most prominent in the first part of the night, and REM at the end.

Though only a few studies have looked at the problem, it does not appear that people can sleep just the first and last parts of the night and learn well. Your biological clocks must be satisfied. Though exercise and temperature changes can increase deep, and perhaps REM sleep, you really need to get enough total sleep in order to learn well.

Most American students do not. The average teenager probably needs in excess of 9 hours of sleep a night, perhaps 9½, to perform at their best. Very few of them get that much. Some teenagers are like Sally, who sleeps about 7 to 7½ hours a night. Too many of her classmates average 6 hours of sleep or less.

It's not because the average high school student is up at night studying physics or reading *War and Peace*. There's Nintendo and the Internet, allowing interstellar battles to be fought with teammates all across the globe, at all hours. There's ICQ, instant communication with a dozen or more friends on the Net. There are television shows and music on disc. Telephone calls to friends. Cell phones with multiple instant messaging. Portable DVD players. Parties. The mall. Part-time jobs to pay for the insurance on their car.

Many schools compound the sleep-deprivation problem. By starting classes early, they cause parents and children to get up earlier and earlier, killing off their last, crucial REM sleep period. Juggling morning jobs with getting the kids off to school promotes households of cranky adults and very sleepy children. Some schools are starting to understand, trying to start classes late enough that students and their families might get enough sleep to function.

Sleep deprivation generally worsens when students go off to university. No longer encumbered with working parents, day shifts into night into day. Many an undergraduate goes to bed at three or four in the morning. Many sleep through morning classes, working on "autopilot" till the afternoon, when they take their involuntary naps.

Students eventually learn that learning requires more sleep. Undergraduates sleep more by senior year. Those who get better grades appear to take sleep more seriously.

However, undergraduates who prefer afternoon and evening classes may have a point. Short-term memory is normally best in the morning, while much of long-term memory is optimal in the afternoon or evening. Students may learn better at later hours.

So may adults.

Here are a few suggestions for improving student performance.

1. School is a marathon, not a sprint. Constant learning and relearning of material is required. You need to study regularly to integrate what you learn into a system you can use.

2. Cramming may help you do well on tests, but it is a lousy way to learn overall. Cramming may cause too much material to be lost from long-term memory.

3. High school students should aim for 9 to 9½ hours of sleep each night. Undergraduates may need almost as much, but 8 hours might be sufficient for most of them to learn.

4. Students, like adults, should try to have very regular times of going to bed and getting up. Reinforcing biological clocks with regular sleep and wake times makes it easier to sleep *and* easier to learn.

5. Though many students learn by what they hear, most learn by reading. Reading is a more profound and useful experience for the brain than is watching television. If students are having a hard time learning, temporarily ban use of the television set.

Taking Tests

Tests require us to learn a great deal of information over a long period of time. This information must make its way into long-term memory, and then we must be able to organize it quickly and use it efficiently in times of stress. Anxiety has a lot to do with how well you test.

Prior to important tests, students should:

1. Take plenty of time for sleep. Nine or more hours a night may help.
2. Exercise in the late afternoons and early evenings (especially larks) in order to feel more relaxed.
3. Cram if necessary. Yet if the material has been studied regularly, a final going-over may be all that's required for optimal performance.
4. Enjoy quiet distractions in the final 12 to 18 hours before a test, in the form of reading, favorite sports, or watching movies, with enough time set aside for sleep. This may produce considerably better results than late-night cramming.

Performance for Adults: The Best Times

Though one-quarter of the working world works shifts, the majority of workers work the day shift.

The day shift is a trial for owls. Most owls view the standard day work schedule as shift work, as well they should. Yet even most owls tend to become alert by midmorning to late morning. Larks are already alert by then.

The late morning may be the best "overlap" time of all. If you want to schedule a short important business or administrative meeting at which all the attendees have a shot at maximal alertness, 11 A.M. is often a good time.

Late afternoon and early evening is also a period when larks and owls have little trouble getting together. While peak alertness for larks may be at 10 A.M. to noon, larks are well over their mid-afternoon sleepiness by 5 or 6 P.M. Most owls are beginning to feel good by 6 P.M.

Early evening is a time when the large majority of people are quite alert. Many also feel sociable. Early evening is a time when alcohol has its least effect, and people, including larks and owls, have their hardest time falling asleep. Early evening is often an excellent time for group work or team building.

The Postlunch "Dip"

Many people across the world complain of feeling tired, sleepy, and wooly-headed in the afternoon. For larks, this period of fatigue and sleepiness usually peaks between 12:30 and 2:30 P.M. Owls are usually hit several hours later, feeling sleepy from 3 P.M. until 4:30 to 5 or later.

The postlunch dip may have nothing to do with lunch at all.

Biological clocks have large effects on sleepiness and energy in the afternoons. When the body temperature curve is flat, people tend to be sleepy. Over a billion people take naps in the afternoon.

Many of these nappers are hard-charging executives and professionals. Midafternoon naps, particularly short ones, may energize many a worker at a time when they do not feel like being anywhere near the workplace.

Though the afternoon dip in alertness will occur regardless of whether people eat or not, food does affect how sleepy and tired you get. Studies now demonstrate that high-carbohydrate meals sometimes contribute to feeling sleepier in the afternoon. Having a lunch that is relatively high in protein may make life a bit easier for those with postlunch dips in attention and energy, as will avoidance of alcohol and caffeine. Alcohol is a depressant 24 hours a day. If you want to drink, try the early evening, when alcohol is best tolerated.

Though caffeine is felt to be essential to many workers to "survive" the afternoon, its effects on sleep may not be helpful. Caffeine is a wonderful drug, but it can be harmful. Many who use caffeine to wake themselves in midafternoon may be lightening their nighttime sleep.

For those who love their midafternoon cup of coffee, try if possible a brisk walk instead. It may not disrupt sleep as much as a cup of coffee will. On the other hand, many people sleep perfectly well at night after imbibing caffeine in the afternoon.

Motivation and the "Conditional Set"

Many people talk of their "peak times" of performance. Particularly for creative work, larks prefer the morning, particularly midmorning and late morning. Working owls often prefer the early evening or late night.

Society has a habit of getting in the way of these "best times."

Most work involves working with other people, often doing things you don't like to do, while trying to fit your schedule with that of larks, owls, and switchers. Work also involves periods of time when there are several overlapping, interesting assignments, contrasted with tasks that are dull or irritating.

Motivation has a lot to do with anyone's peak performance times. Creative people have an advantage here, particularly if they can control all their work periods. Writers know when they are most creative, usually morning for larks, evening or night for owls. Athletes often prefer the afternoon or early evening to achieve their peak performances.

Yet nearly always, other concerns get in the way. Children. Jobs. Commuting times. Meeting friends.

Motivation involves a complex behavioral "set." Motivation engages how much people like their work. How well they are paid. Whether they feel appreciated. How much they like working with their coworkers. Whether they think their work "matters" or "makes a difference."

Fortunately there are an infinite number of ways to motivate people. Bypassing the issue of motivation, peak work times would probably constitute late morning and early evening for much of the population.

That is not how our society is organized. Students spend far more mornings in school than evenings, regardless of when their long-term memory functions best. Much of the workday is spent in the biologically less productive period of the early afternoon and midafternoon.

Though creative, intellectually demanding work is best performed at specific times for larks, owls, and switchers, most day-to-day work is not so intense. Most of us are not fighter pilots or neurosurgeons. We can do a pretty good job throughout the daylight hours.

But only if we get enough sleep. Partial sleep deprivation is a problem for many if not most of us. Sleep deprivation is so common we don't think it a problem at all.

To perform well, most of us will need to average 8 hours of sleep. For many of us, that is a pipe dream.

Too many workers talk about taking work home with them. They need "space," uninterrupted time when coworkers, spouses, or children leave them alone to "get the job done." Too many of us wake early in the morning or stay up late at night in order to get "quiet time" to do our more demanding tasks.

If the whole family understands the importance of sleep, some dents can be made in the sleep-deprivation problem. Division of labor is a requirement for lark-owl couples who want to live together. Often it's a requirement for couples and families whose biological clocks are fully in synch.

There's a time to be together and a time to be alone. Night should be a protected time, not just an opportunity to escape the stresses of the day through entertainment. Sleep is a large part of successful performance through almost all days.

The LENS Program

The best human performance demands sufficient sleep and sufficient personal interest. We want to be rested and motivated to perform our best.

Yet most of us will experience deficiencies in both areas. To improve the odds, consider the LENS program.

LENS stands for four words: **L**ight, **E**xercise, **N**aps, and **S**ocializing. Each of these factors can improve alertness throughout the day and night for students, spouses, and day and shift workers.

Light is a drug. Light improves alertness and mood across the board. Try if possible to have your daytime workplace flooded with light. Sunlight is best. For winter and northern climes, soft, bright lights can improve mood and performance for the entire work force. Light boxes can treat mood disorders and promote alertness throughout the 24-hour day.

Exercise is what we are born to do. Depending on how it is timed, exercise can promote alertness; shift your biological clocks; help you sleep; or control your weight. Most of us should do a minimum of one hour of exercise each day, preferably walking or other aerobic activities, to preserve our physical and mental health.

Naps are an underutilized resource. In a population that is heavily sleep deprived, daytime naps should no longer be shunned. Short naps of 10 minutes seem to do the most for promoting alertness at work, especially in the midafternoon. Naps are even more useful in preserving alertness for shift workers (see Chapter 7). Having a comfortable, quiet, dark place for employees to lie down may be useful for the economic health of all kinds of companies.

Socializing is something humans are meant to do. We are social animals. We like being around each other.

Socializing also appears to keep us alert. Whether doing office work or flying an airplane, socializing with others—talking, joking, and carousing, and yes, discussing items other than work—appears to keep people more alert and happy.

The LENS program—light, exercise, naps, and socializing—can be used in any work context and works best in combination. Putting these factors together can go a long way toward increasing motivation and overall performance, whether by employer or employee.

SUMMARY

- Deep sleep and REM sleep are critical to learning and memory. Test scores and creative work improve when students get more sleep.
- High school students probably need 9 to 9½ hours of sleep in order to obtain their best performances. If students are doing

poorly, remove the television set and computer and ask them to read before bed. Set regular times of sleeping, waking, and exercise.

- Both larks and owls seem to do best in the late morning and early evening, excellent overlap times for business or administrative meetings. Such times also may be best for challenging or creative work, particularly by groups.
- Using the LENS program—light, exercise, naps, and socializing—can help work performance and alertness across the board.

Chapter Seven

Up at All Hours: Shift Work and Overtime

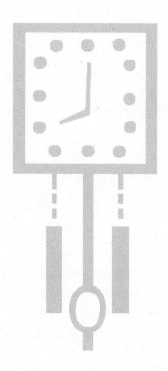

I sabelle couldn't sleep.

She knew what lack of sleep did to people. She had worked as a nurse for twenty-five years. Isabelle had watched patients lie wracked with pain or heavily sedated all those years. Sleeplessness sapped patients of energy and weakened their resolve. There were times she thought sleeplessness killed them. She had never had trouble sleeping herself.

Isabelle had just returned from working overseas. She applied for a hospital job that sounded perfect. She would be a nurse specialist in an area she loved, working in a town she knew well. She would have a chance to reconnect with her old boyfriend. She had missed him more than she expected.

Everything seemed to go right. She worked on the specialty ward she wanted with people she thought competent. The twelve-hour shifts, three times a week, allowed her more free time than any job she had ever had. Until she began working night shifts.

At first night work went well. Like many shift workers, she liked the independence of working at night. She could see patients as she liked without so many supervisors looking on. Isabelle liked having extra time to spend with patients, away from the hours of charting required by her job. Some nights she got in a nap of 10 or 20 minutes, others an hour or more.

Come morning, she could not sleep.

She tried sleeping during her usual nighttime period. That strategy worked only a couple of weeks. Gradually sleeplessness overcame her. She was tired all the time, cranky, irritable.

Her boyfriend noticed. Semiretired, he wanted to spend as much time with her as he could, but he lived in another city. He hated coming into town and finding the woman he loved drinking pots of coffee to stay awake and forgetting where she put her car keys.

Isabelle tried to stop working night shifts. Her supervisor explained that was not possible, at least for a couple of years. Most people get used to it, she said. It just takes a little time.

Isabelle gave it time. Her fatigue and sleepiness worsened. Her boyfriend complained. He remembered their past times together. She seemed like another person now, indifferent, listless. He told her he thought she was depressed.

She asked him to understand. She was not as young anymore. Shift work was hard on her, but she would get used to it. She always grew used to things, she said, she was resilient.

The boyfriend stopped visiting.

It was about that time Isabelle came to my office. She was ashamed, she said, because she believed she was depressed.

I told her that I didn't agree. She was certainly unhappy. But she did not suffer the prolonged mood-lowering characteristic of depression, or much of the other symptoms of clinical depression. She was very capable of enjoying herself, and if life went half-well she did so. Isabelle was a bit anxious, and certainly fatigued. Yet her worst problem was insomnia. In my opinion she was suffering from a maladjustment to shift work.

Isabelle was only working three days out of seven. Unfortunately, all her body clocks were now out of whack. She slept when she could, which was any time of day. Worst of all, she could not sleep the day after her night shifts. It was as if something inside her was preventing her from doing what she needed. She wanted to sleep, but could not.

Her reaction to repetitive sleeplessness was a common one. People without sleep often worry about, think about, and fantasize about sleep. They worry so much about sleep they turned sleep into an impossible job.

The phenomenon is called psychophysiological insomnia. It is especially common among professional people who feel stressed by the demands of work and family life. It is often self-perpetuating, but it was a pattern she could stop.

I told her I wanted her to take home some sleeping pills. Isabelle stared at me with a look of guilt and consternation.

Hers was a frequent reaction on the part of medical people I knew.

Sleeping pills are potentially addictive; they often make for abnormal sleep and may convince the brain that sleep is impossible without them.

Isabelle had seen people "hooked" on sleeping pills many times. "We give it in the hospital, and then they can't get off of it. It's terrible. I don't want to take them."

"Fine," I said. "I just want you to take them home." She did not have to use them. But I did want them around, in her purse, so she could try them when and if she wished.

I talked to her about biological clocks, and about how shift work was a totally unnatural experiment in human biology. How it became more difficult for us as we aged. Her work shifts might be adjusted to, but it would take a lot of planning. She would have to shift her times of certain activities, use light, exercise, and change her sleeping patterns.

Isabelle was willing.

I went over the LENS approach (light, exercise, naps, and socializing). Shifting her biological clocks through light was a poor idea. Isabelle wanted to live in the day world. She only worked night shift one week out of two.

But light at work could keep her alert. Though alertness had not been a problem when she started her job, it was becoming one. I asked her to get a very bright light for her office, and to keep it 14 to 20 inches from where she sat. My only warning was that she not try to use it too late in the night, when the phase-shifting effects of light were greatest.

Next I asked her to exercise on working nights by walking around the ward as much as she could. Whenever there was a chance to walk she was to take it. I also asked her to visit other parts of the hospital—the pharmacy, cafeteria, or administration—whenever she could, and to discuss her business directly rather than on the telephone.

"They'll think I'm wasting time," she said.

"The others will like seeing you," I told her. People like to work face to face, especially nights. Night work can get lonely. Socializing keeps people awake and alert. It also makes them happier.

Isabelle was already taking naps, but haphazardly. I wanted her to program them. I asked her to get 10 to 20 minutes of sleep at 4 A.M. if possible. Having a regular rest break should make it easier to remain awake the rest of the shift. It might also make it simpler to sleep the next day.

"But 4 o'clock is when I get a cup of coffee."

"Which is why you can't sleep in the morning," I explained. "If you're to drink coffee, do it at 11 P.M. or midnight. You'll probably still be able to take a nap later, at 3 or 4 A.M."

"But I won't be able to sleep the next day," she said.

"There are always the sleeping pills. You can use them sparingly, if you wish."

I saw Isabelle several times during the next year. At first she tried sleeping nights, staying up the day after her night shift. Often on those days she felt uncontrollably sleepy by midafternoon, and would nap for an hour or two.

Gradually she realized she could take a sleeping pill on returning from night work. I also told her about the phase-shifting ability of morning light. Morning light would reset her biological clocks earlier, making it harder for her to fall asleep after work. I asked her to use wraparound dark glasses when driving home.

"You mean the kind the old people wear?"

"The kind they give away at car dealerships," I told her. "Exactly right."

Isabelle started to take the sleeping pill as I prescribed. She was to take only a half pill on coming home from her 7 A.M. finishing time, and try to get to sleep by eight. I asked her to read before turning in, and to try to sleep at least until 2 P.M. Then I asked her to take a walk out-side in the late afternoon or evening, in the light.

Her pattern changed over several months. Though never taking more than three a week, she found sleeping pills worked. She began exercising in the afternoon after her night shifts, but still felt sleepy come the evening. Take an evening nap, I told her. Many shift workers do it all the time.

Gradually her pattern shifted to a standard: sleeping pill for sleep until 1:30 P.M. Next, shopping, seeing friends, and doing errands, following by an hour-long nap in the late afternoon. She walked outside or used an exercise bicycle in the hour or two before starting her shift, showering just before work. Caffeine was dosed at midnight, naps anywhere she could get them between 3 and 6 A.M.

The transition was slow, but effective. Isabelle's anxiety rapidly diminished. Partly her anxiety decreased because of the sleeping pills, which were also anti-anxiety agents. Within a month she saw that she functioned better at work, making several new friends among the nurses and staff she met "wandering" the nighttime hallways. Many of these night workers gave her useful advice on how to beat shift work.

Her boyfriend had stopped visiting, but he never stopped calling. After several months, he decided to come by.

It was about that time Isabelle stopped taking the sleeping pills. She still kept them in her purse. She liked the idea that she could use them if she needed them. And she did use them, about once every two or three months.

Managing Shift Work

Isabelle was lucky. She did shift work under controlled conditions, with others around to help if things got rough. She did not have children to take care of, or elderly parents, and she did not suffer from financial difficulties.

Most shift workers are not so fortunate, especially women. Working women are still expected to take care of the kids *and* the home. They must fit the time schemes of school and sports, spouse and extended families, while juggling lark and owl family members and their multiple schedules. Adding night-shift work to those burdens is often too much to bear, even when a husband is supportive and willing to spend many hours helping out at home.

Many studies are done on the precise timing of light and exercise to overcome the rigors of shift work. Too many of these studies miss the point. Shift work is a social problem much more than it is a medical one.

Only a minority of shift workers work a "standard" night shift, able to stay home during daytime hours. However, even these shift workers rarely have a pure "night" schedule.

Their friends, their lovers, their spouses, their families, are living in the day world. They too, must adjust to the day world, a world that does not pay much attention to their problems.

Some shift workers like the idea that they can shop when stores are empty, and have time for hobbies, like fishing, that their friends only dream about. But most night-shift workers are severely sleep deprived in an already sleep-deprived nation. Night-shift workers sleep 2 hours less, on average, than our already sleep-deprived day workers. Shift workers often cannot socialize with their families, because their families' schedules are the opposite of their own. Many shift workers miss watching their kids grow up. Often they miss talking with all the members of their family, including their partners.

The Costs of Shift Work

Anyone who practices medicine will tell you that work stress hits certain organ systems more than others.

People respond to stress in different ways. Yet the most common stress symptoms involve the gut, the heart, and the head. Often certain families will suffer from similar stress symptoms, generation after generation.

For shift workers the most common problem is gastrointestinal. Many a night-shift worker suffers from chronic gastritis, an often painful inflammation of the stomach.

Recent animal studies demonstrate that different organs can develop their own 24-hour clocks. Shiftworkers may develop stomachs and intestinal tracts out of synch with the clocks in their brains.

Shift workers often complain to me about constant gnawing or discomfort in their upper abdomen. They say that they can't eat large amounts of food. Their preferred solution is to eat densely caloric fatty foods, which "comfort" them at night—just the kind of foods available in vending machines conveniently placed at shift-work locations.

So shift workers increase their waistlines. Humans metabolize food much less effectively at night. We keep those calories on our bodies, preserving them in permanent stores of fat. And all those vending-machine-dispensed saturated and trans fat molecules have the chance to migrate into the lining of our arteries, kinking and narrowing them.

Which leads to the next major medical problem for shift workers: high blood pressure and heart disease. Shift workers suffer a lot more from both than does the rest of the population.

Partly it's the stress of shift work: the violation of biological clocks; the inability to sleep in the day coupled with chronic sleep deprivation; and the removal of social support provided by families and friends.

Shift workers try to adjust like everyone else. They use drugs that are sold over the counter, are easy to obtain, and cheap—caffeine, alcohol, and tobacco.

Caffeine has many positive uses in shift work, particularly if given at the start of a night shift. Taken many hours before people plan to sleep, caffeine makes at least the first few hours of the shift easier.

Caffeine taken late is another matter. Caffeine can addict people. Many a shift worker drinks not cups, but pots of caffeine to stay awake. It's not unusual for shift workers to drink ten or more cups of coffee every 24-hour period.

After a while the effects are not benign. Addiction leads to habituation. Caffeine stops working. Truck drivers are famous for "coffee and . . .," coffee and cake to get through the night. One National Highway Safety and Transportation Board study found seven times the fatalities for truckers working at night.

Only one-sixth of truckers work at night. The overall fatality rate was over *forty times* what was expected during the day. Autopsies on truck drivers after these fatal accidents often find gigantic caffeine blood levels of the sort labeled by pathologists "not expected with normal human use." And every trucker who dies takes an average of two other people with him.

Even huge amounts of caffeine can't make severely sleep-deprived people wake up, especially at night.

Difficulties with stress and sleep prompt shift workers to drink more alcohol. Several studies show that this problem is particularly common among swing-shifting police. Alcohol is the most common "sleeping pill" used by the American population. Alcohol use among shift workers often starts as a simple way to get to sleep. Shift workers suffer from far more alcoholism than the average. Worse, alcohol contributes to the already high level of night-shift accidents.

Another shift work "coping mechanism" is tobacco. Tom was a friend of mind who after several years of day work was forced to return to shift work. Unable to stay alert, he quickly returned to cigarettes. Soon his pack-and-a-half habit was back in force.

Tom felt mentally "better" when smoking. He thought he could stay awake more readily, "just like in those old war movies."

However, Tom's blood pressure quickly rose. He was forced to change his medications. Thinking his new antihypertension drugs might bankrupt him, he eventually quit smoking again.

Neither alcohol nor tobacco is a good coping mechanism, certainly not for shift work. Interestingly, both alcohol and tobacco decrease sleep, alcohol directly, tobacco through sleep-time nicotine withdrawal syndromes. The already poor sleep of shift workers is only worsened by alcohol and tobacco.

Women have much greater social costs from shift work, especially when they have children. Role flexibility becomes crucial when bringing up children of shift-working parents. Both mothers and fathers learn through necessity that they must do everything differently when one or both work shifts.

Everything must be reorganized: household work, helping the kids with homework, and taking care of elderly parents.

Often sympathy is not forthcoming from other family members. Many children resent their parents working shifts. Grandparents will often help out, but will not necessarily understand the challenges unless they themselves worked shifts.

Sometimes sympathy is hard to find even in your spouse. Divorce rates are several times higher when a spouse works shifts. This is true whether it is the man or the woman who does the shift work.

Women also face menstrual problems compounded by shift work. Several reports cite increased levels of problem pregnancies, including miscarriages.

With so many problems, why is shift work increasing?

Why Shift Work Will Not Go Away

It's a global world, we are often told. America has benefited from the new global economy. Work is now 24 hours a day, 7 days a week.

And companies are indeed international. Software workers in India continue developments while their American coworkers sleep at night. Just-in-time deliveries of parts and materiel help keep down inventory costs, but must be performed worldwide. For example, the parts in your car must arrive at the factory at the required times, but they often come from several different countries.

Globalization will only increase with the rise of the Internet and global satellite communications. It used to be that truck drivers could take a few hours off and see friends or lovers in between carrying loads. Now global positioning satellites track their path, letting managers know where they are any minute of the day.

The Internet aids globalization. Communication is now easy, cheap, and generally reliable. Work can easily be coordinated over huge distances.

All this makes it easier to treat humans as machines. Shift work originally developed in manufacturing because machinery was expensive. To get back the capital costs quickly, the machines had to be worked 24 hours a day.

Machines have continued to set the pace of our economy and lives. Our hunter-gatherer bodies, requiring frequent physical activity and regular nighttime sleep, are forced to adapt to a technological society in which all the day's 24 hours are demanded for work. Company chiefs are convinced they must utilize all hours of the day if their global corporations are to survive.

However, market economies should not be blamed as the single driver of shift work and other biological clock insults.

People get sick at night. They want to see doctors. They want to travel thousands of miles to visit loved ones. They want to eat fresh fruits and vegetables, foods that might rot if truck drivers and train conductors took their vehicles offline for eight hours each night. They also want to be entertained.

With continuing changes in the international economy, shift work will increase. Companies that used to work the Ohio or Midwest market now cover the entire planet. The goal should be getting employers and workers to recognize the social problems caused by shift work, and to adapt creatively.

Most workers work shifts under duress. They work at hospitals and emergency services, because emergency work goes on around the clock. They work at factories, and the added money from night shifts helps pay for their kids' food and schooling. They don't like working night shifts, but they often like working twelve-hour shifts, which allow them more free time at home.

Not everyone who dislikes shift work should do it. Many of us simply do not adapt to shift work.

Some do.

Who Should Do Shift Work?

In World War II, American troops were performing poorly in the war in the Aleutians.

Located off the Alaskan coast, the Aleutians were no one's tourist destination. The islands were and are bleak, desolate, cold, and wet. The climate was difficult for most to adjust to, even if they were not fighting the Japanese.

Many troops went off to the Aleutians and lost their sense of commitment. Too many became unfit to fight. Different psychological tests were devised to fix the problem. Psychiatrists were enlisted for the task of preparing proper "selection tools."

One sergeant in New York was said, however, to possess a truly superior ability to screen future Aleutian military personnel. The people he sent stayed. They persevered. They worked well.

A delegation was sent to the sergeant to review his methods. How was he doing so well when the experts could not?

The sergeant was quite surprised when the team of officers came by to evaluate his spotting talent. He said he made his decision based on a single question.

"What's that?" his superiors asked.

"I ask them, 'Do you like cold weather?'"

This is an old story. Chances are it never happened quite this way. But the point is made.

Shift working is not for everybody. Some of us adjust to shift work far, far better than others.

Advantage: Owls

Owls often have a horrible time working day shifts. Night work is a different matter.

Owls like the night. Before selecting night-shift workers, the obvious question must be asked: Do you like staying up at night?

Not all owls can work through the entire night. But their natural biological clock differences make it easier for them to adapt to night work. Owls may also adjust better to swing shifts than does the usual lark.

There are other factors that make it easier for people to do shift work. They include:

1. *Age*. Lots of youngsters try to stay up all night anyway, even when they know they have to sleep. Our bodies are more supple and able to adjust to shift work when young.
2. *Physical fitness*. Many a shift worker becomes a junk-food-eating, television-addicted, chronically exhausted "strung out" individual from years of shift work. Exercise can change all that. Exercising at the right times makes people fitter and allows them to stay alert throughout the day. Properly timed exercise can lengthen

your biological clock. Evening exercise before the shift may keep a worker more alert at night and make it easier to fall asleep after work.

3. *Body-clock differences.* Some people will internally shift hours each night they work, while others will keep the same biological clock week after week no matter when they labor. Nobody knows in advance who shifts well and who does not. Working a few weeks of shift work can tell many people that they do not shift time spaces very well.

4. *Short sleepers.* One of my friends requires only 2 to 3 hours of sleep each night in order to feel rested. A medical doctor, he was extremely unpopular with his fellow interns. Frequently working 24 hours straight through the night, his friends would show up for morning rounds looking and feeling half-dead. Yet, my friend would feel nearly as energetic come morning as on nights when he slept in his own bed. For remaining so alert, "the other interns hated me," he says.

When selecting shift workers, employers and employees must think about "fit." For biological and social reasons, people vary greatly in their ability to work shifts. Discussions between employers and employees should be made prior to starting shift work, especially in industries such as health and transportation, where mistakes may prove fatal.

You have to ask questions before you start shift work. It is important to know if you're a lark or an owl, what your family's schedule is, how much sleep you think you need, as well as the lark and owl characteristics of coworkers. Shift work is often a process of selective attrition on the part of many people—particularly the families of shift workers. Some can do it, some can't.

What Shift Workers Can Do to Cope

Adjusting to shift work is difficult and complicated. Biological and medical issues (like when you should take your medications) are just the start.

The social issues of shift work are huge. They demand negotiation within families before they are discussed among employers and employees.

Fortunately there are many small tricks that can help shift workers get through life. Here is a short list:

1. *Become flexible in dividing tasks at home.* Marriages for shift workers survive longest when there is active discussion about division of labor. Work and paycheck are foremost in many people's minds, but living with shift work requires great adaptability, especially where children are concerned. Protecting time with your spouse is crucial. More than others, shift workers must plan their days and nights.

2. *Protect your sleep time and sleep environment.* Yes, wear dark wraparound glasses as you drive home from the night shift. But more important, make sure your bedroom is a sanctuary, a place made safe for sleep. You can start by trying to make your bedroom soundproof and lightproof, particularly by putting up blackout drapes.

   But a dark, quiet bedroom is not enough. Children should not wake you up to help them with homework. Dogs and cats cannot jump onto your bed. Telemarketers must be banished from ruining your sleep.

   Shiftworkers often must turn off the ringers on their phones. Keeping your sleeping place cool, dark, comfortable, and quiet is a formidable task, but do the best you can.

3. *Get fit.* Walk as much as you can during the times you are awake. The fitter and more athletic you are, the better you will survive shift work.

Finally, use the LENS program (see page 131 in Chapter 6) when you work at night:

Light: Many workplaces have experimented with light boxes as a way to keep workers alert. Despite original claims of great success, light boxes have proven to be a mixed boon.

The reason is simple: light changes your biological clocks. And at night there is a time—the body temperature bottom—when light can shift your clocks forward *and* backward. Using a light box all night can really confuse your biological clocks.

The solution is to use bright light only during the first part of the night. Research with twelve-hour-shift oil workers by Torbjorn Akerstedt demonstrated that a specially lit cafeteria, used for 45 minutes to an hour after midnight, improved employee performance and satisfaction.

Light boxes can be used individually as well, at your desk or workplace. But if you are to use therapeutic doses of light, use them early in the night.

Exercise: Isabelle the nurse discovered that exercise greatly helped her to remain alert during the night.

Not every workplace affords you the ability to walk. Adjustments, however, can be made. Workers staring at security cameras can peddle on an exercise bicycle or walk on a stepper. Work "breaks" that include a walk in or near the workplace can be mandated every one to two hours. Stretching and isometric exercises done in place can help.

Exercise in the evening will also "lengthen your day," making it easier to fall asleep when getting home after night shift.

Naps: During the Internet boom, "nappatoria" were popular throughout Silicon Valley.

They were a good idea anywhere. Naps are a great way to provide what night shift takes away from you—sleep.

Short naps may help a great deal. In conditions of stress or emergency in which sleep is difficult, humans adjust by catnapping. Ten-minute naps lead to less "sleep inertia" than do longer naps, a crucial factor in keeping alert during the night.

Learning to nap can help many a shift worker, as well as those who work days and feel sleepy in the afternoon.

Socializing: Many night workers enjoy the "silence" and independence of shift work. They like working the way they want, how they want, without "someone looking over my shoulder."

Yet even independent loners may become lonely. Socializing helps people at work stay alert and alive. Talking with coworkers provides interest and amusement, along with tips on how to survive shift work. Many friendships start on the night shift, especially when owls meet their owl brethren.

Spending time alone can be very efficient. Spending time with others can be even more effective.

SUMMARY

- Shift workers suffer from more gastrointestinal disturbance, heart disease, depression, and menstrual irregularities. But the worst aspects of shift work are social. Many a marriage or relationship breaks up because of shift work. Adjusting to it requires planning, effort, and negotiation.
- The LENS program, using light, exercise, naps, and socializing at the right times, can make shift work more bearable.
- Some people are more adjustable than others. Many owls make excellent shift workers. People who are fit and young also adapt more readily. Workers and their families need to know their own biological clocks to make shift work more manageable.

Chapter Eight

Remaining Alert: War and Security

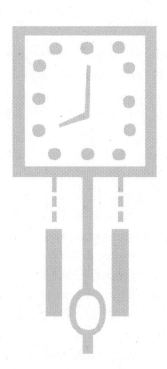

All our capacities and vulnerabilities change constantly over the 24-hour day. It's true whether we are fighting infection or fighting wars. Our vulnerability to terrorist attack and our capacity to survive depend on how well we understand and adjust to our biological clocks. Split-second changes in reaction time can mark success or death. Whether attacking an enemy outpost or defending a nuclear plant from terrorists, timing makes all the difference.

Times of Vulnerability

The disasters of Chernobyl, Bhopal, Three Mile Island, and the Exxon Valdez all took place between midnight and 6 A.M. These six hours are "downtime" for human biological performance. We don't do things well during these hours, and that includes defending ourselves. Many a "sneak attack" against military targets takes place at dawn or in the pre-dawn hours. These hours are a time when defenders are sleepy, slow, and dull-witted.

Until recently, soldiers on both sides of a conflict would feel the same biological effects of fatigue and sleepiness throughout the day. Now, using light boxes, medications, and well-timed training and exercise, personnel can be made highly efficient at any period of the day.

Our airports, transport terminals, and nuclear, fossil fuel, and chemical plants will be vulnerable to terrorist attacks throughout the foreseeable future. Much of that vulnerability will reach its peak between the hours of midnight and 6 A.M.

Fortunately, the American military knows very well that military preparedness must take into account the entire 24-hour environment. The same will now be required for the vulnerable sections of our economic, social, and political institutions. Managing shift work is now a matter of national security.

Preparing for Attack: Fatigue, Sleep, Motivation, and Biological Clocks

Militaries around the world have long been supporters of studies on biological clocks. The U.S. military has recently engaged many universities and research centers for the same task. They have found that the following factors affect the ability to fight and defend.

Fatigue

Fatigue is both mental and physical. Tiredness is a particular worry in combat operations. Fear and terror fill the confusion of battle, a stress difficult to appreciate for those who have never known war. The human body and mind are pushed to their limits, then beyond. People in the finest of physical condition can find themselves mentally broken within a matter of hours, sometimes minutes.

Preparing for such stress requires constant physical and mental conditioning. Soldiers prepare for war far more than they fight it. They are taught over and over the behaviors necessary for combat survival until they become automatic.

Fatigue, however, plays its part. There is just so much the mind and body can do. Every military officer learns to gauge their troops' physical and mental limits, because to exceed them is to invite disaster.

Sleep

Human beings need to sleep. All animals deprived of sleep die. Partial sleep deprivation causes people to learn badly and remember inadequately. Even short sleep deprivation (2 hours less per night) destabilizes overall energy use and metabolism. People deprived of sleep perform virtually any task poorly.

The rigors of combat routinely ruin sleep. Sleep interacts with fatigue to corrode the ability to think and act. Militaries have studied these problems around the world, in field studies and under laboratory conditions. Soldiers in the World War II battle of Stalingrad slept poorly for months. Both the Russians and Germans fired artillery bombardments 24 hours a day, consciously attempting to break their enemy physically and psychologically. Many soldiers slept at most 4 or 5 hours a day. Sleeplessness plays a significant part in "combat fatigue" and posttraumatic stress. Research by Dr. Gregory Belenky and others of the U.S. military demonstrate that combat abilities start to decline within 24 hours. However, truly severe declines occur after 48 hours, even with manipulation by stimulant drugs.

Stimulants

Stimulants, like caffeine and amphetamines, have been used in combat for thousands of years. No matter how they operate biochemically, stimulants have the same properties:

1. Their effects last only so long. Fatigue and sleeplessness make heavy, sustained stimulant use helpful over perhaps only three to five days.
2. By impairing sleep and increasing restlessness, stimulants can decrease as well as improve performance.
3. People vary greatly in their individual biological response.
4. Over long-term use, particularly in high doses, stimulants are addictive.

In research studies, stimulants can make people perform better over the first several days of many experiments. The drugs used are normally caffeine, amphetamines, and modafinil (Provigil). Oddly, long-acting caffeine, the most common and inexpensive treatment, often works as well as amphetamines and more recently developed drugs.

Developed as a treatment for narcolepsy, modafinil is now some-times used in place of amphetamines. Modafinil works at different brain sites than do previous stimulants; whether it is superior remains to be seen. Recent studies are looking positive.

Naps

Soldiers routinely nap before and after battle. Often these naps are involuntary. It is perfectly possible to stand with eyes open and still be asleep.

Under extreme conditions, sleep deepens. Chronically sleep-deprived individuals will preserve deep sleep and REM sleep, perhaps the two most useful parts of sleep.

Catnapping is the normal human response to forced sleeplessness. And though most people want to nap for more than a few minutes at a time, longer naps can create major problems for military operations, largely because of sleep inertia, the lack of complete alertness on awak-ening. A soldier who "wakes up" but is not fully alert may quickly become a dead soldier.

Much of sleep inertia appears tied to which phase of sleep we wake up from (see pages 27–30). People waking from light sleep—stages I and II—*may* have less trouble becoming alert than those waking from REM. Real problems result when people awake from deep sleep. Anyone trying to rouse a sleepwalker will understand: deep sleep got its name for a reason. Often it will take two or three minutes to wake someone in deep sleep into a state of minimal alertness.

The military is actively trying to find drugs to circumvent the sleep inertia problem. Most sleeping pills are benzodiazepines, drugs that touch and connect to special receptors in the brain.

Drugs like Valium (diazepam), Librium (chlordiazepoxide), Dalmane (flurazepam), Xanax (alprazolam), and Ambien (zolpidem) differ in the speed with which they hook onto benzodiazepine receptors, and in how slowly they fall off. Most of these drugs, like alcohol, impede overall per-formance. Balance and memory are diminished.

But drugs that block benzodiazepine receptors also exist. The military is trying to get around sleep inertia by alternately using opposite kinds of drugs: those that actively attach to benzodiazepine receptors, and those that block attachment. They hope to have soldiers fall asleep with benzodiazepines, then be rapidly awakened by drugs that block benzodiazepine receptors.

How well these experiments work remains to be seen. In the meantime, whether in civilian or military life, short naps seem to be the answer for quick rests during night operations. Though longer naps of up to 45 minutes may be used for workers on regular night shifts, conditions of potential emergency may require that nighttime security workers taking a break stick to short 10-minute naps.

Motivation

People fight for many reasons. They fight for their remarkably varied beliefs and ideologies. They fight for decent pay and good working conditions. They fight for their families, homes, and children.

And they fight for their friends and colleagues. What many studies from World War II and after seem to indicate is that in close-knit armies, soldiers fight for the other soldiers in their units. Under conditions that make normal human beings flee or run, soldiers will fight for their fellows in situations that otherwise appear suicidal. The people they live with and fight with are people they will die for.

Motivating civilians who protect civilian targets against terrorist attack is a different matter. In jobs where the enemy is unseen, where actual threat is very infrequent, it is often difficult for people to appreciate the seriousness of their work.

Constant training and continuing practice is one answer. Understanding the threat, particularly the threat represented by events like those of September 11, 2001, requires constant work. Security personnel must work well, and work as teams, overlapping in tasks and responsibilities.

There are no simple answers for prompting people to action. Motivation is a critical part in defending ourselves against all kinds of emergencies, including "common" accidents.

Biological Clocks and Vulnerability in Time

Performance declines between midnight and six are no longer inevitable. One government agency that pays great attention to biological clocks and performance is NASA.

Shuttle space flights are too expensive and difficult to allow human sleep to destroy their efficiency. When weather prevents space shots from taking place during the day, NASA shifts its spacecraft *and* its crews to nighttime capability.

The answer lies in light. NASA has elaborate rooms, filled with light boxes, that allow astronauts to quickly shift from day to night shots. It normally takes two days or more, but people can soon accommodate to eating "breakfast" at 8 P.M., rather than 8 A.M.

Just as NASA does, so can the rest of us. Light boxes, exercise, naps, and socializing—aided by melatonin and properly timed use of caffeine—can make most any group awake, alert, and ready at four in the morning.

Many terrorist attacks will not occur at night, as many targets are more publicly important during the daytime. But we are now and will remain most vulnerable during the night. Even the mid-afternoon dip in human alertness has repercussions for possible accidents and our general safety.

We have to know how to defend ourselves—and we have to know when we are most exposed.

Protecting Ourselves

Almost any public spot may become a terrorist target. Government facilities are especially at risk, but nuclear plants, dams, bridges, transport terminals, and chemical and petrochemical plants are also vulnerable.

Automation can help. The huge improvements in technical surveillance and telecommunications make automatic monitoring more useful and economical. Electronic motion and heat detectors as well as video make it more likely that we can detect attacks before they occur. But humans will oversee all such monitors. The data are only as good as the people watching and interpreting them. To protect ourselves, we need people who can work well and effectively at night.

Nighttime security work is low status and low pay. Many night-shift workers are older, and some have had or continue to have trouble with addictions. They must contend with meager daytime sleep and families that do not understand how hard it is to sleep during the day. Night-shift security workers sometimes self-dose themselves with alcohol to sleep in the daytime, adding large doses of caffeine to keep them awake at night.

Caffeine cuts both ways. It awakens temporarily, but may ruin later chances for sleep. Many night-shift workers are chronically exhausted and terribly sleepy. Too many of the people guarding important installations fall asleep at night.

In the future, night-shift workers must be more alert and more motivated than usual. They will have to remain ready to act despite conditions of boredom punctuated by panic, waiting for unseen enemies who may never come.

Learning from regular night-shift work, several recommendations can be made:

1. *Keep security officers young.* As we age, our body clocks and our capacity to phase-shift change. Youth is an enormous aid to maintaining alertness at night.
2. *Keep shifts constant.* It is best to have night-shift security personnel stay on constant night shift, and not to work swing shifts. Swing shifts are hard on almost anyone. A regular night shift allows those who are working night hours to better accommodate their biological clocks.
3. *Have night-shift security personnel live a reversed night-day cycle.* This is much harder than it first appears. Night-shift workers still live in a daytime society. Time with families and

children, and social and sports activities, normally take place during the day.

However, those who can stay on nighttime schedules should be able to stay more alert at night. That means trying to have security personnel literally reverse the P.M. and A.M. on the clock. This may be easier for people who are young and have not yet established their families.

4. *Give owls a chance.* The people normally most alert at night are owls. Severe owls are those to turn to for nighttime security work. People who feel perfectly alert at 4 A.M. are the people you want patrolling a nuclear plant at that hour.

5. *Exercise and socialize throughout the night.* Walking is helpful in keeping night-shift workers awake. People watching television monitors can pedal away at exercise bicycles or periodically walk on a treadmill. Too often nighttime personnel work alone. Keeping them in contact with others, even if by phone, helps keep them alert.

6. *Allow for short, programmed naps.* Setting up regular 10-minute naps at 3 or 4 A.M. can help many a security worker stay alive until the morning. Short naps prevent sleep inertia, the sluggishness that attends the end of sleep and keeps full alertness from quickly returning.

7. *Use bright light at the beginning of the shift, and keep monitoring areas well lit.* Evening bright light lengthens our biological day. At the beginning of a night shift, using bright lights like those of light boxes allows people to stay awake later and go to bed later (see Appendix 2). Keeping closed, quiet workplaces well lit also helps. Making security workers watch monitors in a dark room is a great way to put them to sleep.

8. *Use caffeine early when it is most effective.* Caffeine used at the beginning of a night shift will help workers overcome the normal 3 to 4 A.M. "hump" of inertia and sleepiness. But too much of any drug may pose a problem. Caffeine use throughout the night can lighten daytime sleep and create anxiety and nervousness

toward the end of shift. Daytime sleep is hard enough to obtain, and nighttime security workers need restful sleep more than most.

We can protect ourselves. To do so requires planning and attention. If we wish to keep ourselves secure, we must recognize the importance of biological clocks. Knowing our vulnerabilities, we can operate safely even under extreme conditions.

Properly adjusting for nighttime security work is difficult and sometimes expensive. Nighttime security work should not be the arena for ill-paid, tired, poorly sleeping individuals. It demands people who are motivated, trained, physically fit, and prepared for the unexpected.

SUMMARY

- We are most vulnerable to attacks and accidents between midnight and 6 A.M., when human performance hits its lows.
- To protect ourselves we need to pay great attention to our nighttime security workers, giving them greater status as well as the tools (such as the LENS program) they need to stay alert at night.

Chapter Nine

Timing Exercise for Health and Performance

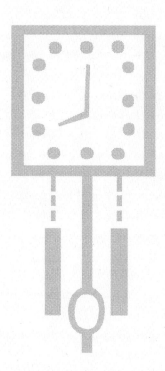

Joe detests exercise. He hated physical education classes in elementary school, and refused to join intramural sports throughout junior high and high school. Before applying to college, Joe demanded to know if physical education was a curriculum requirement.

Yet early every morning Joe wakes up, dresses, and goes out to walk. He does not walk to become fit, aid a long-standing heart condition, avoid future diabetes, or because he secretly likes to march. Joe forces himself to get up and walk because he is an owl. Without exercise and the bright sunlight of morning, he cannot do his job.

Exercise affects health in many different ways. To decide on how much, how, and when you exercise, you have to consider one question: what is your exercise for? For nonathletes, exercise timing can be used to:

- Promote overall health and lose weight
- Phase-shift: make larks more owl-like and owls more lark-like, to fit their work and/or social and family schedules
- Improve overall alertness whether in the morning, afternoon, evening, or night
- Make shift workers more alert and make shift work more palatable
- Improve sleep—whether you are fifteen or ninety
- Improve mood—whether in normal people or those suffering from depression

For athletes, exercise timing has different effects:

- Preparing for peak performances at set times of competition
- Avoiding injury and stress
- Phase-shifting lark and owl teammates to become in synch for competition

Exercising for Overall Health

Because human beings are not naturally sedentary, exercise is a critical part of overall health. Remaining stationary through much of our waking and sleeping life is a reason we often feel sluggish and tired; lack alertness during the day; suffer from heart disease, diabetes, and obesity at high rates; and die earlier than we should.

Many Americans exercise for 10 or 20 minutes a day, tops. In order to promote health and prolong life, how much exercise is enough? Another way to ask that question is: What is the proper amount of exercise that allows us to live the longest?

Several studies, done by Ralph Paffenbarger and others, studied undergraduates and then followed them for decades as they aged. The bottom line: exercise that burns 2,500 calories or more a week appeared to help people reach their longest life spans. How much exercise is that? Quite a lot. Running or bicycling hard may generate 10 to 13 calories a minute. To get to 2,500 calories would require at least four hours a week of tough, aerobic workouts.

Walking is different. Some people walk so slowly that they use perhaps only 150 calories per hour. Others walk briskly enough to work out 250 to 300 or more calories of energy each hour. To obtain 2,500 calories, walking briskly a bit more than an hour a day, every day, should produce excellent results.

An hour a day of exercise turns out to be a useful amount in other ways. It's the daily exercise time that's required for overweight people to keep weight off and remain trim.

But how does exercise work? Exercise appears to modify the set point in the hypothalamus, the weight-control mechanism that keeps our weights relatively constant. The set point is supposed to tell the rest of our brain when we have eaten enough.

If you go out and walk briskly for an hour, expending perhaps 250 calories, you will eat more over the next 24 hours. However, you probably will not eat an extra 250 calories. Chances are good that you will eat less. Perhaps you will take in only an extra 150 calories. The difference between the 250 calories expended in exercise, and the added 150 calories you ate, produces a "calorie debt" of 100 calories.

If you continue to exercise, that "calorie debt" eventually becomes expressed in lower weight. The important word is "eventually." Humans evolved under conditions of food scarcity, and your body is built to avoid starvation. Most of us know, particularly from indulging during the holidays, that weight gain can be exceptionally rapid.

Unfortunately, weight loss is very slow. Even when sedentary people began to exercise, it often takes several months for weight loss to appear on your scale, and that happens only after your body is relatively sure you are continuing to exercise on a higher metabolic level.

No, it isn't fair. It's the way things are. We have to use our bodies the way they are built, which means finding a way to exercise that works for you.

Timing Exercise for Health and Weight Loss

For those of us who attempt exercise, we mainly exercise when we can, not when we like. The usual times are before or after work, and on weekends.

However, to promote overall health, it makes sense to exercise every day. For those who do not have easy access to gyms or health equipment, the safest approach is to walk.

Walking is what humans are built to do. Unless we are afflicted with osteoarthritis—which is unfortunately common as we age—walking is the physical activity almost all of us can do.

Set times of walking such as morning or evening allow you to develop a regular exercise pattern. Such patterns of exercise, eating, and sleeping help reinforce your biological clocks, improving your overall health.

Yet walking is not what many of us like to do. To make it more palatable, try to walk with someone else. Walking with family or friends in the morning or evening has many advantages.

- You'll have time to talk together.
- Spending time with friends, acquaintances, and colleagues is an important factor in overall health.
- If you are in sunlight, walks should improve your mood.
- Exercising together helps put partners' biological clocks in synch.

When to walk is more often controlled by social and economic factors, than by biological ones. In general, evening walks should be easiest from a physical standpoint, as most of us feel best exercising in the late afternoon or evening (an important point for athletes to remember). Evening walks should improve mood. They also have the advantage that children and friends usually can be brought together more easily in the evening.

However, morning walks have their own particular benefits. Usually we are grumpiest in the morning, particularly if we are owls. Morning walks improve fitness and especially mood, particularly when there is sufficient sunlight. And though a bit harder on the joints, morning walks tend to increase alertness for the workday, a real problem in a sleep-deprived society.

Another strategy that helps many people begin and then continue lifelong exercise is to couple exercise and eating—though not at exactly the same time. If you can exercise in the morning before breakfast, you may build up an appetite for that critical but often undesired meal. Walks after lunch can prevent an afternoon dip in alertness. Finally, walks after the evening meal may help us sleep *and* may decrease the tendency of evening meals to stick on our bones and increase our weight.

Please exercise when you can. If at all possible, exercise in sunlight, and with family or friends. The effects on health and weight may multiply when exercise becomes a social affair.

Exercise for Phase-Shifting

Owls have a bad time in a society that has little patience for their habits. Fortunately, light and exercise can help owls stay awake and work through the day with larks, even if they can't pass as larks.

Light and exercise work differently, but in tandem. In the evening and night, light tends to make our 24-hour day longer; in the morning it tends to make our day shorter.

Light's effects are particularly potent around your body temperature minimum. In general, the body temperature minimum is around 4 to 5:30 A.M. for larks, perhaps three hours later for owls. However, each of us is unique.

You could get some idea of your body temperature minimum or bottom by waking up every hour at night for several days, putting a thermometer under your tongue, and recording your temperature. However, it makes more sense to find out your preferred time of waking. If you go on vacation and get to sleep whenever you want, you may find a time when you really prefer to wake. (Unfortunately, this may take a *really* long vacation, as many working owls and larks are profoundly sleep deprived.)

Let's say you are a lifelong owl who awakes on vacation days at 10 A.M., feeling moderately refreshed. Your body temperature bottom is probably around 90 to 150 minutes earlier. This means that 7 to 8 A.M. may be a critical point of light exposure. Light before this time should shift you later (more owl-like), light after that time should make you shift your biological clocks earlier (more lark-like).

People shift differently with different amounts of light. You will find what works for you. But if you are a severe owl who works by an owl's late schedule, you may not want to get up very early for light exposure at 5 or 6 A.M. Light at this time may make you even *more* owl-like than you already are. In this case, light after dawn, particularly after 8 A.M., may be a safer bet.

Light can be obtained from the sun by walking outside or from a light box. Fortunately, the desired phase shift in your biological clocks can be enhanced by exercising and using light at the same time.

The beauty of light and exercise is that they both work *in the same direction*. Evening and night light and exercise make most of us more owl-like; morning light and exercise make most of us more lark-like. Shift workers are different. Many shift workers have highly disordered biological clocks, making it difficult to really know how their overall cycle functions from day to day.

The issue also varies with whether you need to shift yourself temporarily or permanently. Temporary effects are in some ways easier.

Linda is a lark friend of mine married to a musician. Her husband, Fred, is a true lifelong owl; he loves to take time out and socialize after finishing his sets, generally around midnight or later.

When she was younger, Linda had less trouble keeping late hours to stay up with Fred. However, as she ages, she finds herself, like most of us, more and more lark-like. Fred has hardly changed at all.

Linda keeps to a lark schedule most days. However, on nights when she wants to engage with Fred and his friends, she gets on the treadmill or exercise bicycle at around 9 P.M. After a steady workout of 40 minutes or longer, she showers, dresses, and heads off to join her husband.

Most nights she can continue until around 12:30 or 1 A.M. without feeling "totally wasted." However, if she socializes beyond that into the later hours, "I'm ready to crash—whether I want to or not."

If she wishes to stay awake further, Linda either tries a short walk, or small doses of caffeine. Her major problem, however, is sleep. Like many larks, Linda will wake at a set time no matter what time she gets to bed. Generally, she wakes at 6:30 A.M., regardless of the time she went to sleep.

As Linda rarely can sleep past 7 A.M., I advise her to get up at her usual hour. I ask her to take a brisk walk around noon following such late nights if possible. This walk allows her to feel a bit more alert in the early afternoon when "I'd really feel like hell and just crash."

Her noontime walk has another useful result. Following this brisk walk, Linda generally feels sleepy about 3 hours later. The midafternoon becomes a perfect time for a nap, particularly on weekends. Since she has slept so little the previous night, I advise Linda to try for 45 minutes to an hour of sleep.

Though the naps help, Linda often feels "really tired" the next evening. If she went out with Fred on a Saturday night, I sometimes ask her to try melatonin Sunday night. Late Sunday melatonin tends to shift people earlier. It also helps Linda fall asleep at night and prepare for work on Monday.

Shifting owls or larks on a permanent basis has the advantage of causing people to look at many parts of their lifestyle: socializing, diet, exercise, and sleep. Yet for owls adapting to lark time, or larks adapting permanently to nighttime, the same simple rules apply: evening light and exercise make us more owl-like, morning light and exercise more lark-like. Whenever possible, obtaining exercise with family and friends, particularly on a regular basis, makes it much easier to establish the lark or owl pattern you desire.

Exercise Timing to Increase Alertness

Exercise, fitness, healthiness, and alertness all work together. Each reinforces the other.

Alertness is increased by physical activity. Heavier physical activity, such as aerobic exercise in which most heart rates go well over a hundred, causes many people to feel refreshed and alert in ways they cannot otherwise achieve. Our improved feeling of healthiness and alertness is one reason U.S. senators play squash at noontime, and CEOs place treadmills in their offices or even on the executive jet. Aerobic exercise makes people sharper, more mentally alert, and better able to adapt to the stresses of the day and night.

To know when exercise can best be used to increase your alertness, track your overall alertness throughout the day. Just take out a set of ruled paper, and write at the top "Alertness Scale."

Now, split the paper with five vertical lines, and label them Monday, Tuesday, Wednesday, Thursday, and Friday. If you work on weekends, add Saturday and Sunday. On the left-hand side of the paper, use a line each for 12 P.M., 1 P.M., and so on through 5 P.M.

For a full work week, write down your level of alertness for each hour, noon through 5 P.M. Alertness of zero equals "I'm ready to fall asleep standing up" while alertness of 10 equals "I'm as sharp and alert as I ever felt." The event producing such alertness might have been a planned meeting with a romantic partner, or just an annual physical.

Check your overall alertness. Usually there will be a regular period of an hour or two when you feel least alert. These are the times pre-emptive exercise and light can help you. If you find that you are desperate to snag a pillow at 1:30 to 2:30 P.M., try to walk and get bright light during the half hour or hour before. Walking with friends should be particularly helpful.

All right, you say. I walk. I march in the sunlight. I work out with friends. I still feel sleepy and lethargic in the afternoon.

If exercise and light do not help keep you alert in the afternoon, start writing down on the same sheet of paper what you had to eat for lunch—and when. If you find that lunches of bread and pasta make you feel half dead two hours later, consider high protein meals with reasonable helpings of fish, chicken, or soy. Try if possible to couple exercise with eating by walking before or after you dine.

If your brain still feels like soggy straw come the afternoon, try to take a little time to visit colleagues. Walk and socialize as you go. Often midafternoon is a time when it's best to get out for a little while, looking at the sunlight as you take a walk to visit a work acquaintance or customer.

Unfortunately, many office workers feel chained to their desks. If that is the case, try to avoid doing your most demanding and creative work in the midafternoon. Leave your most important work to the times when you are at your best, generally mornings for larks and late afternoon or early evenings for owls.

Alertness is temporarily improved by exercise no matter what the time of day. The exercise need not be severe or particularly sustained to help people stay sharp.

But scheduling exercise usually requires creativity. Humans, especially employers, are sometimes convinced that workers only work when sitting at a desk. Try whenever possible to disabuse your boss of this view. Keeping yourself alert, especially walking before and after mealtimes, may pay dividends in work performance for all concerned.

Shift Work and Exercise

Most people who engage in shift work don't think about exercise. They're too tired, too sleep deprived, and too overwhelmed by their children's and partner's schedules to even bother thinking about exercise.

All the more reason they should.

As you saw in Chapter 7, working shifts is a task for which the human body is evolutionarily unprepared. Shift workers have a chance to fight back and adapt their biological clocks using the LENS program: light, exercise, naps, and socializing. However, as in all other things, timing is key.

For those swinging shifts from day or evening into the night, exercise can prove very helpful. If you are planning to work graveyard shift, which is generally around 11 P.M. to 7 A.M., exercise just before the shift (often after a nap) can make the first few hours of shift work much easier to bear.

Aerobic exercise, generally pushing your heart rate well above 100, is best for keeping someone alert in the middle of the night. If you can do aerobic cycling on a stationary bike, or brisk walking, running, or exercise machine workouts, your 11 P.M. shift may convert from a sleep time to an alert time, and not just for severe, night-loving owls. Caffeine dosed between 11 P.M. and midnight can also be very useful.

One of the tricks to surviving nighttime shift work is to try to be in motion as much as possible. Walk, fidget, move on the balls of your feet, even if you're forced to stare at a security monitor most of the night. Socializing helps, but planned exercise may help much more.

Night workers often adjust to their shifts by learning isometric exercises, or yoga techniques. Simple in-place exercises, particularly stretches, are often useful. But don't stretch too strenuously, as your nighttime muscles and tendons will not be as flexible as they are during the afternoon or evening.

In work assignments that are primarily sedentary, walks with coworkers should be scheduled as often as possible, preferably once an hour. Taking 5 minutes to walk around and talk with a coworker can revive many a nighttime shift worker.

Nighttime caffeine must be used carefully. Too much late-night caffeine and you won't sleep in the morning. When in doubt, take a walk or perform isometric, in-place exercise, before you reach for the coffee mug or chocolate bar.

Exercise, talks with friends and co-workers, and midnight caffeine may keep shift workers going until 3 or 4 A.M. However, many shift workers then find themselves "hitting the wall." In some Japanese workplaces, 4 A.M. naps are mandatory. Except for owls, 4 A.M. is a time when human function reaches its performance lows.

Exercise can also be used by shift workers to keep themselves in shape. Shift workers sleep poorly to begin with. However, athletes of all kinds sleep better than does the rest of the population. Mental fatigue can often be overcome by physical effort, even when we feel half-dead. Shift workers need to remain fit to protect their health from the stresses of gastrointestinal and heart disease, as well as improve their chances of obtaining decent sleep.

When should shift workers exercise? Usually whenever possible. The main exception is not to exercise too close to times of going to sleep, especially for those who find exercise highly stimulating.

Exercise and Sleep

Timing of exercise to promote sleep is somewhat controversial. Like many controversies, the difficulties lie in normal human variation. Just as people vary 2,000 percent in how well they metabolize different drugs, there is great variation in exercise timing and its impact on sleep. I found this out in my own personal experience.

Many years ago, when teaching at the University of Texas Medical School, I joined an Ultimate Frisbee team from Rice University. Ultimate Frisbee is a game with rules similar to soccer. The basis of the game is teamwork and sprinting; Ultimate players are nearly always engaged in constant, breakneck motion. As the oldest, and generally the worst player on the squad, I needed more practice than anyone.

Our captain decided that we should have team practice starting at 7:30 P.M. It was a time most of us could make, students as well as professionals. I came to practice regularly, working out in the night until about 9 or 9:30.

When I returned home, I could not sleep. I read, took baths, and tried to relax, but I still could not fall into sleep until midnight or 12:30 at the earliest. When I woke in the morning I felt awful. I knew that I had awakened many times in the night, arousing repeatedly at times when I normally slept.

I continued with team practices for a while, until I found I could no longer function at work the next day. I tried to have our captain schedule practices at other times, but change proved difficult. Finally we began practicing before our usual Sunday-afternoon matches.

Back in the 1980s, Professor Jim Horne demonstrated that people seemed to sleep best 4 to 6 hours after heavy aerobic exercise. However, this is not true of everyone. It is particularly not true of athletes, who normally are extremely fit. Many athletes can exercise in the evening and still fall asleep an hour or so later. Some people I see exercise almost until sleep time, take a hot bath, and quickly find themselves asleep.

Do late-night exercisers sleep as well as they could? My guess, based on what I see, is no. Those who exercise late at night seem to have decreased sleep times on the nights they work out.

For those who are planning to go to sleep between 10 P.M. and 11:30, early evening exercise is probably best. Walking with the family or friends in the hour just before or after a meal seems to help many people "de-arouse" and relax. Evening exercise prepares people to enjoy their evenings, and if brisk, appears to help people fall asleep and obtain deeper sleep.

The key here is human body temperature. Heavy exercise causes our body temperatures to go up. The higher they go—and they go quite high in athletes—the more rapidly they may descend. This rapid deceleration may sometimes provide quick entrance into sleep.

Exercise in the evening also appears to increase deep sleep, probably the most important part of sleep. Evening exercise is particularly helpful to the sleep of older men.

Sleep When We Are Older

When we are young, deep sleep may constitute 15 to 20 percent of total nighttime sleep. By the time men reach 70 years of age, even healthy males obtain only 1 to 3 percent deep sleep per night. The decrease is not as dire among women, but the decline with age is still extreme.

When we are older, sleep is hard to get. Sleep efficiency declines and awakenings increase, as do rates of sleep apnea and nighttime leg kicks, all of which worsen sleep quality. Older women and men need as much help with sleep as they can find.

Two aids to sleep for older people are ones you know well: exercise and light. Several studies show that evening exercise helps older people to fall asleep and stay asleep. Bright light therapy at night also helps older people sleep longer and more comfortably.

There is nothing wrong with combining the two. One man I see, presently in his eighties, has had insomnia for thirty years. He exercises in the evening, outside if possible to gain the advantage of light. Once back in his apartment, he sits in front of his light box from 8 to 9 P.M., watching television or reading.

The combination works moderately well for him. Walking for a half hour and sitting by the light box for a half hour or an hour every evening has added about 2 hours of sleep to each of his nights. He feels better, he tells me, but not well enough.

I've also tried to add passive body heating (hot baths) to his regimen. Though he dislikes baths, he has tried that regimen with some success. I'm still trying to obtain better sleep for him.

Evening exercise helps many people sleep. Making evening exercise social, engaging your partners and children in walking or sports, often makes the experience more rewarding.

Exercise and Mood

If you watch television, you might think the main treatment of depression is antidepressant drugs. For many people, antidepressants may be lifesaving. But they are only one way to treat depression, and often not the most significant one.

Much of the population suffers from long-standing minor depression. People feel unhappy, sad, disinterested, and unmotivated, but still work fairly effectively and lack suicidal or guilty feelings. For this large group, exercise may be as effective or more effective than antidepressants. To work, the exercise should be consistent, meaning daily, and preferably involve an hour or more of activity.

Many a depressed patient I know has felt far better simply by taking long morning walks. Morning is the time mood is at its low for most of the population. Morning walking or other exercise, especially where you can obtain exposure to light, can decrease or eliminate this feeling of unease.

Morning is often the time when light exposure has the greatest impact on mood. A quarter to half of the population of the northeastern U.S. notes a large decline in their mood every winter. The worst period seems to be late November into March.

For several million Americans, this change in mood is severe. Many people find that much more than their sense of pleasure in life disappears. They feel tired, listless. They want to sleep, a lot. Many eat more. Many mornings, they feel they can't drag themselves out of bed. Some say they feel half-dead, like "hibernating bears."

This yearly event, called seasonal depression, or seasonal affective disorder, affects a very large number of people worldwide. Using light boxes in the morning has a major impact on improving people's mood. Morning light appears to be more effective than evening light.

People with seasonal depression experience differences in their biological clocks. Unlike most other human beings but in common with many mammals, their nighttime melatonin levels shift with the seasons. They also experience profound improvement of mood with bright light therapy.

It is important to know that light improves the mood for everyone, not just those with seasonal depression. Overall mood correlates well with how much light exposure people have. Light is one reason why people move to sunnier climes like Florida and California or come south for vacations.

Morning exercise can improve mood even without sunlight, making people feel alert and alive at a time when their bodies otherwise feel half-asleep. Yet for those who exercise outside, much of their improvement in mood comes from morning light.

Unfortunately, stiff ligaments and joints present a problem for those who exercise in the morning. Our biological clocks decree that muscles, joints, and ligaments are more stiff and prone to injury in the morning. Whether lark or owl, your joints tend to work better in the afternoon and evening. Particularly for people who suffer with arthritis, late afternoon and evening exercise may be preferred.

Mood improves in most people come evening. Perhaps that is why many people feel that evening exercise improves their mood more than morning exercise does. Evening exercisers also experience fewer injuries.

Exercise improves mood, as well as overall health, in both morning and evening. So what should you do?

If you're lucky enough to be able to exercise at different times of day, morning exercise is probably preferable for owls and people with seasonal changes in mood. People needing to become alert enough for early jobs probably benefit more from morning exercise. There is some small evidence that morning exercise might be slightly better for those trying to lose weight.

Evening exercise tends to make people feel far more alert and sharp. Walking or working out in the evening also has the advantage, for most people, of separating the work day from the social day, and increasing people's energy to socialize with family and friends. The best possibility may lie in exercising both in the morning and evening, walking or playing sports with family and friends.

When possible, exercise in bright light. It aids your mood, and can be used to reset biological clocks any way you wish (just be sure to use sunscreen when outdoors).

Exercise Timing for Athletes

Even before Roger Smith and colleagues wrote about the impact of timing on professional sports, professional teams had taken biological clocks seriously. Now they routinely schedule their practice sessions and practice games at hours that will best prepare them for major events.

Jet lag is less and less a factor for teams flying across time zones. Especially in professional football, teams have learned to arrive at their destination early, often by two days or more. Though human biological clocks generally adjust better going west than east, most people will reshift their inner time clocks 40 minutes to an hour each day towards the time zone where they land. This shift in inner clocks may be quicker on average for professional athletes, who are very fit and capable of enjoying and using several hours of light exposure.

Most athletes feel at their best in the late afternoon to early evening. They recognize that strength and speed are also superior at these times. Injury rates also appear to be lower in the late afternoon and early evening.

Less commented upon is that both larks and owls naturally tend to have high alertness in the late afternoon and early evening. The hours between 4 P.M. and 7 P.M. are excellent "overlap times," when most larks and owls on any squad should all be alert, reaching relative peaks in their own performance cycles.

Yet not all athletes obtain peak performances at these hours. Nor will most athletic events, especially for nonprofessional athletes, take place at hours when people are just leaving work or starting to prepare dinner.

Peak Performance

Your peak athletic performance is affected by far more than biological clocks. Time of eating, form and number of calories, overall mood, interest in the sport, importance of particular events, family affairs—these all have an impact on performance. The quality of motivation, generally high in professional athletes, shifts rapidly with psychological factors, even in professionals who have trained at their sport daily for a decade or more. Anyone who has watched professional tennis can see how shifts in confidence from one moment to the next may determine who wins or loses a match.

Biological clocks are one factor among many in determining how well you perform. Fortunately, they can be put to good use by just about any athlete.

Peak Performance for Larks

Larks prefer the morning. Though morning injuries are more common than evening ones due to biological shifts in connective tissue tension and resiliency, larks who habitually stretch and prepare their muscles and joints should be able to avoid major injuries. They should also be able to perform well into the late morning.

Larks have one clear advantage: they will tend to do better than owls during the morning. In sports like track and field, golf, or tennis, larks should be able to perform *relatively* better than owls, particularly in the early morning to midmorning.

Problems arise when larks must perform in the early afternoon, and are especially acute at night. Though evening exercise over time makes larks more owl-like, nighttime performance can be a particular burden for larks.

The way to improve lark nighttime performance is to consider the use of a light box (see Appendix 2). If there is a single major nighttime event to prepare for, larks can work with up to one or more additional hours of evening light for two or more days prior to the match. By shifting their biological clocks later, they will make themselves more owl-like, and be better able to perform at night.

If there is little time to prepare for a nighttime match, larks need not despair. Warming up that evening under bright light may improve performance. The reasons for this improvement are twofold: evening exercise *and* evening bright light tend to make our biological clocks later.

The combination makes it easier for larks to prepare for night matches. Best of all, bright light tends to improve alertness and mood. Many a lark will feel mood and competitive spirit increase from bright light exposure before a night match.

Female athletes in particular should use light to their advantage. Though some women who are serious long-distance runners do not menstruate, most female athletes must deal with premenstrual stress and tension. Regular exercise can help prevent some premenstrual symptoms, but light exposure may be more helpful.

Working in ways different from their antidepressant effects, serotonergic antidepressants such as Paxil (paroxetine), Prozac (fluoxetine), Celexa (citalopram), and Zoloft (sertraline) are effective for the majority of women suffering premenstrual mood shifts. However, many women, especially athletes, do not want to take antidepressants for a week or two each menstrual period. For those who do not, bright light is a possible alternative. Many women feel much better the week before menstruating if they sit in front of a bright light box for an hour or more each day.

Light boxes can be used by male as well as female athletes. Working out under bright light improves motivation and mood for many athletes. Using evening bright light can phase-shift lark athletes to perform at their best even at night, and improve their mood.

Peak Performance for Owls

In many professional sports, owls have the advantage. Professional sports make a large part of their revenues from television. Media sponsors prefer night games, when audiences are largest.

Owls usually need not do much to prepare for night games. When their lark opponents and teammates will want to prepare for bed, many owls will feel at their best. Owls have a much larger problem preparing for morning matches. As with larks, light can come to their rescue.

If you are an owl playing early morning matches, you must doubly beware. Your body may be ill prepared. Joints, ligaments, and muscles may respond as if you are still asleep. You may feel clumsy, and act it. Morning is the time you will be at greater risk of injury.

Morning light—whether provided by sunlight or by light boxes—phase-shifts owls to become more lark-like. Doing warm-ups, reading, or eating breakfast under a light box before an early morning match can help owls increase their alertness and preparedness.

Midafternoon may also be a trying time for owl athletes. Preparing with bright light an hour or two before a match should dispel some of the "afternoon blues" that afflict so much of our sleep-deprived population. Though athletes sleep more efficiently than does the rest of the population, there is no antidote to sleep loss besides sleep. Athletes in particular need to protect their sleep time. Some athletic abilities will correlate directly with how many hours of sleep you've received. There are reasons coaches ask players to keep nighttime curfews.

Peak Performance: Team Sports

Inevitably sports teams are combinations of larks, owls, and switchers. Getting the entire squad "in synch" can help most teams perform at their best.

Individual athletes can test their larkness or owlness with the tests explained in Chapter 1 and Appendix 1. Owls can prepare for morning practice and matches with morning light, while larks can use evening light to help them prepare for night matches.

Most teams, however, practice at times that are convenient. Practicing consistently at the same times allows team members to adjust their performance to those hours. Late afternoon and early evening are periods when injuries will be least, and overall performance for most members of a team near their best, whether lark, owl, or switcher.

However, getting larks and owls in sync is a different matter if matches are scheduled at times that ill favor either group. In college sports, early morning games, as in junior varsity soccer or lacrosse, can make life difficult for owls. Owl athletes, especially normally short-sleeping college students, have to be sure to protect their sleep times before morning matches. They will also be served by morning bright light exposure, preferably for several days before a match so they can properly entrain their biological clocks.

Night matches are a different story. Many players on teams that play during nights declare themselves owls. In part this is because most athletes are generally young and very fit, able to shift their biological clocks with relative ease.

Not everyone is so lucky. For teams that normally practice and play during the day, night matches represent a different challenge. Night play is not something they normally attempt. And their lark team members may feel and perform far below their norm.

To prepare for night matches, sports teams, especially college teams, should try to practice at night. Night practices will prepare athletes for the different stresses and requirements of the night, including different lighting and field conditions, and the differing abilities of their teammates, particularly those who are larks.

Night practices are inconvenient for many. They interfere with family, social, and scholastic life and may also interfere with some athletes' ability to sleep that night. However, night practices, especially for nonprofessionals, will help a team prepare for the special environment of night play.

SUMMARY

- Exercise needs to become an ordinary activity; we should walk, bike, stroll, and run every day we possibly can.
- For weight loss, exercise, such as walking, should be linked to eating and done before or after each meal.
- Morning exercise and light make us more lark-like; evening exercise and light make us more owl-like.
- Exercise is often critical for keeping shift workers awake and alert. It is also useful for shifting their biological clocks.

- Evening exercise often helps people sleep, particularly older insomniacs.
- Exercise can improve mood throughout the day. Morning exercise, particularly combined with light exposure, is best for overcoming winter blues.
- For most athletes, peak sports performance is generally in the late afternoon and early evening. Using light exposure and changing exercise times before matches can improve performance for both owls and larks.

Chapter Ten

Medical Treatments: Changing Times, Changing Results

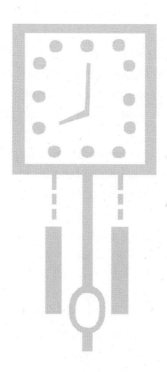

M

r. Lipton was scared. His wife was frantic.

Five days earlier Mr. Lipton had started taking monoamine oxidase inhibitors, an older type of antidepressant. His doctor had told him that MAOIs, as they are commonly known, are unusual drugs. He would need to follow a special diet. No Chianti wine, no blue cheese. He would need to carefully watch his blood pressure. If he ate the wrong foods, his blood pressure could go sky high. He might even have a stroke or heart attack.

Mr. Lipton went out and bought a new blood pressure cuff. Soon he was proficient at using it.

I had the good luck to be on call to cover Mr. Lipton's doctor the weekend after he started taking his new antidepressant. The emergency call came on Saturday evening. I took the number and dialed.

"Hello," Mrs. Lipton answered. "I think my husband is about to have a heart attack."

When I found out the treatment circumstances, I asked to speak with Mr. Lipton. I heard heavy breathing before he came on the phone.

"My blood pressure is going up and up and up. I think I'm having a reaction. You know I'm on MAOIs."

Mr. Lipton's blood pressure was increasing. A retired engineer, Mr. Lipton had recorded his blood pressure. Now he was charting its progress through the day.

At nine in the morning, his blood pressure, right arm standing, had run 138/90. A little on the high side, perhaps, but quite normal for him. He decided to check his pressure again at lunchtime. His noon blood pressure clocked in at 150/95. Though he had strictly followed his MAOI diet, Mr. Lipton became worried. He decided to check his blood pressure again at two o'clock.

"I've been checking it *every* hour since then," he told me. "It's going up every hour. Every hour. Up and up and up."

"You're checking it *every* hour?" I asked.

"Of course. I have to know if I'm getting into trouble."

I tried to explain to Mr. Lipton that blood pressure *normally* goes up during the morning. It often will continue to rise later in the day, reaching its peak about ten to twelve hours after the time he woke. Normally systolic blood pressure, the top measured number, goes up 10 to 20 points, while diastolic, the more important lower number, increases 5 to 10 points.

Mr. Lipton wasn't buying it. "Look, I'm on a dangerous medication that increases blood pressure. My blood pressure is rising and rising. What are you going to do about it?"

"Ask you to stop taking your blood pressure."

"What?"

"That's right. You're sure you didn't eat anything that might cause trouble. Please stop taking your blood pressure."

"My blood pressure is already 175 over 103. That's dangerous. My doctor told me it was dangerous. I'm taking a dangerous drug. You've got to do something about it."

"I will. But probably the main reason your blood pressure is rising is because you're taking it so often."

"What?"

"Your blood pressure is rising for two reasons: first, it's supposed to rise during the day. Much of the rise you've described happens normally, until you reach evening or night. Second, you're so worried about your blood pressure that you're causing it to rise further. If you stop taking your blood pressure, it should go down."

The conversation that followed was long. I told Mr. Lipton a little of the history of MAOIs, how they had originally been devised to *lower* blood pressure. Which is exactly what they did in many people, even when eating the "forbidden" foods.

Next, I explained again about biological clocks and how blood pressure, like every element of his biology, had cycles. Blood pressure was not supposed to be the same from morning to evening. If it stayed the same, that itself might be abnormal. Finally I described to him "white coat syndrome," how blood pressure may rise dramatically when taken by doctors. He might be inducing white coat syndrome on himself by frequently taking his own blood pressure, especially since he had been given very good reasons to fear what his new medication might do. Anxiety could markedly increase blood pressure within a very short span.

After we talked, Mr. Lipton told me he felt a little more relaxed. He still wanted to take his blood pressure, but I persuaded him to wait a few hours. When he did, it had dropped down to 135/85. When we spoke later, I was happy to hear less tension in his voice. I told him to stop taking the new drug, which had caused him far too much distress. I did not explain to him that his blood pressure lowering was normal and expected. Blood pressure normally went down during the night.

Everything in our body is cyclic—everything. Your blood pressure, heart rate, glucose levels, the speed with which your cells divide and repair themselves, how fast you walk or run, all changes throughout the day.

The same is true for your symptoms, your diagnostic tests, and all your potential medical treatments. Any therapy you take will have different biological-clock results through the day for both the therapeutic effects *and* the side effects.

Nothing in the body is constant. Just as your intake of food and its effects change throughout the day, so will the effects of any drugs or treatments you use. Unfortunately, for several reasons I will describe, how these changes affect your health care are unknown to many of your doctors. To protect yourself, you have to know about your own biological clocks.

Good Health Is Not the Same as Good Health Care

Too many Americans think their health is mostly bound up with the quality of their health care. Sadly, they are wrong.

Health is the ability to survive and thrive under different environments: physical, environmental, psychological, and spiritual. The real measure of healthiness is how well you respond to changing environments, particularly environments you don't like or have never experienced. When faced with a challenge, whether a group of cold-virus particles coughed towards your face or losing a new job, do you get sick or stay well?

Health is a measure of your resiliency, the ability of your body and brain to adapt. Flexibility of response is key.

At the beginning of the twentieth century, the average age of death in the United States was about thirty-five. The vast majority of people who died young died of infectious disease. Most people I know think the doubling of average life span in the twentieth century was due to antibiotics and improved health care. That is a myth.

The effect of antibiotics on increasing our population's life span was very small. Most of the improvement in the national health had already occurred due to changes in sanitation and nutrition. Health improved due to changes in the way people went about their lives, the cleanliness of their water, streets, offices, and homes, and their overall diet. Vaccinations further helped increase life expectancy by decreasing deaths in the very young.

The same is true today. *How* we live determines how long and well we live far more than our health care does.

People now see healthiness and life span limited by chronic illnesses like heart disease, stroke, and cancer. The major impacts for decreasing these illnesses come from quitting smoking, improving diet, and increasing exercise levels—not from health care.

The effects of health care on increasing life spans have so far been limited. The war on cancer has not appreciably increased longevity in most cases. Surgery has improved the population's cardiac mortality, but only marginally. So far, up till now health care has not been very effective at increasing overall life span. It is, however, excellent at improving quality of life for sufferers of illness.

Yet overall quality of life is still governed by the same factors discussed in Chapter 4: genetics, diet, exercise level, amount of social support, and your outlook on life.

Plus the regularity and patterns of your days.

Circadian Health

Everything in our body changes all the time. Our inner environment undergoes constant flux. So does the environment beyond, outside us. The temperature and light levels change, as do the levels of allergens, carcinogens, and viruses in the air. Our social, work, and emotional life all possess their own frequently shifting environments.

Our health is determined by this clash of inner and outer lives. Why you get a cold but your daughter doesn't may have as much to do with when the virus reached your respiratory system (and what your immune function was that hour) as with how many virus particles flew in the air.

Everything changes, yet most natural changes are cyclic and predictable, like the movements of the sun and moon above the rapidly rotating earth. Because these changes are predictable, we can prepare ourselves for them. The changes in our biological clocks are also cyclic, and we help them work by adopting regular patterns in our lives.

Because our bodies are cyclic, it pays to live within the boundaries of our clocks. Living well means living regularly: Going to sleep at the same times of day; waking at the same times; exercising and eating at regular times; and socializing and playing at regular intervals.

Life is about balance. We need to balance our desires and our means, our wants and abilities, our capacities and actions. We help balance our lives by leading regular lives.

Leading a regular life is particularly important for those of us who are ill. Living within our biological clocks gives our bodies the chance to function at their best. It allows us to develop and use the most adaptable, adjustable systems for fighting off disease and illness. Just as we are always fighting off colds and flus, we are trying to destroy the cancer cells we constantly produce, and open the narrowed vessels that compromise our heart and brain.

Living with a regular pattern puts us in sync with whatever health treatments we require. Just as we change, so do the effects of all health treatments change, hour by hour.

With constantly changing internal and external environments, our bodies need patterns to make sense of life. We have evolved those patterns by embedding time in our biology, preparing us for the changes of day and night. Keeping that pattern constant gives us the chance to fight off illness and keep ourselves well.

Circadian health is based on the ideas that:

1. Our ability to maintain our health changes during the day.
2. Our health is very much a matter of how we live our lives. Balance in our lives goes a long way toward making us healthy.
3. Prevention of illness is the major goal. No matter how excellent, most medical treatments come too late, when illness has already developed.
4. Our symptoms change during the day, and they have to be treated in line with those changes.
5. The effects of treatments, along with medical test results, also change throughout the day.
6. A regular pattern of action preserves us by making it easier for our body to adapt to changes in both inner and outer environments.

Know Your Symptoms—and How to Record Them

Doctors talk about symptoms as subjective measures of distress. Fatigue and sleepiness, depression and pain are symptoms. "Sign" is the medical term used for changes that can be directly measured, like blood pressure and heart rate.

Some illnesses have an evident cause, like pneumonia caused by a specific bacterium or virus. So-called minor illnesses, like colds, often have clear causes, though knowing which virus causes your particular cold is presently considered too difficult and expensive to determine.

The large majority of chronic illnesses do not have clear-cut causes. Though risk factors have been established, like cholesterol levels or homocysteine levels for heart disease, in most cases we really don't know what causes the illnesses associated with those risk factors.

The chronic illnesses that most of us suffer or will suffer are groupings of symptoms and signs called syndromes. Syndromes have particular patterns, forms, and life spans all their own. Early-life diabetes (type I) is a syndrome, as is chronic obstructive lung disease, coronary artery disease, chronic pain or depression, and many, many others.

Though doctors and others may be able to help you treat your illness, you will know its manifestations better than anyone. One of the most useful things you can do to help yourself is to record the pattern of your symptoms.

Creating a personal record of illness is not difficult. Mostly it requires patience, and a little effort. The simplest way of looking at symptoms is to note what they are. With a syndrome like osteoarthritis, the illness of painful joints that afflicts most of us with age, you need to know where you have the pain, when you have it, how severe it is.

Osteoarthritis is generally considered a disease of the daytime. Most sufferers have their worst symptoms in the afternoon and evening. This pattern, however, may not be true for you.

First, buy a notepad. For several days, use it to note when your symptoms are worst, when they occur, and how painful they are on a scale of 0 to 10 (0 means absolutely no pain; 10 is pain you consider unbearable).

You should be able to see a pattern after only a few days. Now, start a fresh page on your notepad. Draw a series of vertical lines. Each vertical line represents a day. On a horizontal line, write down *Times*.

Let's say most of your symptoms occurred between 2 and 8 P.M. Over the next several days, set yourself to track your symptoms hourly from 2 to 8 P.M. A digital watch with an hourly time chime can help, or you can look at a clock. At each hour, write down the severity of each symptom.

Let's also say you suffer most from wrist pain, neck pain, and fatigue. For each of those hours, rate those three factors. At 2 P.M., you might score 0 for wrist pain, 2 out of 10 for neck pain, and 3 for fatigue.

Record your answers over a few days. Look at the results, and notice any patterns you can. If you are going to visit a doctor, give the record to her. That record will help both you and your doctor to figure out what is ailing you, how to treat it, and *when* to treat it.

Although all treatments have different effects and side effects throughout the day, your concern is for your own unique health. Every medication and treatment works differently in you than in someone else. Having a record can help you track your symptoms. It also helps you find the correct diagnosis.

Having a record also allows you to track and evaluate your treatment. Treatment is a broad term. It includes far more than medical treatments. Any changes in your life that you make can be evaluated. For example, if you suffer from arthritis, you can check what morning aspirin versus afternoon aspirin does for your symptoms. You can also check to see whether exercise helps or hurts, massage helps or hurts, taking a short nap helps or hurts.

If you suffer from an illness, try at some point to have a record of what that illness does to you. Having a record can help you in many ways, including avoiding side effects of treatments.

Most people do not keep records of this sort, but they should. When people keep symptom records they notice the importance of timing in their symptoms and therapies. It allows them to plan their treatments, and their days, more effectively.

Dangerous Diagnostics

Everything in the body changes through the days and seasons. The results of lab and medical tests do as well.

Most doctors are taught that circadian (24-hour) body rhythms exist, but they have a hard time paying attention to them. For one thing, biological-clock effects are sometimes expensive to study. Medications, many of which cost hundreds of millions of dollars to develop, change their effects from hour to hour. Plotting those changes would increase drug development costs. It is probable that such information will not routinely be kept unless mandated by the government.

The end result is that for many treatments, the biological-clock effects are unknown. People often ask me when they should take certain medications. Is it better to take at night or in the morning? I can track part of the answer from the timing of their symptoms, the timing of treatment effects and side effects. Unfortunately, I don't know if certain drugs are overall more effective if taken in the morning, evening, or night. The overall timing of effectiveness for many treatments is simply not known.

Another problem is that people vary a lot in how they respond to medication, in what kinds of side effects they have, in how careful they are in taking the treatments that are offered, and in how regular they are in applying them.

Medicine is often wildly complicated. Doctors have a hard enough time figuring out what to do with their patients, and then they must also consider whether patients will actually do what they suggest. Additional considerations for physicians include the crazy quilt of medical insurance; the costs of treatment to the patient financially, occupationally and socially; the demands of running their own business; and worries about malpractice. The difficult-to-evaluate effects of biological clocks may lose relative importance. Figuring out whether you are a lark or owl and whether you should take nighttime aspirin at 8 P.M. or 11 P.M. is not going to be highest on many doctor's lists. Considering biological-clock effects in what happens to their patients and treatments may add too much complexity to a doctor's rushed work day.

The same is true of diagnostics. All the tests you are given by doctors have results that change with the time of day. Don't expect your doctor to know what those biological-clock changes are.

Diagnostic tests are never foolproof. Many tests will not have the same results even if performed perfectly. For example, if you take two blood samples at the same time, don't expect the test numbers to be exactly the same. Testing machines sometimes produce significant error factors.

Next, many tests look at markers of an illness, rather than the illness itself. Someone with rheumatoid arthritis might have his or her rheumatoid factor checked. But rheumatoid factor, despite its name, will vary with many other elements other than the actual progress of rheumatoid arthritis.

Many people who have positive tests for rheumatoid factor never have and never will have rheumatoid arthritis. Such "false positive" tests are frequent in medicine. Because doctors were until recently not instructed in basic statistics, and are taught that mistakes "may kill the patient," they often test and test until they find something wrong. Often what they find is a false positive test. Which leads to more tests, and more false results. Sometimes these incorrect results miss *true* positives, the kind of test results that allow you to make a proper diagnosis.

Unfortunately, biological-clock factors can lead to both false positive *and* false negative tests. Blood pressure is one example. Many physicians know that blood pressure changes during the day, increasing in fits and starts until the few hours before we fall sleep. However, many will not note the time of taking your blood pressure at each succeeding visit.

Your blood pressure may be "better" or "worse" as a result of *when* it was taken. Doctors treating high blood pressure may not notice that your last blood pressure was sampled at 9 A.M., while you arrived for your present visit at 4:30 P.M. They may change your medication based on these differences, even though your actual baseline blood pressure may not have changed at all.

Similar results occur when testing your eyes. Glaucoma affects many men and women as we age. Glaucoma can be tested by looking at visual field defects, how well we detect and see objects at the edges of our vision. However, most testing for glaucoma is done by taking ocular pressure. Pressures within the eye are usually worst in the early morning hours. They decrease thereafter, usually reaching their low in the early afternoon.

When are you most likely to see an ophthalmologist or optometrist: 2 P.M. or 2 A.M.? It is the very rare doctor who will call you into her office to test your eye pressures at two in the morning.

As you see, one reason biological-clock effects are not considered is because they interfere with the normal flow of life. It is not possible for you to meet your doctor at the exact same hour for every visit, nor at the same point in your menstrual cycle. Nor is it possible for you to take your diagnostic tests at the absolute best times for sorting out disease from unpleasant but innocuous symptoms.

All the more reason for *you* to take notice.

When having tests that you know are cyclic, like hormone levels or blood pressure, carefully note the time of the tests along with the test results. Most medical reports, especially chemical blood tests, already do this.

Next, compare your results with what is known about medical test results. An excellent book for this and many other health purposes is Michael Smolensky and Lynne Lamberg's *Body Clock Guide to Better Health*. Their book recognizes how variable body-clock effects are on health, and provides more useful information on that subject than any other book does.

Though most medical tests change with time of day, many of these changes are unimportant. Anatomic tests, like x-rays and computerized axial tomography (CAT) scans, do not change much with time of day.

Treatment, however, is a different story.

Drug Treatments: What Your Body Does to Pharmaceuticals

When people think of medical treatments they rarely consider exercise, diet, social support, and good sleep habits as the primary determinants of health. We tend to pay attention to our health only when we are losing it. For most of us, medical treatment usually means the treatment of illness, involving everything from surgery to massage to light therapy, though when people think about medical treatments, they usually first think of drugs.

Whenever possible, drugs are delivered like food, through our gastrointestinal tracts. Oral drugs are easiest for people to use. However, large-molecule drugs like proteins cannot make it through our alimentary canal. They must be injected, which is painful. Other drugs, like insulin, break up under the assault of our gut enzymes. Constant injection of medication is one thing many diabetics grow to hate.

If a chemical solution is available—such as the small modification to salicylic acid that makes aspirin ingestible—we prefer to take our drugs through the mouth.

Food and drugs are similar in many ways. Both involve substances that may aid or hurt our overall health. Both are treated by the body as potentially foreign substances and are carefully scrutinized by our immune system. Both are metabolized in very much the same ways. For the beginning of their travels in our body, oral drugs are treated pretty much the same as food.

As those who have read Chapter 3 already know, there are hordes of digestive enzymes waiting to work on anything we ingest. Drugs are protected by their coatings and fillers—materials like talc and resin—that help them survive at least as far as the stomach before really nasty things get done to them.

Many drugs, like alcohol, are absorbed through the stomach. However, the major absorption of most drugs takes place lower down in the gut, in the small intestine and colon.

As with food, ingested drugs are picked up and rapidly sent to the liver. Depending on their size and whether special liver enzymes quickly move to attack them, medications are then transformed into substances that are either useful drugs or inert flotsam that is quickly dumped out through the gut or kidneys.

Many pharmaceutical drugs are not immediately detoxified by the liver, though that is where most will ultimately meet their demise. Instead they are either dumped back unchanged into the gut or sent through the bloodstream. In the blood they go pretty much all over the place.

This phase of drug metabolism, called distribution, is the period when drug levels in the body are usually highest. Depending on many factors, drugs will either go where they are supposed to or they find themselves floating about in interstitial fluid, pumped into muscle, fat, connective tissue, and the brain; locking onto big blood proteins; or wending their unattached way back through the blood towards the liver.

The relatively rapid distribution phase is a time when side effects are sometimes worst. Much of the "rush" people feel from medications comes from this quick, short-lived period when drugs have the chance to roam just about everywhere. Some useful therapeutic effects will occur as well. Most of the time, however, the distribution phase is the prologue to further manipulation of ingested drugs.

While there are some drugs like lithium that are small and diffuse throughout the body, drugs usually work by connecting or attaching to something. Some drugs look like other substances normally present in the body, and act as surrogates for them. Other drugs push themselves into places where they are not normally welcome, or stick onto molecules that provide information services to organs or cells.

Many drugs work by connecting to receptors. Receptors are usually complexes of protein and sugar that hook on or around membranes on the surface and insides of cells. Receptors act as a kind of lock to which drugs act as a key.

Some drugs work by jamming the lock. Others work by opening the lock. Some set up a flow or cascade of separate information molecules that tell a cell what to do.

Opiates, drugs like morphine and codeine, operate by attaching to opioid receptors. Connecting to opioid receptors turns off pain. These cell-surface receptors have been around for a long time, perhaps hundreds of millions of years. Opiates are molecules that fortunately for us happen to attach to the same biological receptors that have been there all those millions of years.

The receptors are fooled. To them, drugs like morphine or codeine look chemically just like the natural pain-reducing substances normally produced by the body. However, unlike the substances created inside our bodies, most drugs produced by humans stick around, lasting a lot longer than their natural kin.

But the receptors start to know that. They don't just sit there. They are manufactured and erased, used and discarded. This explains why people get "used" to addictive drugs like opiates.

When receptors are exposed to large amounts of a drug, they start to become manufactured differently. Often they are less "sensitive," and sometimes their production falls off. And of course their levels of production and destruction shift with biological clocks, just like everything else.

Receptors control a lot of things, including fat cell metabolism. Researchers have looked for many years to find receptors that turn off production of fat. What they have found instead is that fat cells are smart. Depending on how many nutrients they see, fat cells produce their own hormones to determine how quickly they and other fat cells grow. They communicate with each other, effectively sending out their own drugs to control fat production in different organs. All those hormones and receptors are changing in sensitivity and number, minute by minute and hour by hour.

Most oral drugs do not last much more than a day. Eventually they are dumped out through the urine, or more commonly, make their way back to the liver. The liver is waiting for them. A whole host of enzymes reside in the liver, ready to detoxify drugs. These enzymes add or subtract different chemical groups.

The result may be a new batch of active drugs. More often, however, the liver eventually turns most drugs into useless substances that are then excreted through the gut or urine.

The process by which the liver detoxifies drugs most often is the critical step in determining how long they last in our bodies. Different people have different enzyme groups. Each one of us is quicker or slower at detoxifying certain drugs.

This process of drug detoxification is an exponential one. It is expressed in scientific shorthand as "half-life." A half-life is how long it takes for half the drug you took in to disappear from your blood. Half-lives vary from person to person. They also vary from hour to hour. That is because the detoxification enzymes, like everything else, cycle in activity to the tune of biological clocks.

Aspirin has a half-life of about four hours. Following its rapid distribution phase, four hours after you ingest your aspirin tablet, half of it is gone. Four hours more and a quarter more of the aspirin is gone, leaving only one-quarter left at eight hours. At twelve hours, only an eighth of your aspirin dose is left.

All the phases of drug distribution, detoxification, effect and side effects, run according to different biological clocks.

No wonder the results are complex. Now add on the effect of different foods on drug absorption; exercise; other drugs (the average eighty-year-old is on twelve different medications).

It is not a surprise that given these complex changes, most doctors do not consider biological-clock effects.

Timing Your Treatments

One of my patients was told to take aspirin to prevent further heart attacks. She also felt pain in her joints when she woke most mornings, usually around 6 A.M. She thought this pain was due to her "old arthritis."

Soon after she woke she normally ate breakfast. She wanted to be able to take her aspirin "on a full stomach." Five hours later her stomach would start "reeling."

I told her that aspirin usually caused less stomach irritation if taken at night rather than in the morning.

"What about the pain I wake up with?"

I told her it was better to prevent pain than to treat it *after* it appeared. For her, aspirin took thirty minutes or more to start to work. She would experience pain for at least an hour after taking aspirin. It might be better to take aspirin earlier and prevent her pain from occurring.

She started taking aspirin at night. At first she thought "it was irritating my stomach then, too," but gradually she felt less stomach upset. Her morning pain also lessened, though it did not disappear. As she also had stomach reactions to other aspirin-like drugs, the NSAIDS, or nonsteroidal anti-inflammatories, such as Motrin (ibuprofen) and Aleve/Naprosyn (naproxen), Tylenol (acetaminophen) took care of her morning pain on those mornings when nighttime aspirin was insufficient.

Most anti-inflammatory drugs cause fewer side effects at night. However, many people experience their worst symptoms in the morning and afternoon. Unfortunately, they must take medications at times that are less than optimal for diminishing side effects.

Biological clocks also subtly interact with the desired effects of drugs. Twenty years ago I was working in Manhattan in the Bellevue Hospital emergency room, having moved from training in internal medicine into psychiatry. An older man arrived complaining of severe and very frightening hallucinations.

He had been sent from the internal medicine section of the emergency room, where he had been diagnosed as "schizophrenic." He was considered chronically psychotic, and it was now up to the psychiatrists to treat him.

The man was not clear-headed. Nevertheless, he was still able to explain to me that his hallucinations occurred every night, usually about 3 or 4 A.M. Then he told me that he was diabetic.

"What kind of glucose levels do you run in the morning?" I asked.

He could only tell me that his numbers were high. Very high.

"Did they change your insulin dose recently?"

Yes, they had. They had doubled his nighttime dose of short-acting insulin.

"Did the hallucinations start after that?"

Yes.

His history saddened me. One reason I had moved from internal medicine to psychiatry was because I saw very few internists willing to treat "crazy people." Now I was seeing a man whose "craziness" had been partially created by his doctors.

His high morning glucoses were not normal. They had probably been caused by *too high* a nighttime dose of insulin. Too much nighttime insulin had caused low glucose levels, a condition named hypoglycemia. My guess was hypoglycemia then caused his frightening hallucinations.

Because too much nighttime insulin had brought his glucose too low, his body compensated with a massive stress response. This massive stress response then caused his organs to produce hormones that immensely increased the glucose in his blood. When measured at the time he woke, his morning glucose would then be very high—the paradoxical effect of *too much* insulin the night before.

Hypoglycemia has many severe effects. Since the brain runs exclusively on glucose, low brain glucose levels are truly dangerous. They cause brain damage, a result that leaves many diabetics demented early in life. Low glucose also causes extraordinary physical and mental symptoms, including the frightening hallucinations this man experienced.

Rather than recognize that the insulin doses were too high, the medical resident had looked only at the man's morning glucose levels. In his mind, high glucose meant the patient needed more insulin. It was a classic medical mistake.

The man took the doses as prescribed. The result was more hypoglycemia and more hallucinations.

I called to the medical attending physician and asked that he come over. Late, and very reluctantly, he did. Sensing his irritation, I went over the case as I normally did on medical floors, noting how the hallucinations probably were due to the timing of his insulin dose.

The attending physician knew where I was going. He started shouting: "You're turkeys! You're turkeys! So we're turkeys and you're turkeys!"

He stomped out of the room before I could say anything. Talking about the timing of medication actions was unpopular then, and it remains unpopular today.

Effective Dose: Same Person, Different Effect

How drug effects change over the 24-hour day can be estimated with a single measure: effective dose. Effective dose looks at the same dose in the same person, and gauges how much the effect changes with time. For example, a drug with twice the effect at its peak time of day compared with the low would have an effective dose of two. Sometimes these dose effects are large, sometimes small.

The drug haloperidol was long a mainstay for the treatment of psychosis. Twenty years ago Ross Baldessarini looked at its effective dose. He found a seven-fold difference in the studied effects of haloperidol between 4 A.M. and 4 P.M. Same dose, different time, seven times the effect.

The problem was that the study was done in animals. It's difficult to study psychosis in the rat. Effective dose was inferred indirectly, by looking at changes in muscle tone and receptor changes.

It is expensive and difficult to study effective dose in people. Still we know that substances have very different effects depending on time of day. We know that alcohol at midnight has two to three times the effect on sedation and muscle coordination as does alcohol at 6 P.M. We know that digoxin has a twofold effective dose for its action on heart arrhythmias. We know that insulin will clear far more glucose in the morning, perhaps 40 to 50 percent more, than it will at night.

But studying drug effects is complex. For most drugs, we don't know the effective dose—but we should.

Recently, the Institute of Medicine, an elite group of academic doctors, did a study of hospital care in the United States. They concluded that perhaps 100,000 hospital deaths were preventable. Some of those 100,000 deaths, as well as others, might be prevented if we knew more about drug-effect changes with time of day.

A problem for such studies is that effective dose has to look at more than one effect: the desired medical effects *and* the side effects. It's unclear exactly what the effective dose of anti-inflammatory drugs like ibuprofen is. It may be that nighttime ibuprofen (Advil, Motrin) is twice as effective in relieving pain symptoms as morning ibuprofen. What is known is that the unpleasant and often painful stomach effects of ibuprofen are one-quarter to one-half as severe for nighttime doses as compared to the morning. The effective dose of side effects for ibuprofen is two to four times in morning compared to nighttime. For most of us, it is safer to take anti-inflammatory drugs like ibuprofen at night.

Similar side-effect profiles exist for cancer drugs. It has been known for many years that tumor cell number increases at different rates during the day. Many cancer drugs kill tumor cells best during "S-phase," when the cells reproduce.

It might make sense to deliver the medications when they would have the most effect—when tumor cells are dividing. But most cancer drugs also kill rapidly dividing normal cells. These include many of the immune cells that fight infection. In the past, chemotherapy often decreased immune cells to such low levels that patients died. If they did not die, the pain and distress they experienced frequently was horrifying.

For some tumors it is possible to balance the desired and side effects of cancer medications. There are best times to give drugs—to maximize effects and minimize side effects.

These treatment procedures, however, are complicated. They demand pumps and sensors and exquisite timing. Often they are sufficiently complex that they are only carried out in a few research centers.

One reason effective dose is so little thought of in the daily practice of medicine is this additional level of complexity. Looking at the effective dose of a medication as it changes during the day is difficult enough. Knowing the effective dose for side effects adds another wrinkle.

Then there is the question of work schedule and convenience. Electroshock is a publicly unpopular but surprisingly effective treatment for truly severe depression. Often patients who are near death can be brought back to health with electroshock. The more afflicted the patient, the more effectively the procedure works. The vast majority of depression sufferers never become candidates for electroshock, which should be reserved for those who have severe medical conditions, or who are very ill and have failed most available therapy.

Electroshock has nasty side effects. One is loss of memory. Another is sedation. Electroshock works by inducing seizures, and seizures leave people unconscious. Normally, people "sleep off" their electroshock treatments.

Because it caused seizures, it made sense to researchers to try electroshock at night. If patients were going to sleep immediately after therapy, why not treat them at night?

Pilot studies were done. The overall results were excellent. Patients tolerated nighttime procedures well. The overall decrease in depression was greater.

Yet, morning is the time electroshock is given in the United States. The reason is work schedules. Anesthesia is required for present-day electroshock. Anesthesiologists and operating rooms normally operate in the mornings, not the middle of the night. All the work and supply schedules for electroshock makes morning treatments far more feasible than nighttime treatments.

Effective dose will have its day. Eventually cheap sensors will become available that will track drug blood levels through days and shifting menstrual cycles. Computerized drug delivery will make it possible for intravenous medications to be given when they are most useful. In the meantime, there are several principles you can use to protect yourself.

Why Effective Dose Should Matter to You

In any medication treatment, the goals should be the greatest improvement for the least cost—to your health and to your pocketbook. With every treatment there is a tradeoff.

To make that tradeoff work for you, it makes sense to follow these principles:

1. Know your symptoms and especially when they appear, increase, and decrease. Remember that prevention of illness should be the goal of medical care. Preventing pain is much better than treating pain.
2. Evaluate the effects of treatment in three areas: usefulness, side effects, and time of day.

If, for example, you suffer from a chronic illness like osteoarthritis, you want to know when your symptoms are most severe; when treatment, as with anti-inflammatories, gives you the greatest relief; and when treatment is expected to have the worst side effects (anti-inflammatories often cause the most stomach upset in the morning) and whether that is also true for you.

Many people have their worst arthritis symptoms in the afternoon. These folks want to take their medications several hours before the symptoms, attempting to prevent them, even though they might have the worst side effects from anti-inflammatories taken in the morning.

However, if your worst arthritis symptoms are in the morning, taking medication at night may be preferable. You might also get the better side-effect profile on your side.

The point is to evaluate *your* body and *your* treatments. The best way to do that is:

- To survey your symptoms hour by hour, recording the changes using the method outlined above
- To see how much treatment decreases the symptoms you have, hour by hour
- To note what side effects you have, hour by hour

Most people think these evaluations will take them too much time. They should not.

If you have a chronic illness, especially one that afflicts you for months or years, it pays to track symptoms, treatment effects, and side effects for at least a few days. You can then bring the results to your doctor. With your help, she should have a much better handle on how to treat you in the future.

Whenever possible, do what you can to promote your health. Exercise, diet, and stress management achieved through humor and interactions with friends and acquaintances all have a large impact on health over time. Your goal should be staying healthy and avoiding illness, not having the best insurance or access to health care.

However, when your health needs require medical care, it is worthwhile to see exactly what problems you have and when you have them. Then you will be able to treat your symptoms at times when *you* have them, and treat them with the greatest efficiency and least worry.

All illnesses vary throughout the day. Yours will vary differently from others. But many illnesses have a pattern of appearing worse during the day or night. It's worth knowing a bit about the differences between night and day diseases.

Night Diseases

Many illnesses are at their worst at night. Some of the common ones are colds, peptic ulcer disease, and asthma.

Colds

Colds are virus-caused illnesses that normally last less than a week, and they make most of us miserable with sore throats, runny noses, fever, low mood, and marked fatigue. Often people have "prodromes" (preliminary symptoms) that occur before major cold symptoms strike. Such colds cause people to become tired, listless, angry, and irritable before they get their "real" cold.

Hundreds of viruses cause colds, which has made treating them difficult. New medications have come out that cut perhaps 24 hours from the standard length of cold symptoms, and may work for as many as dozens of winter-virus colds. How well they work overall remains to be seen, but progress has been made.

Most colds cause their worst symptoms at night. Nighttime is a period when immune function shifts. People are most debilitated by cold symptoms of coughs, clogged noses, and fever when those symptoms prevent them from sleeping.

If people can sleep with a cold, they usually say their symptoms are worst when they wake. Come morning, their natural immune functions become more active, and symptoms usually continue to improve until the late afternoon or evening before becoming worse the next night.

As many cold viruses cause sedation, you might not want to take sedating treatments, which are only for symptomatic relief anyway. Antihistamines, which help dry out mucous membranes, are often sedating. However, using drugs like Benadryl at night can help you sleep through a cold, and perhaps not feel horribly fatigued when you wake.

As many people work all day with colds and find that sedation, tiredness, and stuffed, nonfunctioning noses are the worst daytime problems, stimulant-type drugs like caffeine and pseudoephedrine (Sudafed) make sense to use during the day. Morning is the best time to use such stimulants. Be careful about using "round the clock" cold medications that last twelve hours or more. The stimulants that are part of such drug cocktails often keep you awake during the night. You need comforting, restful sleep to fight off a cold.

The best choice of cold treatment, of course, is to avoid getting colds. Obtaining enough sleep is important. People with insufficient sleep appear to have compromised immunity, particularly for "minor" illnesses like colds. Resting after exposure to colds may help.

However, come winter and your job as an elementary school teacher, getting a cold is nearly inevitable. Having kids makes getting colds almost automatic for many parents. Recognize that:

1. *Prevention helps.* Getting enough sleep and keeping fit help your immune system. Washing your hands a lot may be useful, but cold viruses are so ubiquitous it is very hard to avoid them.
2. *The most debilitating symptoms generally occur at night.* Use sedating drugs, like many antihistamines, only at night, when they can help you the most. If you need stimulants, use them mainly in the mornings (shift workers must adjust for their shifts).

Peptic Ulcer Disease

Most of us think that ulcers cause us abdominal pain during the day. Often that is true. However, most ulcers actually *form* at night.

Treatment of ulcers has a long and bizarre history. Ulcers can kill you, and until recently they frequently did. An ulcer that went through the stomach lining, perforating into the cavity behind the gut, often led to seepage of stomach contents. If people did not bleed to death, the infections caused by food and acid dumped into the abdominal cavity murdered them later on.

In the nineteenth century, William Halstead, a renowned surgeon at Johns Hopkins, devised an operation for cutting out the offending ulcerative part of the stomach. Though a chronic morphine addict, Halstead was a highly innovative and creative surgeon, and his operation was performed routinely for over a hundred years.

Throughout the last two centuries, diet was a mainstay of ulcer treatments. Most diets were no help. Then gastric freezing came into vogue in the 1960s, and was used by many thousands until clinical treatment trials found gastric freezing to be utterly useless.

Finally, effective drugs that prevented stomach acid secretion were devised. These drugs, like Prilosec (omeprazole), Zantac (ranitidine), and Aciphex (rabeprazole sodium), have gone through several generations of development. They remain very helpful today.

However, the unthinkable occurred: researchers discovered that most ulcers were caused by bugs. Bacteria were not supposed to survive the harsh, acidic environment of the stomach.

But bugs are smart. If organisms can live in Pacific hot water vents, where the temperatures reach hundreds of degrees Fahrenheit, they can certainly learn to live in your stomach. Bacteria called helicobacteria are now believed to be the main cause of ulcers. The definitive ulcer treatment is to take antibiotics.

However, many billions of dollars are still spent each year on anti-ulcer drugs and antacids. Even though acid production falls at night, the ability of your stomach lining to buffer acid falls even more.

If you suffer from peptic ulcer disease, you want to use anti-ulcer drugs *at night*. Taking medications like Prilosec or Nexium in the hour before you sleep tends to do as much for you as treatment at any other time of day, and with fewer side effects.

However, ulcers are not just caused by stress-induced stomach acid production. Alcohol and tobacco are major risk factors. So if you have an ulcer problem and must have a drink, take it early in the evening, when alcohol's effective dose is low. And cut down your smoking whenever you can. Stomach bacteria may die today, but they know how to return tomorrow.

Asthma

Asthma occurs much more commonly at night, especially if you look at severe asthma symptoms. Particularly around 2 to 5 A.M., asthma can provoke a disaster.

Asthma has come back into the news with the realization that improvements in treatment have not decreased asthma death rates. Instead, deaths from asthma recently have increased. If you want to treat asthma effectively, you must recognize that it is a nighttime disorder. Many of the deaths due to asthma, particularly in children, occur in the middle of the night.

Asthma is best treated by prevention. Figuring out which allergens set off asthma is not easy. Nor is it easy to avoid such allergens, especially when they are items like house dust or mold, or common irritants like exercise and cold air. Keeping your bedroom clean and cleaning it during the daytime, well before you go to sleep, may help. Replacing carpeted floors and dust-absorbing textiles may also help, but avoiding allergens is often a trial for many asthma sufferers, as it is for their families.

Most asthma drugs mimic epinephrine and cortisol, two major hormones in your body. Epinephrine, called adrenaline in Britain, has major effects on heart rate, vessel constriction, airway size, and glucose levels, among many other effects. Cortisol's effect on cells are incredibly wide-ranging, modifying our immune response in nearly every imaginable way. Cortisol effects easily deserve a book of their own.

Asthma sufferers usually take their drugs in the form of inhalers. Since asthma is worst at night, many feel they should take asthma medications at night. However, side effects from asthma medications also are frequently worst at night. Often the best time to take asthma drugs is during the late afternoon.

You can track the results yourself. Check the times you have symptoms, and the times you take your medications. See if changing your medication's timing affects your symptoms and ability to withstand side effects.

And pay careful attention to sleep. Sleep, especially certain stages of sleep, are times when asthma is exacerbated. Asthma itself can worsen sleep, as can asthma drugs, particularly those that mimic epinephrine.

Please don't wake yourself up to monitor your asthma symptoms. But if asthma is waking you, make sure to track that change with a written record and inform your doctor.

Treating asthma effectively at night not only prevents unnecessary deaths, but all the problems that come with poor sleep. Timing your medications correctly is crucial. Just like any illness, that timing will differ from person to person. Try to set the treatment times that work best for you.

Daytime Illnesses

Other diseases and ailments are more likely to have greater effects during the daylight hours.

Heart Attacks

Heart attacks can strike day and night. During the night, REM sleep, when respiration and heart rate vary most (see Chapter 2), is a time when heart attacks are quite common. However, the worst time for heart attacks is in the morning.

Morning is a special time for your circadian clocks. Just as dawn appears, your body prepares for the new day. Levels of epinephrine and cortisol go up, while growth hormone goes down. Blood pressure starts its most rapid rise. Insulin secretion increases. Platelets, which help your blood clot, get stickier, preparing for the time you will wake from bed and become physically active.

The morning's biological-clock changes create a perfect scenario for causing heart attacks.

Many researchers believe that heart attacks start with platelet clots. Increased by risk factors like smoking, extremely small platelet clots can start a cascade that produces clots that surge in size until they finally clog up an artery.

Heart attacks also occur when blood vessels become reactive and suddenly narrow, or constrict. Just as an asthmatic's airways constrict in the middle of the night, so can coronary arteries narrow come morning. When these arteries constrict a lot, blocking off fair-sized amounts of blood flow, we feel that constriction as the chest pain of angina.

Morning exercise does not immediately help. Heart attacks increase very slightly as people are exercising. Fortunately, the long-term results of exercise are so overwhelmingly positive that you are much better off exercising than not.

Monday morning is a particularly bad time for heart attacks. Much of the population has gone to bed late and awakened late over the weekend. The number of cardiac deaths multiplies.

Some of you may suspect that the best way to decrease morning heart attack risk is to stay in bed. Not so. Regular exercise helps. Exercise will open up the coronary arteries, and create "collaterals," new blood vessels that naturally bypass old, clogged, or clotted-up arteries.

Collaterals keep many of us alive, a fact that has been known for hundreds of years. In the eighteenth century a wood cutter walked into the Royal Society in London. The wood cutter suffered from angina, painful constriction of his coronary arteries. Angina was a rather rare illness at the time, probably because so much of the population was physically active. The good London physicians told him their diagnosis, and they asked the wood cutter to donate his heart at the time of his death.

They had to wait quite a while. When the wood cutter died at a relatively advanced age, his heart was found honeycombed with new coronary arteries, formed to bypass his old, clotted-off vessels. Woodcutting was effective therapy for blocked coronary arteries.

For those of you who have a hard time exercising every day, eating a lot of vegetables and fruits should help. Foods with high quantities of folate and B vitamins lower a substance in the blood called homocysteine, which can be as large a risk for heart disease as cholesterol. You can eat fruits with any meal, but they will be metabolized most effectively in the morning and early afternoon.

If you do have any risk factors for heart disease, nighttime aspirin may be helpful. The dose need not be large, only 81 or 162 milligrams, one or two baby aspirins. The enzyme blockade provoked by aspirin seems to prevent platelet clots, and may prevent the greater tendency to clot that occurs when you rise up from bed in the morning.

There is no need to fear the morning. A morning walk under healthy morning light can improve your mood, decrease your weight, and markedly lower your risk of heart attack. It's more enjoyable and useful to walk if you can take along a spouse, sibling, child, or friend.

Narcolepsy

Narcolepsy is a strange and fascinating disease that causes people to fall asleep all day long.

The sleep of narcoleptics is not normal. Narcolepsy, which now appears to be the result of a lack of a specific brain neurotransmitter called hypocretin/orexin, is a disease in which REM sleep appears to intrude itself into wakefulness.

All the effects of REM sleep may be present: lack of muscle tone, dreams (read as hallucinations by the brain), and uncontrollable sleepiness. Probably the oddest part of narcolepsy is cataplexy, the loss of muscle tone and control. Cataplexy can be brought on by strong emotion. Anger, fear, terror, sadness, and laughter can all provoke cataplexy; in fact, it is most commonly provoked by jokes.

A narcoleptic hears a wonderful joke, laughs, and falls flat on the floor, asleep. Often they watch dreams flow through their minds, provoking the daytime hallucinations so many of them despise.

Lots of people have narcolepsy without cataplexy. One person who does was a former resident I taught while at the University of Texas Medical School. I ran into him years later, in the city where I took my Sleep Medicine Board exam. A smart and delightful fellow, he complained of mild daytime sleepiness to a friend, who offhandedly suggested he obtain a sleep study.

Thinking he had nothing to lose, he went to sleep one night in the sleep laboratory. The next day he remained in the lab for the Multiple Sleep Latency Test, devised by Dr. Mary Carskadon. The MSLT asks people to fall asleep at two-hour intervals following a night's sleep. If during these daytime "naps" they fall asleep quickly and go into REM sleep repeatedly, they probably have narcolepsy.

My former resident was surprised to learn he had narcolepsy. "The only problem I really had was falling asleep in lectures. I thought it was because the lectures were boring."

He was soon taking stimulant medication. Stimulants did not bother him, and made him more alert. I asked what difference his diagnosis and treatment had made in his life. "Well, I used to work twelve hours a day. Now I work fourteen to sixteen hours a day."

Not all narcolepsy sufferers are so lucky. Many people with narcolepsy have abnormal sleep. They go into REM sleep very quickly, have long stretches of abnormal REM, and also experience leg kicks that wake them during the night, making them feel ragged and sleepy come morning. And narcoleptics need sleep. Without restful sleep, narcoleptics will fall asleep again and again throughout the day. For many narcoleptics, normal work life is impossible.

Today people are more effectively treated for narcolepsy than was true before. New drugs like modafinil have appeared, and the old standbys of treatment, stimulants like Ritalin and amphetamines, are given in higher doses, doses that make it possible for narcoleptics to stay awake throughout the daylight hours.

But sometimes stimulants are dosed too high. If taken too late in the day, stimulants lighten sleep. They may prevent narcoleptics from falling asleep, staying asleep, and obtaining the deeper, more restful stages of sleep.

Good timing is required. Fitting the doses earlier in the day, especially to keep people awake during the midafternoon "hump," often works best. Morning stimulant use is usually most effective.

SUMMARY

- Biological clocks time your health. All our biology changes throughout the day, minute by minute and hour by hour—and so do the effects of medical treatments.
- Healthiness is about regularly pursuing activities that prevent disease and preserve health, like exercising, eating plant-based diets, seeing and conversing with friends, and keeping your sense of humor.
- When you do fall ill is strongly determined by when you were exposed to the illness-causing agent or agents.
- All medications and treatments work differently at different times of day. Called effective dose, these differing effects can multiply or diminish the effect of any treatment you take.
- Timing your medications by tracking your symptoms can markedly improve their effectiveness.

Chapter Eleven

Jet Lag: Resetting Your Clock

J anet would never visit Europe again.

The dream of her farm childhood was to visit Paris. Realizing this dream had taken her more than seventy years. She had married after high school, raised a family, and watched her husband die. In her seventies, her children had provided her the money for a ten-day tour of European capitals.

Janet read and read. Each city—London, Paris, and Rome—merited a separate book. The tour guides she borrowed from the library read to her like adventure novels. She could not believe that so many people and so much history existed in such small spaces. She could not accept that so much of the past remained.

The flight was delayed. She never liked planes, those "long sardine cans" holding stale air and stale food. She equated flying with medical procedures, an hour's jet flight as pleasing as a doctor pushing an endoscope down her throat. Though not frightened of air travel, she had never flown more than two hours in the air.

They arrived in London at seven o'clock in the morning. Following the sensible suggestions of her tour books, she had shifted her watch to London time the moment she sat down on the plane.

They disembarked. Customs, baggage claims, discomfort, and confusion as the tour bus picked them up and drove to the hotel. Their schedule was so packed the tour guide invited them to start early, after the hotel breakfast. Though many others went directly to bed, she ate her second set of scrambled eggs of the morning, and climbed back into the bus.

"That was when I started to feel bad," Janet said. "I didn't know if I was sick, but I felt sick. Well, not really sick, but tired, so tired. My arms and legs felt heavy as a rock. I couldn't think. It was like somebody had banged me on the head."

Janet was told her travel fatigue would go away, but it did not. The next few days "I saw these amazing things, but I couldn't remember them. Things went by in some sort of blur."

By the end of the tour, "I was feeling more myself. Some of it was fun. But then I got this terrible cold." Returning home, "it took me two weeks to recover. Maybe more."

Even if you have never been in a jet, many of you know what jet lag feels like: the sleepiness and leaden fatigue, the mental and physical sluggishness, and the weakness and sense of ill ease. You'll know what jet lag is like if you've ever experienced shift work.

Jet lag is shift work performed by plane. Our bodies did not evolve to work day and night. Nor are we designed to travel and function well across separate time zones.

A "minor" form of jet lag we all know is daylight savings time. Every spring and fall, clocks magically spring forward or backward, disregarding the movements of the earth and sun.

The clocks change that morning, but not your body. Many people dislike daylight savings, saying it takes them days to more than a week to adjust to the manipulated hour. In my experience, daylight savings is particularly hard on shift workers and people suffering major depression.

Fortunately, what works to adapt to shift work also works for jet lag—the LENS program of light, exercise, naps (or sleep), and socializing. But the peculiar burdens of jet travel and the changing length of day and night demand their own forms of adaptation.

Changing the Length of Your Day

Jet lag is about crossing time zones, the differing patterns of day across the surface of the earth. Traveling east means making a 24-hour day shorter. A trip from Miami to Paris normally flies across six different time zones. Your 24-hour day is abruptly cut down to 18.

Our body clocks are precisely set by light and daily routines to a strict 24 hours. They do not adjust well to days that are shorter or longer. Even the small changes that occur with astronauts' space travel, days that may last 23½ hours, cause multiple physical, mental, and psychological disruptions.

For those of us remaining on earth, traveling east is an especial hardship. If left without cues, human body clocks run a bit longer than 24 hours. Shortening our days to less than 24 hours is harder than lengthening them. Since traveling west makes the day longer (flying from New Jersey to California makes a 24-hour day 27 hours long), adjustment is normally better flying west than flying east, at least for most people.

The rule of thumb is that body clocks adjust about an hour for each day one spends in the new time zone. The amount adjusted may be a bit longer when traveling west. Our body clocks adjust, but at different speeds—your body temperature rhythm shifts to the new time faster than does your cortisol level, for example. Different organs adapt at different speeds. Usually the worst part of jet lag is the first two to four days in the new time zone. Just as you would expect, larks adapt differently from owls.

Larks have it easier on flights east. Owls have the advantage flying west. As with shift work, comparative youth and fitness help. Jet lag is less a problem for well-rested twenty-year-olds than for middle-aged businesswomen. Short sleepers, particularly those who normally sleep less than 4 hours a night, have less trouble with jet lag than the rest of us.

Motivation, Pleasure, and Jet Lag

Not everyone experiences jet lag. Recently Charlene Barshefsky, the hardworking and long-traveling trade representative of the Clinton administration, told the *New York Times* that jet lag was "a myth" she did not personally encounter. According to this report, Ms. Barshefsky could fly to Tokyo, a twelve-hour time-zone shift, and start trade negotiations with the Japanese as easily as she would start a workday in Washington.

Most of us are not so lucky. Some people I know who formerly worked in the State Department believe that jet lag was the cause of many of the unfavorable trade pacts the United States concluded with Japan in the 1980s. A friend explained why:

"You get this guy who's all puffed up because he's leaving to negotiate in Japan. Rather than prepare for jet lag, he'll go into work the day of his trip and stays till the last minute in case the Secretary or Assistant Secretary have final instructions. He waits by the phone patiently. Of course they never call. Then he's zooming to the airport, flying right straight to Tokyo and starting negotiations the next day when his body's half-dead and his brain can't think. No wonder we ended up giving them the store."

Individual variability responding to jet lag varies widely. Much of the variability is due to motivation. People tell me that jet lag is "much less of a problem" if they are going to a destination they like, especially for a vacation. Young Americans experience partial sleep deprivation as a way of life. Many experience little jet lag on their first trips to Asia or Europe. Often they are so excited on arrival that they forget about sleep and immediately begin nonstop sightseeing.

Frequent business travelers experience jet lag differently. One executive I met in Hong Kong explained to me that he had five homes across the world and traveled so often "I have no idea what time my body is at. When a client calls, I go." His firm had considered developing different sets of "teams" to deal with businesses in different time zones, but it "didn't work." Personal relationships were too important, and competition too intense to allow a "second team" to perform the intricate and difficult financial negotiations. "The client wants to deal with someone they know."

Six months later I learned that the same executive, a healthy man in his mid-forties, had taken a long leave of absence.

Jet lag is about much more than flying across time zones. International travel is difficult today, and its future may prove even more troublesome. Increasing security requirements cause necessary but unpleasantly long waits. While airlines worldwide skirt financial insolvency, airport attendants worried about keeping their jobs try to manage flustered and frustrated passengers. Never noted for their relaxed, "homey" feeling, airports force travelers to trek endless hallways that appear to have been designed by moonlighting horror movie directors. The long walks and waits create perfect conditions for back and neck injuries in passengers who do not want to be held up for hours by hand-scanning of checked luggage. (Massage therapists have not yet opened offices in airports, but their day is coming—if they can afford the rents.)

For those waiting for their delayed, altered, or cancelled flights, airport restaurants combine many of the dining touches of fast-food emporia and sports bars while dishing up expensive, non-nutritious, fattening food. People who try to sleep are lucky to find seats, but will then find themselves rocking back and forth in benched unison as they try to slumber under the drone of strategically placed televisions broadcasting the "Airport News Network."

Airport "travel" is especially ghastly for smokers. Unwelcome in most public spaces, airport smokers are herded into cube-shaped glass cages where they nervously puff away, watched by passing nonsmokers as if they're animals in a zoo. Or perhaps the nonsmokers are fascinated by the extraordinary stalactite-like tar formations accumulating on the ceiling tiles.

Then there's the flight.

Tips for Surviving Airports and Air Travel

Do not expect jet travel to improve anytime in the near future. As the Stoics wrote two thousand years ago, we humans cannot change our fate. But we can change our *response* to fate.

Whenever you plan on jet travel, expect the unexpected—delays, inconsistent security arrangements, bad weather, and harassed airport and flight personnel. Though it is convenient, it is pointless and often unfair to blame the airlines. Deregulation made them like any other stock-market-influenced business. Poised for "growth," they are sinking under enormous debts, and they are doing what they can to make people comfortable while they fight to survive.

Here are a few suggestions for your own survival:

1. *Expect to wait.* Then expect to wait a bit longer. Business-people and professionals may bring laptops, notepads, and handheld computer devices that allow them to work no matter what happens at the airport or in flight. For the "casual" traveler, this is your opportunity to read all the trashy novels and fashionable magazines that have been accumulating near your bedside. This is also the time to read the things your mother or grandmother would never let you buy. Long novels may be stored up for jet travel, and self-help books on managing stress are frequently a must. Classic novels can be immensely helpful. Great literature allows us to understand human fears and strengths with the forbearance and wisdom required to survive jet travel, and in many cases can act as a surprisingly effective sleep aid (in other words, read books you should have read in high school but didn't).

2. *Bring toys for the kids.* Airports and planes are especially difficult for children. Bring the most entertaining toys and reading materials you can, and expect to spend lots of time playing with your children. Security concerns scare kids at least as much as adults. Paying your children lots of attention should help.

    When carrying electronic toys, try to find models that make minimal noise. Lots of people need and try to sleep on planes, and they often complain about clacking laptops and clanging electronic games.

3. *Bring your own food.* As their budgets shrink, airports and airlines try to do more with less. The "less" includes any attempts at healthy nourishment—or nourishment altogether.

    If you are not concerned that foreign customs officials will confiscate your food stash on arrival, make plenty of space in your handheld luggage for your individual nutritional needs. Remember that space will then be available for all those gifts you must buy for those you will see on your return.

It is not impossible to eat healthily during air travel. Some airline fare is quite passable. Yet most of us are not pacified by 2 ounces of petrochemically flavored "snack mix" combined with a quarter can of metallic-tasting orange juice.

Raw materials that travel well may be preferable for long trips, particularly where space is a premium. Consider:

- *Grains.* Granola can be a marvelous snack food, especially mixed grains to which sugar is not added. If you don't like tipping your spoon or hand in a small sack of muesli, consider less nutritious, sugarized granola bars.
- *Fruits.* Bananas bruise and apricots may drip, but apples, oranges, grapefruit, and pears have skins that resist the rough handling of air travel. If you pack well, virtually any fruit can help you survive airports and planes.
- *Nuts.* High in "healthy" polyunsaturated fats, nuts like walnuts, Brazil nuts, cashews, and many others are relatively efficient air-travel fare.
- *Vegetables.* It is possible to snack on broccoli, cauliflower, carrots, and other vegetables, but they must be cleaned and dried in advance. They make a great combination with grains and fruits.
- *Soy, balance, and protein bars.* Though often stuffed with sugar and made to taste like candy, high-protein bars are particularly useful for long flights, balancing the nearly pure carbohydrate content of airline "snack foods" and drinks.

And please don't forget:

4. *Drink lots and lots of water.* Going into an airplane is effectively walking onto a 6,000-foot mountain plateau filled with virus-infested, recirculating air. Our bodies dry out in such environments, and hydration is quite important to maintaining health and fighting off infections. Many people get sick after long airplane flights. Colds are especially common, and smokers in par-

ticular may have a very rough time. For smokers, airplanes are great places to try nicotine gums. If you need to be close to a bathroom, try to obtain nearby aisle seats.

5. *Try to get lots of sleep before, during, and after jet travel.* Most of us are sleep deprived anyway. The stress of air travel, especially across time zones, demands we prepare. Getting plenty of sleep in the nights before travel, and enough after, can help. Sleeping on planes is also helpful; for those of us who can't sleep on planes, sleeping pills may work.

6. *Walk.* Airplanes do not make it easy for you to exercise. If placed in a window seat, you may need to wake up two fellow passengers in order to get out to the aisle. Still, it's well worth the try. Our bodies are not designed for lengthy, enforced sitting. While we sit, our blood pools. Many a traveler experiences blood clots, though fortunately most clots are small, short lived, and do not cause permanent medical problems. Prevention is key. If you are taking a long flight, make sure to get out into the aisle and walk, preferably every hour or two.

   If you know other passengers, go and visit them. Socializing is one means for avoiding jet lag. It's also helpful for making plane flights easier.

7. *Look out the window.* Air travel gives us some of the most astonishing vistas we may witness in our entire lives. Where else can we see for hundreds of miles, take in the full stretch of mountain ranges, or watch gigantic storms cross oceans? In the daytime, windows also supply sunlight, a wonderful opportunity to help you overcome jet lag.

Tips for Jet Lag—Short Trips

Hundreds of articles and books are written about how to "beat" jet lag. Yet the majority of seasoned travelers make little or no attempt to adjust. Part of the reason is that correcting jet lag "just right" demands a bit of effort (you'll see how it's done with the Two-Watch Technique, on page 227).

Still, many techniques exist that can help you adapt to jet lag. Most of them do not require much effort or thought. Here are some:

1. Try to adjust to the new time zone by taking your destination time as your new clock time. (Biological time is the time your body clocks were at when you *began* your trip.)

   When in Rome, think like the Romans.

   Shifting to the time zone you arrive in is often difficult, but it is exactly what most travelers attempt. For short trips over one or two time zones, adjusting yourself to the new local time, eating and sleeping and exercising at times fitting the new location, works for most of us. However, longer trips almost always cause some disruption, which requires more effort on your part to adapt.

2. Consider a low dose of melatonin. Melatonin is the hormone of darkness. When it is night, melatonin secretion begins deep inside the pineal gland of the brain. Light stops melatonin production.

   Melatonin is commonly used as a sleeping pill in the United States. Doses of 1 mg to 3 mg thirty minutes before bedtime will cause perhaps one-third of the population to feel quite sleepy. However, melatonin also shifts our body clocks. One method for overcoming the "Monday morning blues" is to take 1 to 3 mg of melatonin on Sunday night. Normally you will wake up a bit earlier the next morning, and more attuned to the lark work world.

   Melatonin and light shift our body clock rather differently. The effects of melatonin are weaker, and work at opposite times of day. When light is relatively ineffective at shifting our clocks, as occurs in the early afternoon, melatonin works to make our body-clock length *shorter*. The amounts of melatonin required to shift our body clock are also, according to Professor Al Lewy at the University of Oregon, considerably smaller than what is needed to make us sleepy.

When taking trips eastward, this fact can be used to advantage. A 1 mg melatonin pill can be sliced into quarters and taken at 1 or 2 P.M. Such a small dose of .25 mg should not make us sleepy. Still, you may want to try it out before a trip, as some people are very sensitive to melatonin. Remember, afternoon doses of melatonin should shorten your body clock.

Alternatively, you can use melatonin as a signal to the body that "night has arrived" and it is time to go sleep. In this fashion, you can use melatonin as a sleeping pill each night in your new destination. Here you will want to use higher doses of 1 to 3 mg.

3. Consider the *brief* use of short-acting prescription sleeping pills. Jet lag is a form of shift work. Just as shift workers often do not sleep well during the daytime, travelers often cannot sleep well on reaching their new destination. Whatever the local clock time, their body's biological clock thinks it is still daytime.

Most people who travel across time zones are casual travelers who do not fly to Europe or Asia every week. They are reasonable candidates for sleeping pills, which are most effective and least dangerous when used infrequently and intermittently. Also, many people find they cannot sleep on airplanes without some sleep aid.

Sleeping pills can turn addictive. They do not provide normal, regular sleep. However, they can help most of us overcome jet lag.

Sleep and biological-clock researchers, especially from countries like Australia, frequently use melatonin and sleeping pills when traveling long distances. Though most sleeping pills will work, short-acting ones like Ambien (zolpidem) and Sonata (zaleplon) may have a small advantage over the others, unless you are taking a truly long flight, like Los Angeles to Hong Kong. Sleeping pills, including melatonin, can also be used to "acclimate" to the local time once you reach a destination.

Especially when shifting twelve or more time zones, I often bring melatonin to help me fall asleep on a flight, and a sleeping pill for the first "night" I sleep under the new local time. If there's trouble coming home, a sleeping pill the night after your return can also help you adjust to normal work life.

Sleeping pills are helpful for jet lag, but only up to a point. Usually they provide only partially effective sleep on flights, and some people complain of oversedation once they finish their trip—even with the short-acting sleeping pills. By themselves, sleeping pills will do nothing to reset your inner biological clocks.

Still, sleeping pills have an important place in treating jet lag. Even 3 or 4 hours of sleep on a 15-hour flight can make jet lag much easier to handle. Obtaining sleep at your new destination, particularly for the first one or two nights, is often extremely helpful. For those of us who do not readily adjust across time zones, sleeping pills can make a long-distance pleasure trip much easier to handle.

Using the LENS Program to Beat Jet Lag

Shift workers adjust their biological clocks by using light and exercise, accompanied by planned socializing and specially timed sleep. The same techniques can be used to help you master jet lag.

Though light can act as a two-edged sword, particularly when obtained around the times of our body temperature minimums (see the Two-Watch Technique on page 227), light and exercise remain the most effective means for changing your inner body clock. The rule that works best for larks and switchers is this:

When traveling east, obtain late morning light at your destination. When traveling west, try to obtain late afternoon and evening light.

For example, when flying from Miami to Los Angeles, your 24-hour day becomes 27 hours. Needing to lengthen your day, you can usually obtain lots of bright southern California light quite late into the evening, when it will work best.

Exercise shifts inner clocks in the same direction as light. Taking a walk in the late-afternoon to evening southern California sun makes it easier to adjust to the longer, 27-hour day. When you return to Miami a week later, reverse the process. Go out and enjoy a fine morning walk. Your body should adjust back to Miami time that much more quickly.

If you can't sleep on arrival at your destination, consider short-term use of melatonin (1 to 3 mg) or sleeping pills.

Socializing helps jet lag in any form. Though less powerful than light, social factors are also powerful adapters, and usually more fun. All of our regular activities during the day, like eating lunch and dinner, working a standard 8- to 9-hour day, conversing with our family, are *social cues* that help keep our clocks stable. The same kinds of activities can be used to adjust to jet lag.

When in Rome, socialize. Talk with your friends, fellow travelers, and the Romans, who will talk with you even when they can't speak English. Adjusting yourself to the meal times, television times, and strolling times of the local population will help your inner clocks adjust to the time zone. Though you may not want to go to bed or eat at the late hours common in Madrid or Rome, you will probably still want to wake, sightsee, and work at about the same hours as the locals, regardless of what your biological clock tells you.

Socialization is normally the first part of motivation. Humans are social animals. Falling "in synch" with the local population is usually fun for all concerned, and makes jet lag a far smaller concern.

Tips for Long and Frequent Travel— the Two-Watch Technique

Jet lag changes your day. Going east, it becomes shorter. West, it becomes longer. Slowly your body will drift into the new time zone. But if you wish to rapidly shift your inner clocks, you need help. The first thing to do is buy a second watch.

The Two-Watch Technique is how you can overcome frequent or severe jet lag. If you like, you can buy a watch with two separate sets of hands. However, it is usually easier to buy a second "travel" watch that will allow you to shift your body clock across any number of time zones.

When buying a second watch, find something that is inexpensive with a quick, simple hour change. Some of the digital watches on the market carry a huge range of features, but are as difficult to program as a VCR. Stick to the less expensive models of large manufacturers.

As you sit down in the plane before your long trip, keep your easy-to-reset travel watch at your present time, which should also be your *biological-clock time*. You do not have to wear your travel watch, just have it easily available. Next, set the watch you normally use to your *destination clock time*.

Biological-clock time originates in the time zone where you live and work. It is the time you normally operate in, day by day and night by night. For most of us who do not do much shift work, it is relatively constant—until we take a long flight. Destination clock time is the "artificial" time your body will need to become used to at the end of your flight.

Biological-clock time varies for larks and owls. Its most important and treacherous period is the body temperature bottom, or minimum, the time when your internal temperature hits its daily low. This low is critically important because it determines how powerfully and in which direction light and exercise will shift your biological clocks. At the body temperature bottom, you will be most sensitive to changes in light and exercise. Both light and exercise will have their largest effects at the body temperature bottom. (See the figures on pages 10 and 12 in Chapter 1.)

But beware. The body temperature bottom is also when light changes its phase-shifting direction. Before the body temperature bottom, light and exercise will make your day longer. After the body temperature bottom, light and exercise will make your day shorter. *The effect does not just vary; it also changes direction.*

So when is your body temperature bottom?

International Travel for Owls and Larks

Most days your body temperature hits its low point while you are asleep. Outside of special laboratories, it is difficult to know exactly when your body temperature reaches its minimum. Instead, many researchers use a rule of thumb, figuring that the minimum is reached an hour to an hour and a half before you get up in the morning. For larks who normally get up at 5:30, the minimum is thought to be around 4 A.M. For owls who get up at 9, the minimum might be around 7:30 A.M.

For most of us, *morning light makes our body clock earlier; evening light makes our body clock later.* But that is because we are normally obtaining light long before or after our usual body temperature minimum. For both larks and owls, we are normally asleep when the body temperature minimum is reached.

Not so when we fly across time zones. If you are a lark flying from Washington to Paris, you may arrive there at 9 A.M. That time is 3 A.M. on your biological clock.

If you get out of the airport before 4 A.M., you will experience light at the point where it is most powerful at making your body clock lengthen. Since you are in Paris, where your day has abruptly shortened to 18 hours, this is the opposite of what you want.

The end result of walking into morning light at 3 A.M. biological-clock time is to make jet lag worse. Larks and owls both would want to wear very dark glasses if going out into the Parisian sunlight when their inner clocks tell them it is so early.

Since it is difficult to know exactly where your body temperature bottom is, it makes sense to give yourself leeway in determining when to exercise and obtain light. Here is what you can do:

1. Find out your habitual home wake times, and average them up.
2. For a week or two before your flight, record when you wake up. If you're a lark who must get to work early, and you wake at 6 A.M. most mornings, put that time down. If you are an owl theater director who normally wakes between 9 and 10 A.M., put that down.
3. Subtract 90 minutes from your habitual wake time. This represents your supposed body temperature bottom. For the lark who wakes at 5:30, 4 A.M. is your minimum; for the owl who wakes habitually at 9:30, it's 8 A.M.

Going East

If you are lark or owl, you want to get light and exercise after your body temperature minimum. You do *not* want to obtain light and exercise exactly at the minimum, as this will unpredictably shift your clock forward or backward. Here is where the two-watch technique helps out. Your travel watch helps tell you your body clock's real time.

If you fly from New York and arrive in Paris at 9 A.M. Paris time, your travel watch tells you your body clock time is 3 A.M. This is far too early for you to get light or exercise. If you do, whether lark or owl, you will make your jet lag problem worse.

Fortunately, you now have the two facts that make it simpler for you to correct jet lag—your body-clock time, staring at you on your travel watch, and your averaged body temperature minimum. Using those two numbers, you can shift your body faster than the hour a day that we normally adapt to jet lag.

You need to use light and exercise when it's helpful, and keep out of bright light when it's harmful. Once you have reached your destination, follow these simple rules: When outside wear dark glasses until your travel watch tells you that you have reached an hour past your body temperature minimum. Then take off the glasses and take a walk.

Let's illustrate with examples for both larks and owls.

Larks

You arrive at Paris at 9 A.M. local time. Your travel watch tells you your *body-clock time* is now 3 A.M. Your averaged body temperature bottom, estimated by following your normal wake time (5:30), is 4 A.M.

You want to wait two hours, until your body clock time is at least 5 A.M. (one hour after your body temperature minimum), before you go out in the sunlight and walk or do heavier exercise. Sunlight and exercise at 5 A.M. body-clock time and later should help your inner clock shorten its day and adjust to local time. Remember, when you arrive, 5 A.M. on your body-clock travel watch equals *11 A.M.* Paris time. Until 11 A.M. you want to wear dark glasses if you are outside. Really dark glasses. The kind that do not admit a lot of light, but still allow you to see.

Owls

Your arrival in Paris at 9 A.M. leaves your *body-clock time* at 3 A.M., the same as your lark friend. But your body temperature bottom is much later—8 A.M., equaling 2 P.M. Paris time.

Since you need to give yourself at least an hour's leeway to make sure you do not obtain light at times which make jet lag worse, you cannot take off your sunglasses until 9 A.M. on your travel watch—which equals normally 3 P.M. Paris time.

The Second Day

The next day in Paris is also important for shifting your body clocks. Since you have spent a day in the new time zone, and you have obtained sunlight and exercise at the proper times, your body should have shifted at least one hour toward local time.

Take out your travel watch. For each day spent in the new time zone, set the watch one hour *later* if you have traveled east, or one hour earlier if you have traveled west. Now when you go out and obtain Parisian sunlight, you can enjoy it *at least* an hour earlier than the day before. Your travel watch tells you the optimal times for light and exercise exposure.

Your travel watch should tell you that your inner body-clock time is now five hours ahead of New York, not six. If you are a lark, you still want to get light and exercise after what your travel watch tells you is 5 A.M. If you are an owl, you want your light and exercise after what your travel watch tells you is 9 A.M.

For every day you are in Paris, you want to set your travel body-clock watch at least one hour earlier. Using these techniques, you may adjust much faster. Some people shift body clocks three, four, or five hours a day when using two-watch technique, combining bright light and exercise.

The two-watch technique works, but it is a little complicated. Most people find it simple to use after their first day in a new location. They say that knowing their inner clock time versus the local time helps them understand when they should schedule everything, especially business meetings and sleep.

For especially long trips, light and exercise are markedly helped by melatonin. Especially when traveling between North America and Asia, melatonin before sleep helps you shift the long twelve-hour time difference.

For those who do not want to buy a second watch, the Bio-Brite corporation is now selling travelers' light boxes with special "jet lag" software. It's a good idea whose technology should only improve with time. More tips on how to use light, exercise, and timing to adjust to jet lag appear in the book *How to Beat Jet Lag* by Dan Oren, Walter Reich, Norman Rosenthal, and Thomas Wehr.

SUMMARY

- Jet lag is an unusual form of shift work, where body clocks no longer align with the times set by the sun. The LENS program—Light, Exercise, Naps, and Socializing—diminishes jet lag.
- Once on the airplane, drink lots of water and make sure you walk as often as is socially and physically possible. Expect the unexpected: delays, long waits, and unreliable service.
- To sleep on flights, try using melatonin or occasional sleeping pills. Adjusting to local times and customs may help on arrival.
- For long and frequent travel, the Two-Watch Technique allows you to precisely plan light and exercise to minimize jet lag, as well as schedule your most important events.

The Horne and Ostberg Morningness–Eveningness Scale Test

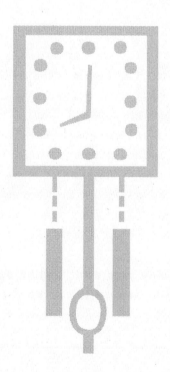

The following test will provide you with a Morningness–Eveningness score that gives a very good indication of where you fall on the lark/owl scale.

This test, written by James A. Horne and Olov Ostberg, originally appeared in the *International Journal of Chronobiology* 1976:4:97–110. (The journal's Web site can be found at *www.tandf.co.uk/journals*). It is reprinted here by permission of Taylor & Francis Ltd.

Instructions:

1. Please read each question very carefully before answering.
2. Answer ALL questions.
3. Answer questions in numerical order.
4. Each question should be answered independently of others. Do NOT go back and check your answers.
5. All questions have a selection of answers. For each question place a cross alongside ONE answer only. Some questions have a scale instead of a selection of answers. Place a cross at the appropriate point along the scale.

1. Considering only your own "feeling best" rhythm, at what time would you get up if you were entirely free to plan your day?

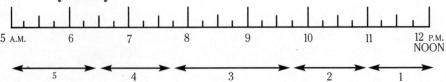

2. **Considering only your own "feeling best" rhythm, at what time would you go to bed if you were entirely free to plan your evening?**

8 P.M.	9	10	11	12 A.M. MIDNIGHT	1	2	3

5	4	3	2	1

3. **If there is a specific time at which you have to get up in the morning, to what extent are you dependent on being woken up by an alarm clock?**

Not at all dependent	❏ 4
Slightly dependent	❏ 3
Fairly dependent	❏ 2
Very dependent	❏ 1

4. **Assuming adequate environmental conditions, how easy do you find getting up in the morning?**

Not at all easy	❏ 1
Not very easy	❏ 2
Fairly easy	❏ 3
Very easy	❏ 4

5. **How alert do you feel during the first half-hour after having awoken in the morning?**

Not at all alert	❏ 1
Slightly alert	❏ 2
Fairly alert	❏ 3
Very alert	❏ 4

6. **How is your appetite during the first half-hour after having awoken in the morning?**

Very poor	❏ 1
Fairly poor	❏ 2
Fairly good	❏ 3
Very good	❏ 4

7. **During the first half-hour after having awoken in the morning, how tired do you feel?**

Very tired	❏ 1
Fairly tired	❏ 2
Fairly refreshed	❏ 3
Very refreshed	❏ 4

8. **When you have no commitments the next day, at what time do you go to bed compared to your usual bedtime?**

Seldom or never later	❏ 4
Less than an hour later	❏ 3
1–2 hours later	❏ 2
More than 2 hours later	❏ 1

9. **You have decided to engage in some physical exercise. A friend suggests that you do this one hour twice a week and the best time for him is between 7:00 and 8:00 A.M. Bearing in mind nothing else but your own "feeling best" rhythm, how do you think you would perform?**

Would be in good form	❏ 4
Would be in reasonable form	❏ 3
Would find it difficult	❏ 2
Would find it very difficult	❏ 1

10. At what time in the evening do you feel tired and as a result in need of sleep?

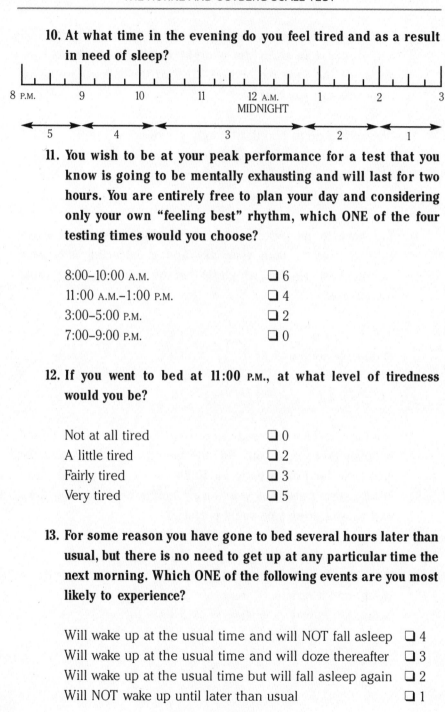

11. You wish to be at your peak performance for a test that you know is going to be mentally exhausting and will last for two hours. You are entirely free to plan your day and considering only your own "feeling best" rhythm, which ONE of the four testing times would you choose?

8:00–10:00 A.M.	❑ 6
11:00 A.M.–1:00 P.M.	❑ 4
3:00–5:00 P.M.	❑ 2
7:00–9:00 P.M.	❑ 0

12. If you went to bed at 11:00 P.M., at what level of tiredness would you be?

Not at all tired	❑ 0
A little tired	❑ 2
Fairly tired	❑ 3
Very tired	❑ 5

13. For some reason you have gone to bed several hours later than usual, but there is no need to get up at any particular time the next morning. Which ONE of the following events are you most likely to experience?

Will wake up at the usual time and will NOT fall asleep	❑ 4
Will wake up at the usual time and will doze thereafter	❑ 3
Will wake up at the usual time but will fall asleep again	❑ 2
Will NOT wake up until later than usual	❑ 1

14. One night you have to remain awake between 4:00 and 6:00 A.M. in order to carry out a night watch. You have no commitments the next day. Which ONE of the following alternatives will suit you best?

Would NOT go to bed until watch was over	❑ 1
Would take a nap before and sleep after	❑ 2
Would take a good sleep before and nap after	❑ 3
Would take ALL sleep before watch	❑ 4

15. You have to do two hours of hard physical work. You are entirely free to plan your day and considering only your "feeling best" rhythm, which ONE of the following times would you choose?

8:00–10:00 A.M.	❑ 4
11:00 A.M.–1:00 P.M.	❑ 3
3:00–5:00 P.M.	❑ 2
7:00–9:00 P.M.	❑ 1

16. You have decided to engage in hard physical exercise. A friend suggests that you do this for one hour twice a week and the best time for him is between 10:00 and 11:00 P.M. Bearing in mind nothing else but your own "feeling best" rhythm, how well do you think you would perform?

Would be in good form	❑ 1
Would be in reasonable form	❑ 2
Would find it difficult	❑ 3
Would find it very difficult	❑ 4

17. **Suppose that you can choose your own work hours. Assume that you worked a FIVE-hour day (including breaks) and that your job was interesting and paid by results. Which FIVE CONSECUTIVE HOURS would you select?**

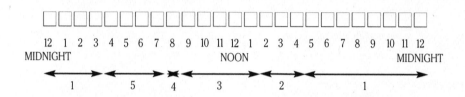

18. **At what time of day do you think that you reach your "feeling best" peak?**

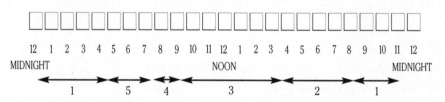

19. **One hears about "morning" and "evening" types of people. Which ONE of these types do you consider yourself to be?**

Definitely a "morning" type	❏ 6
Rather more a "morning" type than an "evening" type	❏ 4
Rather more an "evening" than a "morning" type	❏ 2
Definitely an "evening" type	❏ 0

Scoring:

- For questions 3, 4, 5, 6, 7, 8, 9, 11, 12, 13, 14, 15, 16, and 19, note for each response the appropriate score displayed beside the answer box you marked.
- For questions 1, 2, 10, and 18, refer the cross you made along each scale to the appropriate score value range below the scale.
- For question 17, take the most extreme cross on the right-hand side as the reference point and take the appropriate score value range below this point.
- Add together the scores and compare the sum to the Morningness–Eveningness scale below:

Definitely Morning Type	70–86
Moderately Morning Type	59–69
Neither Type	42–58
Moderately Evening Type	31–41
Definitely Evening Type	16–30

Sample Sleep Monitoring Chart

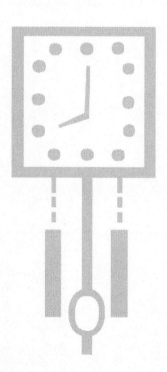

NAME: _____

WEEK BEGINNING: _____

Please respond after waking up.

	MONDAY	TUESDAY	WEDNESDAY	THURSDAY	FRIDAY	SATURDAY	SUNDAY
When did you actually try to fall asleep?							
What time did you actually fall asleep?							
How many minutes did it take you to fall asleep?							
How many times do you remember awakening?							
When did you wake up?							
How long did you actually sleep (in hours)?							
What woke you up? Alarm Spontaneous Other							

NAME: _____   WEEK BEGINNING: _____

Please respond after waking up.

	MONDAY	TUESDAY	WEDNESDAY	THURSDAY	FRIDAY	SATURDAY	SUNDAY
On a scale from 1 to 5, with 5 as excellent, how was your sleep last night?							
Was it refreshing? (same 1–5 scale)							
Did you nap yesterday?							
Start							
End							
On a scale from 1 to 5, was it refreshing?							
Did you take any drugs yesterday?							
If so, please list time and dose.							

How to Use a Light Box

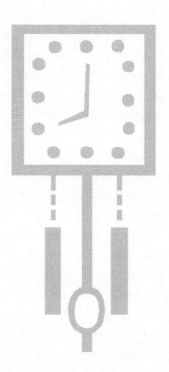

Light boxes are manufactured lights that simulate sunlight. Since sunlight sets so many of our biological clocks, light boxes can be used to do what the sun does: reset our time spaces, make us more alert, improve our mood, and treat depression. Light boxes have extremely varied uses, from helping larks stay up late for a party to preparing athletes for big games, as well as treating insomnia or fixing jet lag.

Light boxes normally produce full-spectrum white light. Though they are more expensive than the sun's rays (particularly when you consider rising electricity costs), light boxes have many advantages over sunlight.

First, they contain no harmful ultraviolet (UV) light. People forget that sunlight is probably the most significant cancer-causing natural element in the world. As the world's population ages, skin cancers are now epidemic. Melanoma, also caused by UV light, is increasing rapidly, and has a much higher death rate than do the more common skin cancers. Cataracts are also related to sun exposure.

Studies of light boxes demonstrate that UV light is not needed to maintain their therapeutic effect. Though there have been worries about light boxes' effect on eyes, no one has yet demonstrated anything serious to worry about. (One area that needs more study is how high levels of light interact with certain drugs.)

Light boxes have other advantages over sunlight. Even in sunny places like southern California, global warming is changing the weather. Sunlight is not as predictable as it once was.

Nor does sunlight arrive at night near the body temperature minimum. If you have a source of electricity, light boxes can be used to provide bright light anywhere, anytime. Light boxes can be set up as small devices next to your computer (as the one I'm using as I write these words) or in huge arrays, as NASA has created for resetting the body clocks of astronauts.

Where to Use Light Boxes

Light boxes produce light that is meant to be placed approximately 1 to 2 feet away from your eyes. Some manufacturers and researchers recommend that light boxes be set about 14 to 22 inches (about 40 to 55 centimeters) away from the face. At this level, most light boxes will produce 5 to 10 thousand lux, or lumens, of light.

Ten thousand lux is a lot of light. On a bright, sunny, southern California noon, sunlight might provide 50,000 to 100,000 lux. However, in most northern homes lit by artificial lights, the light exposure is often only about 100 lux. Light boxes produce fifty to a hundred times more light than most of us obtain indoors.

This high-intensity light is needed to create the brain changes that shift our inner clocks and markedly improve alertness and mood. Light intensity falls off rapidly as you move away from your light box. The fall-off is extremely rapid, following what scientists define as the second power, or distance squared.

What this means is that if your light box is putting out 10,000 lux 2 feet from your eyes, at 4 feet from your eyes the dose is 2 squared, or four times *less*—a mere 2,500 lux. It's important that you keep your light box relatively close if you want to feel its effects.

Keeping a light box close to you does not mean you should make it *too* close. Some people think they need to look directly into them, but that is not the case. Looking directly into a light box for a half hour or more often causes a "bleaching" of the cones in the eyes that allow us to see colors. Looking straight into a light box may cause you to feel "bug-eyed" and cut down on your full appreciation of color.

Keeping a light box off on the side at about a 45-degree angle works quite well. The light can strike your eyes from the side and still accomplish its therapeutic effect. You can look directly at the light box on occasion. Many of us do that automatically, glancing quickly at the light box, then going back to reading, watching the computer monitor or television, or continuing conversations at the breakfast table.

Where to put a light box is really about finding a place where it will be used. If you are an owl using a light box to become alert for morning work or school, putting your box on the kitchen table while you eat a worthwhile breakfast should be fine.

If you are a young lark trying to stay up for a big date, you can put your light box on your desk, next to the computer or the pile of books you plan to read, or to the side of your television. Put it in a place where you will use it.

Exercising with a light box demands a little bit of ingenuity. If you are running on a treadmill or working out on an exercise bicycle, light boxes can be placed on tables or chairs at or near eye level. If you plan on exercising under bright light most days, it may pay to buy a bigger light box with a surface width of at least 2 feet. Also, models with adjustable heights are very useful when exercising with light.

Older people sometimes object to their insomniac spouses watching television near a light box. They feel the light hurts their spouse's eyes. First, those not using a light box should avoid staring straight ahead into it. Though looking directly into a light box for a brief time will not hurt them, staring straight into a light box may make some people feel "hyper," or very temporarily decrease their color vision. Sitting or standing at an angle from light boxes usually so decreases their strength that "bystanders" have little or no trouble. Since the power of light falls off so rapidly, most spouses get used to light boxes. Often they begin to start using them themselves.

If you are using light boxes primarily when reading or sitting at a computer monitor, small light boxes with surface areas of 6" x 12" may prove sufficient. For those who use light boxes while watching a large-screen television, sizes of 1' x 2' may work best. If you plan to exercise with a light box, the large, freestanding units, some of which are several feet or more in height, may be suitable.

Where to Obtain a Light Box

Many people I know look at light boxes and assume they can make one themselves. It's just a bunch of bulbs in a box, they say.

No, it isn't. Light boxes produce very concentrated, intense light. It is not light normally available in fluorescent tubes or ordinary light bulbs. Nor will stacking regular light bulbs together produce the same effect as standard light boxes.

Most light boxes built by manufacturers have intricate arrangements of lights and reflectors that produce their high-intensity light. Manufactured light boxes do not produce enormous heat as do many "homegrown" varieties, and they are usually very portable and easy to use. Particularly in terms of safety, they have many advantages over the light boxes people build themselves.

As of this writing, there are several producers of therapeutic light boxes that have been in business for years, have had good responses from consumers, and appear to be reliable sources of parts and service.

Please make sure that the light box you're buying is for *direct human use*. Most of these boxes were developed for treating seasonal depression. The light boxes used for artist tracing or reading enveloped mail are not appropriate for personal, daily use.

Many people seem to like light boxes made by Bio-Brite, SunBox, Apollo Box, and Northern Lights over those of other manufacturers, though others prefer products by Advanced Light Products and Hall. In the next few years, other companies will likely build personal light boxes, and it is possible they will produce a less expensive, more reliable product. Generally, however, the four companies noted above produce items that work well over time and are easy to use.

SunBox and Bio-Brite have been leaders in this field. Their light boxes come in many sizes, but they also produce many smaller models. Bio-Brite now makes lights that use LED diodes. How well these lights work remains to be seen; one advantage is that they can be programmed to combat jet lag. For traditional uses, SunBox's Sun Light Junior is light, very portable, and easy to use, especially on the desktop.

Apollo Box has produced light boxes for many years. Their cabinet-style light boxes have many uses, and they are particularly good for placing next to televisions. Northern Lights has a fine curved model that is very efficient for reading, as does Advanced Light Products.

Light boxes generally run from about $200 to $400. When obtaining them through physicians, various rebates are sometimes offered. New deals come up all the time. Since the mainstay of light box manufacturers has until recently been treating seasonal depression, bargains may be obtained around Christmas time.

However, many people prefer to obtain light boxes over the Internet. Checking out the frequently changing models is easy on the Net, and light boxes can be shipped within a few days, though some people tell me it takes one to two weeks to obtain the light box they want. Unlike video recorders or computers, light boxes are very easy to use and normally no assembly is required. You plug them in and can begin to use them within seconds.

When to Use a Light Box

The specific uses of light boxes are covered throughout this book. Here are a few examples:

- *Alertness*: Light boxes can be used to improve alertness at almost any time throughout the day or night, especially when alertness is lagging. Light boxes are efficient at decreasing normal afternoon sleepiness and increasing wakefulness for nighttime shift workers. Usually at least ten minutes of light exposure is required for improved alertness, though many of us require a half hour or more in order to feel sharp.

    If alertness is all that you are after, be careful not to use your light box around the body temperature bottom. If you are a lark, your body temperature usually hits its low around 4 A.M. to 5:30, in owls perhaps three hours later. If you're not sure whether you are lark or owl (check Chapter 1), your body temperature bottom is usually 90 minutes to 2 hours *before* your habitual waking time.

- *Insomnia*: Light boxes work well for many insomniacs. Generally the best time to use them is in the evening, somewhere between 7 and 9 P.M. for larks, perhaps two hours later for owls. Many insomniacs who use light box therapy find an hour or more of light exposure is required, but again, beware of timing—light in the evening will push your body clock later. That means you will wake a bit later than you do normally. For many insomniacs, this is precisely what they want.

- *Body-clock shifting*: Light boxes have been intensively studied for their ability to shift human body clocks. The basic rules are simple:

  Evening light shifts your body later.
  Morning light shifts your body earlier.

- The largest effects for light are around the time of your body temperature bottom. If you obtain light just before that bottom, you will most effectively shift your clock later. If you obtain light after the temperature bottom, you will shift your body clock earlier.

- With the exception of shift workers and those undergoing jet lag, most people are not going to use bright light at 3 or 4 A.M. The main problems come if people use bright light *precisely* at the time their body temperature hits bottom. If you do, you may phase-shift yourself later or earlier, or not at all.

- Since most people use light boxes at night or after they arise in the morning, the problem rarely presents itself outside of correcting jet lag. Still, you do not want to use a light box much earlier than your usual wake time.

- Remember, exercise works to shift your internal clock *in the same direction as light*. The effects of light can be increased by exercising under bright light—either light boxes or sunlight qualify.

- *Depression*: For those who suffer from seasonal depression, light boxes work best in the morning. This may have something to do with the unusual body clocks of those who are susceptible to seasonal depression, which appear to change with the seasons more than those of others. Walks under morning light may also help.

For those without seasonal depression, morning light may produce a bit more mood elevation than evening light. However, for most of us, bright light can mildly improve mood at almost any time of day or night.

Bright light boxes work for many different problems, but function differently with different people. Though they take a little getting used to, working, studying, or socializing under light is usually easy, and often fun. Try your light box under different conditions. Put it on your desk, your breakfast table, next to your television. See what works best for you. Chances are very good you'll find more than one good reason to use your light box.

Suggested Further Reading

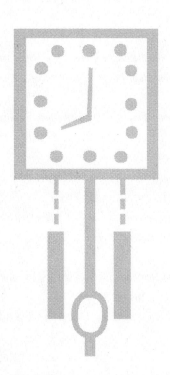

An excellent book on the health benefits of paying attention to body clocks is *The Body Clock Guide to Better Health* by Michael Smolensky and Lynne Lamberg (Henry Holt, 2000). It is informative, well written, and remarkably complete. Robert Arnot's *The Biology of Success* (Little, Brown, 2000) also discusses how to use body clocks for the promotion of individual health, as does Sue Binkley's *Biological Clocks: Your Owner's Manual* (Taylor and Branch, 1998). Sidney MacDonald Baker and Karen Baar's *Circadian Prescription* (Putnam, 2000) emphasizes the relationship between body clocks and diet.

Other more specialized books worth a look include:

No More Sleepless Nights by Peter Hauri and Shirley Linde (John Wiley, 1996)

Birds of a Different Feather by Carolyn Schur (Schur Goode, 1994)

How to Beat Jet Lag: A Practical Guide for Air Travelers by Dan Oren et al. (Henry Holt, 1993)

Wide Awake at Odd Hours by Torbjorn Akerstedt (Swedish Council for Work Life Research, Stockholm, 1996)

Inner Time: The Science of Body Clocks and What Makes Us Tick by Carol Orlock (Birch Lane, 1993)

The scientific literature on body clocks is vast. A small selection of the articles of interest includes:

Mitler, M. et al. "Catastrophes, sleep, and public policy." *Sleep* 1988; 11:100–109.

Smith, R. et al. "Circadian rhythms and enhanced athletic performance in the National Football League." *Sleep* 1997; 20 (5):362–365.

Panda, S. et al. "Circadian rhythms from flies to human." *Nature* 2002 16; 417:329–335.

Sack, R .L. et al. "Use of melatonin for sleep and circadian rhythm disorders." *Annals of Medicine* 1998; 30:115–121.

Focan, C. "Chronobiological concepts underlying the chronotherapy of human lung cancer." *Chronobiology International* 2002; 9:253–273.

Arendt, J. "Biological rhythms: the science of chronobiology." *Journal of the Royal College of Physicians of London* 1998; 32:27–35.

Dinges, D. et al. "Cumulative sleepiness, mood disturbance, and psychomotor vigilance performance decrements during a week of sleep restricted to 4–5 hours per night." *Sleep* 1997; 20:267–277.

Meerlo, P. et al. "Sleep restriction alters the hypothalamic-pituitary-adrenal response to stress." *Journal of Neuroendocrinology* 2002; 14:397–402.

Wright, K. "Times of Our Lives." *Scientific American* 2002; 287 (3): 58–65.

About the Author

Matthew Edlund, M.D., Director of the Gulf Coast Sleep Institute, is the author of *Psychological Time and Mental Illness*. He has had multidisciplinary training—in internal medicine (University of California; Massachusetts General Hospital), psychiatry (New York University; Bellevue Hospital), sleep medicine (Brown University), and occupational health (Harvard University).